The Management Profession

McGRAW-HILL SERIES IN MANAGEMENT

Keith Davis, Consulting Editor

The Management Profession

LOUIS A. ALLEN

President
Louis A. Allen Associates, Inc.

McGRAW-HILL BOOK COMPANY

New York

Toronto

London

THE MANAGEMENT PROFESSION

For Mike, Ace, Steven, Terry, Debby

Preface

The purpose of this book is to present a fully validated statement of the concepts and principles of modern, professional management. Taking as its purview the entire field of knowledge concerning leadership and management, it attempts first to evaluate and preserve the best of what is already known and used successfully in practice. With this it reconciles and integrates the varying and often conflicting viewpoints and theories that have developed in the behavioral sciences, decision theory, automation, and the use of the computer and related areas.

In substance, the contents summarize the new findings of our continuing research in the management of leading companies. Originally begun in 1954 as a three-year study of 150 business enterprises in the United States and Canada, it now reflects the results of further studies embracing 385 business, governmental, and institutional enterprises throughout the world.

Our research leads us to conclude that the ability of *leaders* to *manage* is the most important single factor in group undertakings today. From Standard Oil to Ford to United States Steel, from Finsider to Mitsubishi to Tata, the history of leaders in commerce and industry is the story of growth and improvement in management. Because of this, business enterprises throughout the world are giving new thought and effort to the identification of the true nature of management, and to the concepts and principles that underlie its professional practice.

But the demand for management goes beyond business. The critical need in the world today is for people to learn to work effectively together. As individuals, enterprises, governments, and nations, we search for more effective ways of pooling our efforts with those of others for the greater good of the whole. Misunderstanding, expediency, and lack of knowledge stand as formidable barriers. The answers will not be found wholly in politics or economics, in psychi-

atry or science.   Many of them lie in the development and perfection
of the science and art of management.

The manager is a new kind of professional, destined to take his
place with the scientist and the educator in shaping the society of the
future.   Expert in a complex, difficult, and most demanding kind
of work, the role of the professional manager is critical and his
potential is unlimited.   In the years ahead, competence in management
will mark the difference between the leaders and the also-rans.   This
will hold true not only in business, but also in government and education, and in all those situations in which people wish to maximize
their efforts for their common benefit.

To the individual interested in getting ahead in business, perhaps
nothing is more important than an understanding of this new status
of management.   Until very recently, management in most organizations had been practiced rather haphazardly.   This situation is fast
changing.   We are discovering that management is a special kind of
work that can be identified and defined.   It can be practiced in terms
of verified principles and can be learned as a classified body of
knowledge.

Much of this information has been hidden or buried in the administrative processes of many of our leading companies.   In some cases
this was by design, for alert executives have realized that leadership in
management is even more important than leadership in technology.
Often, managers have evolved new and effective ways of handling
management problems without being aware that their solutions were
applicable to similar conditions in other companies.   Principles of
management have been applied in response to the pressures of competition and growth and, in most cases, without having been formalized.

The present volume is designed to do three things: (1) to outline
in practical form the best information now available which will tell
us how to provide most effective leadership for organized endeavors,
(2) to classify this information so it can be taught and learned as a
coherent body of knowledge, and (3) to provide a logical framework
of theory within which will be developed principles, concepts, and a
precisely defined vocabulary of management.

We would like to explain these three points in more detail.   In
identifying the best information available about leadership and management, we have attempted to focus on those practical conclusions
that will be of help to the manager concerned with the problems of
running the socioeconomic entity we call a business enterprise.   Many
new theories have been offered lately with respect to organizations, the
people who work in organizations, and the best way to integrate the
two.   Some of this thinking is helpful; some is pure speculation; some

is obviously designed to attract attention rather than to advance useful knowledge. Once it is in print, most of this information is ingested with undiscriminating celerity by managers hungry for assistance.

How to ensure practicality? Our approach has been to present the ideas and conclusions here outlined in seminar sessions to practicing managers in what amounts now to a large proportion of the industrialized countries of the world. Each concept, principle, and definition offered has been reviewed critically by a minimum of 12,500 managers located from Chicago to New Delhi, from Melbourne to London, from Rome to Tokyo. In this effort, disagreements have been resolved, contradictions identified, idle theories abandoned. What is left, we hope, has the hard muscle of practical fact and will apply with validity to the manifold problems of management wherever they may be found and in whatever language they may be voiced.

On all sides we have been confronted by the bewildering variety of categories into which management knowledge is crammed. We have undertaken a classification of this management information which is based upon logic, yet consistent with the actual needs of business. To this end, we have identified as many applicable points of view as possible in each major area, reconciled them so far as possible, but in the end have, with some temerity, arbitrarily arrived at our own conclusions and established these as final. Again our justification is the almost unanimous acceptance which these findings have had from practicing managers.

The theoretical framework we have developed to accommodate the realities of management practice is based upon the assumption that management is a specialized kind of work which represents a maturation of leadership. A manager is a particularly competent, knowing, and, hopefully, most effective kind of leader. His purpose is to enable the people he leads to work most effectively together with him. To accomplish this, he devotes most of his time and energy to performing certain kinds of specialized work which only he is organizationally capable of performing with maximum efficiency. The four functions and nineteen activities of management are identified and defined, their logic is established, and the major requirements of successful practice are developed in the body of the book.

This book is neither definitive nor exhaustive; it attempts to represent, as accurately as possible, the best of our current knowledge about the art, science, and profession of management. Other research now in process will be validated and published in later editions.

To our readers we offer the book in the hope that it will encourage those in management positions to look at the work they are called upon to perform from a new point of view and to study, adopt, and advance the principles, standards, and ethics of what will eventually become a profession of management. To students of management, we hope that this will provide an up-to-date summary of what managers in leading companies of the world are actually thinking and doing in the practice of their demanding tasks. To managers in fields other than business, we trust that the lessons learned in competitive enterprise may have useful application to similar problems in their own organizations.

Because most of the viewpoints here expressed have been presented vigorously to all manner of executive groups, it is hoped that any missionary fervor that may still seem to flavor the work will be forgiven. If to some of our readers there may seem to be too much of a personal staking of claims in the tracts and territories of management knowledge, we ask forbearance and recognition of our human frailty.

Finally, the author wishes to extend his grateful appreciation to the literally thousands of executives in many countries who made this volume possible. Their free and frank participation inevitably searched out the untenable theory, the impractical conclusion, and the personal bias that otherwise might have colored the work. The author, however, accepts full accountability for interpretation of the data and the conclusions drawn from them.

Louis A. Allen

Palo Alto, Calif.

Contents

Part Five MANAGEMENT CONTROLLING

PART ONE

Leaders and Managers

CHAPTER 1   *A Challenge for Leaders*

Some labor with their minds, and some labor with their physical strength.   Those who labor with their minds govern others; those who labor with their strength are governed by others.   MENCIUS

The great question of our times is how to reconcile and integrate human effort so people everywhere can work for their common good and not their common disaster.   The answer depends most largely upon the capabilities of leaders in all positions in all segments of society.   The task of leadership literally is to build the kind of world in which we live.

Yet vitally important as is effective leadership, it is startling to realize how little we know about it.   Compared to the breadth and precision of our knowledge in many other fields, our understanding of leadership is primitive indeed.   Consider for a moment: we can visualize the interior of a 2-ton forging and predict to a fraction the volatile distillate that can be secured from 1,000 barrels of crude petroleum.   We can measure the molecules necessary to cover the point of a needle.   With increasing confidence, we can project and return human beings from space.

A review of our knowledge of leadership presents a different picture. As minute and detailed as is our understanding in other fields of science and technology, the information we have about leadership is limited indeed.   We do not know with any certainty what are the characteristics of a good leader.   We find it difficult to identify the work a leader should do.   We do not know how to measure with precision the results he secures.

Leadership, most vital of all human skills, is still learned by trial and error.   The leader finds it difficult to make himself understood when he talks to others about leadership.   The purposes of his work are often obscure to him and his techniques tend to be improvised from day to day.

Whether in business or government, in labor unions or hospitals, the leader of group endeavors today does not have the tools he needs for his demanding tasks. Most often his leadership is highly personal. It tends to be intuitive. The rules and axioms he follows are often a hardening of precedent and an updating of folklore rather than a logical statement of verifiable principles.

The remarkable fact is that few leaders in the world today, even those of great undertakings, have had formal, disciplined training in the work of leadership in the same sense that a physician is trained to practice medicine or a scientist to work in his specialty. Most heads of state, governors, company presidents and managing directors, and a majority of church, educational, and institutional leaders are experts in such things as politics, finance, preaching, teaching, selling, or investing. Few, however, are trained and expert in the work of leadership.

This is, perhaps, the most pressing challenge of our times. We need, as never before, a systematic and orderly understanding of leadership. As surely as there are universals in the other sciences of man, we need to discover the principles that will enable people in all kinds of endeavors to work more effectively together. Because the problems of leadership repeat themselves endlessly in their larger dimensions, from business enterprise to military to governmental undertakings, we should not find it necessary to repeat interminably our past experience and our past mistakes.

A scientific approach to leadership will enable us to capitalize upon the accumulated knowledge of the past, to learn from our common experience, and to build more effective techniques upon a foundation of logic.

THE NEED FOR A NEW LOOK AT LEADERSHIP

Leaders have been with us since history began and we have taken the institution so much for granted that we have rarely given it the same kind of analytical dissection we find necessary for the discovery of new knowledge in other fields. Since leaders are, by definition, authority figures, we tend to invest with signal importance almost any statement by a recognized leader with respect to leadership. Presumably the individual who builds a great nation, establishes a large business enterprise, or heads a sizable and complex undertaking has consciously mastered the techniques of leadership in the same way that a famous surgeon has become expert in surgery or a great engineer has learned to excel in engineering.

However, we have found that the parallel rarely holds. Most outstanding leaders have accomplished greatly because of what they are; their competence is intuitive and not learned; to emulate them often is to try to adopt a quirk of character or an ability that is highly singular and works only because of the unique kind of person the leader in question happens to be.

How can we learn about leadership? We propose that there is not much point in theorizing what a good leader should be and criticizing existing leaders because they are not what the theory says they should be. Far better to rely upon logic. By this we mean that our first need is to determine what we want to accomplish through the efforts of leaders, to study leadership as it is practiced, to determine what deficiencies exist and why they exist, and then to identify the specific methods, principles, and techniques that can be used to improve.

Since leadership is as broad as humanity, our question now is: Where shall we begin? What leaders shall we study to determine the purpose a leader should serve and what makes for effective leadership? A few minutes' thought will help to establish that if we are to focus upon the essentials, we should study a situation where demands made upon leaders are great, competition is keen, pressure for success is unrelenting, and weakness or failure is identified quickly and positively.

THE BUSINESS ENTERPRISE AS A MODEL

We can best satisfy these criteria if we use the business enterprise as a model. Long belabored, castigated, and looked upon with scorn, competitive enterprise provides the best testing ground for leadership and furnishes the most acceptable model for analysis. Rather surprisingly, before we complete our study we shall conclude that if leaders in politics and government, in education and religion, were as competent in accomplishing their purposes as those in business have proved to be in achieving their objectives, the progress of humanity in producing spiritual and moral wealth, the wealth of the mind, would more closely approximate the gigantic strides it has made in producing material wealth, the wealth of the flesh and of the appetite.

Business provides the harsh environment of reality which becomes the proving ground of nonmaterial values for those who must live in the real world. In business and industry, leadership is subjected to the merciless scrutiny of customers, stockholders, government agencies, and competition. Natural selection operates most freely. The fittest survive. Over the years, those enterprises that have advanced fastest in the stern competition of a free market have been foremost in developing and applying the skills and techniques of scientific leadership—

which is management. These are the companies that have learned how to manage their affairs most effectively. Ford Motor Company, Armco Steel, Standard Oil (N.J.), E. I. du Pont de Nemours, General Motors, Unilever, Philips Electric, Procter & Gamble, International Business Machines, American Telephone & Telegraph, General Electric, Sears, Roebuck, among others, stay at the top not because they are large, but they are large and successful because they have the most effective leadership.

THE ARGUMENT

As we discuss leadership, we shall try to determine what it is, how it *is* practiced, what is the most logical way it *should* be practiced, and how we can improve our current methods of leadership.

Seemingly we shall approach this backward, for we shall begin by examining not leaders, but followers. We shall find that the groups being led are the most important force in determining what kind of leadership can be successful. The needs of followers change as they work together in organized groups and these evolutionary changes *demand* corresponding changes in leadership. As we approach leadership from this point of view, many of the questions that have perplexed us in the past will begin to resolve themselves.

With this evolutionary pattern of group maturation as a background, we shall look at leaders. We shall establish that leadership is the work a person does to enable people to work most effectively together. The question that arises will be: Work for what? We work together to accomplish on earth what the great myths and most of the great religions would provide for us only in the hereafter: satisfaction with ourselves and with the world in which we find ourselves living.

Having disposed of this essentially philosophical question in the most material way possible, we shall look at the process of leadership. In this analysis we shall find that a most important characteristic of leadership is its dynamic quality. Leaders must change to meet the changing needs of their followers. To the present, much of the evolutionary changes that occur in leadership have been spontaneous and intuitive.

Here we shall tread new ground, for we shall identify a regular and predictable pattern of change in leadership. While this may seem strange at first glance, a moment's thought will help set the background.

The Pattern of Change

We know a great deal about biological changes in human beings. Many are regular and predictable, such as the progressive changes in nerve tissue as it grows and the development of the individual from a few undifferentiated cells to that most complex organism—the matured adult. We are beginning to discover also that there are regular and predictable changes in behavior, in culture, and perhaps even in history and religion.

Most important to our current study is the idea of biological evolution, the concept that living organisms undergo a continuous genetic adaptation to their environment, utilizing such integrating agencies as selection, hybridization, inbreeding, and mutation. The concept of evolution tells us that living things tend to change in order to adapt better to the requirements of the world in which they live.

Living things evolve in many ways. The largest tree was once a seed; every butterfly at one time was a caterpillar; each human was once a few cells and grew through the stages of undifferentiated notochord, gill clefts, and vestigial tail.

Such evolutionary changes as these are universals and can be predicted with certainty. Not so commonly recognized is the fact that there are regular behavioral changes in human beings which can also be predicted.

Every normal human being, for example, tends to make an increasingly efficient adaptation to his environment as he grows and matures from childhood to adolescence to maturity. We can predict with assurance many characteristics of the child from four to six, the adolescent from twelve to fourteen, and the mature adult.[1]

There is also an evolutionary development of total cultures or civilizations. Egypt, Rome, Greece, the Aztecs and Incas of Central and South America, the Khmers of Indo-China, and a great number of other civilizations have had their time of infancy, their maturity, and their deterioration. What causes these progressive changes has long been the subject of speculation and analysis. Historical, anthropological, biological, and social reasons have been presented. We find now that progressive changes in leadership occur and that these significantly affect the survival and success of the group being led, be it large or small.

Evolution of the Business Enterprise

In our studies we have found that the evolutionary development of organized business groups is very characteristic. Some companies evolve successfully and are long-lived, with many productive years in their time of maturity. They have survived the vagaries of the market and the challenge of competition in good times and in bad, in war and in peace. Other organized undertakings die early. Where are such

---

[1] See especially the outstanding work done by the Gesell Institute of Child Development. A good popular treatment is Frances L. Ilg and Louise B. Ames, *Child Behavior,* Dell Publishing Co., Inc., New York, 1955.

former giants as the Central Leather Co., American News, Hupmobile, International Mercantile Marine, and a thousand others? Some have faded; others have merged to find support; still others have disappeared. Of the twenty largest companies in the United States forty years ago, only two are still among the first twenty in size. Of the one hundred largest companies in the United States twenty-five years ago, almost half have disappeared or have declined substantially from their peak.

Commonly, we consider each such organized group and its life cycle an individual phenomenon. But our research has led us to conclude that there are universals in the way groups grow and die. We can now identify a predictable pattern of growth in the organized endeavor, much of it influenced by its leadership. Looking again to the business enterprise as a model, we find that, as is true with human beings, each company *is* unique, but all have their similarities. Our task is to find the common pattern.

The Importance of Understanding

There is a fascination in the study of the life of an organization. Like an individual, it has its drama, its frustrations, its triumphs. Inevitably, it faces its crisis and either meets the challenge successfully or fades to mediocrity or failure. Consider Fruehauf Trailer Company, largest manufacturer of trailers in the United States. Under the dynamic impetus of a strongly sales-oriented president, the company boomed its sales by almost 75 per cent from 1954 to 1956. Anticipating continuation of the upsurge, the company built an inventory large enough to meet its anticipated volume. Sales fell short of the target, a recession set in, and the glowing profit picture dimmed to a deficit.

Here, the leader who had invested his career in the organization he had built found his efforts endangered, his leadership in question. The security and income of hundreds of families were threatened. Several of the banks and insurance companies that had loaned the company money began to close in to safeguard the funds of *their* investors. In 1958, a new chief executive assumed command. Now what happened? The recovery of Fruehauf is a story more graphic than that found in most novels and it repeats itself almost daily on the stage of world business.

But reporting the drama of business is not enough. More important is analysis and interpretation of what has happened in an attempt to find the universals that prevail. Our knowledge that the Fruehauf story is a repetition of a theme found also in General Motors, Du Pont, International Business Machines, Goodyear, and hundreds of others highlights the importance of identifying and stating the principles involved so that other companies can anticipate and prepare for their crisis before it occurs.

If we can do this, we should be able to identify the leadership reasons why Montgomery Ward, the great mail-order house, outgrew Sewell Avery, its highly capable chief executive.   Avery desired above all else that the great enterprise he founded should continue to prosper, but he, in effect, became the unwitting obstacle to its further progress.

If we can identify the requirements of this evolution of leadership, we should be able to determine why the Underwood Corporation, once the king of typewriter manufacturers, sold out to Olivetti; why S. W. Kress & Co., the retail chain, failed to realize its true potential; and why other companies beyond counting failed because they outgrew a leadership that did not change.

This would help us better understand, on the world stage, why Russia outgrew the leadership of Stalin; why mainland China requires its Mao Tse-tung; and why each of the emerging African nations will need its dictator before it can become a democracy, for the same logical reasons that autocracy ruled in England before democracy became tolerable to the people and their rulers.

Leaders to Managers

We shall establish that there is an infancy, an adolescence, and a maturity of leadership.   We shall identify the immature leader as a *natural leader* and shall trace his place and his impact upon the group he leads.   As organized endeavors grow, we shall find, a different type of leadership is required.   Upon the basis of logical analysis we shall describe the necessary characteristics of this new type of leader, and we shall identify management leadership as the work of the leader who leads in a conscious, disciplined, and most effective manner.   We shall also point to the reasons why it would be well for management to become a profession.

Upon this foundation we shall construct a logical structure of leadership theory, centering it upon the work a manager performs in leading. We shall identify four functions and nineteen activities of management, establish a body of principles and a variety of concepts, define several hundred management words, outline a unified concept of management that applies to all types of undertakings, and in general, attempt to provide in organized and classified form a systematic statement of what management is and how it can be practiced in a professional manner.

These conclusions will be stated as universals.   For this reason, only the broad framework will be outlined and in such manner that the concepts, principles, and vocabulary will apply to business, government, military, institutional, and other types of organized endeavors. Details of technique and the mechanics of management will be omitted for fear of obscuring or confusing the large outline which must first be developed.

All of this, quite clearly, would be of small value if it were based completely on theory or were only personal opinion. We have been able to establish the validity of these conclusions by personal presentation to well over 12,500 practicing managers from business, government, and institutions. This number has included some 1,100 presidents, managing directors, and board chairmen. The presentations have been made to groups in the United States, Canada, Great Britain, France, West Germany, Italy, Japan, India, Hong Kong, the Philippines, Indonesia, Australia, and Africa.

This experience has amply confirmed the universal nature of these concepts and principles. Further endorsement is found in the adoption of the principles and the vocabulary of professional management which are here defined by a growing number of businesses and other enterprises in many different countries.

The identification of an additional activity of management, the development of additional concepts and principles, and further definition of management terms have been completed and are now being validated. Research on the evolutionary pattern of group development is well under way. As these new findings are confirmed, they will be made part of new editions of this volume.

Points of View

In this approach there are varying points of view to be reconciled. Many different disciplines are concerned with leadership, management, organization, and people. Unfortunately, each tends to adopt its own insular viewpoint and ignores or condemns all who do not agree or who see it from another perspective. Keeping in mind that facts tend to differ depending upon the point of view from which they are observed, we have attempted to make a full circle, carefully studying and assessing the ideas and conclusions of behaviorists, psychologists, psychiatrists, anthropologists, and sociologists. We have evaluated and updated the classical concepts which still are valid and important, and we have analyzed decision theory, information theory, the theory of rationality, and others that are relevant.

Our conclusion is that much is to be learned from each of the major fields of related interest. Looking at the total accumulation of knowledge from the practical viewpoint of "How can this be used to help a leader work more effectively with his followers?" we have developed what we hope is a logical and understandable synthesis that will provide a practical guide to managers who must put this information to work and to students who need to differentiate between what is useful in real life and what is not.

Before we proceed, we should now point out that in our analysis of management we shall have to piece together many seemingly unrelated parts of a puzzle which will be visible as an integrated whole only after it is finished. Of our readers we ask patience as the puzzle unravels, in the certainty that there will be an end entire because we have already constructed it.

SUMMARY

Leadership is an activity that has been practiced since the beginning of history; however, we still know very little about it.

This study has been designed to determine what makes for effective leadership and to identify the concepts, principles, and techniques of leadership as practiced in the most successful organizations. The business enterprise has been selected as a model for study because of the great stresses placed upon leadership in a competitive situation and the pragmatic nature of the results that would be obtained.

CHAPTER 2

The Evolution of Groups

Everything is in a state of change. Thou, thyself, art in everlasting change, and in corruption to correspond; so is the whole universe. MARCUS AURELIUS

Change is a universal. People and things tend to change with time. Some changes proceed in terms of basic forces and laws such as the rotation of the earth, the growth of a plant and of a human being. Other changes occur haphazardly. If we can identify a series of changes that occurs repeatedly and in much the same manner for any natural phenomenon, it enables us better to study and to work with that occurrence.

In this chapter we shall discuss the changes that occur when people working together as a group modify their own behavior so that they can improve their chances of benefiting more personally from the group effort. Perhaps you went back to read the preceding sentence for a second time to be sure you understood its true meaning, but what we want to show is that each of us has as his purpose in life to secure the greatest personal satisfaction from the world in which he lives. We shall show that much of our potential for personal satisfaction comes from our ability to work with others. We must feel that we can do better for ourselves as a member of a group than we can by going it alone; otherwise we remain a member of that group only through pressure. It follows that each of us will be willing to subordinate his personal desires to the needs of others to the extent we feel we gain more for ourselves thereby.

Groups evolve. When people work together in groups, the group takes on a character and a personality of its own, much as if it were an individual. When a group persists as an organized entity, it tends to grow in much the same fashion as an individual human being. Each group, if it survives and continues in its development, will have its infancy, adolescence, and maturity.

It is provocative to consider that the giant Metropolitan Insurance Company was once in its infancy and showed all the symptoms thereof; Russia is now entering its adolescence; and the United States is adolescent but not yet matured as an organized group.

WHY DO GROUPS EXIST?

Before we attempt to identify the evolutionary pattern of change in groups, we must answer some basic questions. First we want to know why people work together in groups. Why do groups exist?

To find the answer, let us begin with the largest perspective. Visualize with us the world spinning majestically in space, the blackness of its turning surface brightened by the great fires of the sun. Some three billions of human beings move purposefully on its continents and seas. Come closer and follow one of these people. You will find that he works at many and diverse tasks all of his days. He is endlessly industrious, putting forth mental and physical effort to create and produce wealth both tangible and intangible.

This man works because he is hungry. He is hungry for many things—for food, shelter, and material goods, for luxuries and baubles that satisfy, educate, amuse, and entertain him. He is hungry for companionship and admiration, for knowledge and achievement. He is hungry in his body and in his spirit. He works to satisfy these varied needs.

By himself, one of these human creatures can accomplish little; therefore he learns to join his puny efforts with the complementary strengths and skills of other people who want similar things. In their hundreds and thousands, working together, men achieve greatly.

The Unnatural Necessity. These teeming human beings are gregarious, but they are gregarious for a reason.

People join together in groups because they realize that *the pooled efforts of many will produce greater returns for each than the uncoordinated efforts of individuals.* To illustrate, let us look at a group of people organized to work together for some common objective, as seen in Figure 2-1.

Here we have six people. They are farming, manufacturing, selling, teaching, or working together in some other way toward some goal they hold in common. The cement that holds the members of the group together is the conviction that participation in the team effort holds promise of greater personal reward than working as individuals. To the extent that an individual member of the group sees promise of sharing from the total output, *he will be willing to make concessions to maximize the effectiveness of the group.*   To the extent that he fails to see that there is something in it for him, his interest and support will tend to diminish.

Not to belabor the point, at first each individual is interested primarily in his own goals, not the objectives of others.   People work most willingly and productively *for what others want* when they see a satisfactory return for themselves from the group efforts.   Groups, then, exist to provide a framework within which individuals can contribute to common effort in the expectation of securing more from the total of what is produced than they could accomplish by themselves.

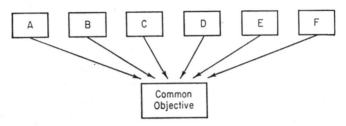

FIG. 2-1. A group working toward a common objective.

WHY DO GROUPS CHANGE?

Evolution is not blind; as is true of everything else in this ordered universe, evolution has its purposes.   Our failure to recognize or understand the purpose does not mean that there is none.   We have concluded that the purpose of the evolution of a group of human beings is *to provide for the optimum personal satisfaction of the largest number of the members of the group.*

As members of a group, we do everything we can to make it change so that we can get the greatest possible personal satisfaction from our membership in the group.   Groups change because members of the groups want more of what the group provides.   The greater the disparity and the stronger the need, the greater the pressure for change.

THE PRINCIPLE[1] OF GROUP EVOLUTION

Dynamic disequilibrium leading to change will tend to exist within an organized group until personal satisfaction is enjoyed by the largest possible number of members of the group.

---

[1] We define a principle as a fundamental truth that will tend to apply in new situations in much the same way as it has applied in situations already observed. A principle does not tell us what we "should" do.   Too many management principles are simply admonitions.   A principle should state, so far as possible, a logical cause and result.   It tells us that if we do something, we can reasonably expect something specifically identified to happen.   Drop a stone, it tends to fall *down.*   Put a person in a management position, he tends to operate, not manage.

The human tendency to work to secure greatest satisfaction from group participation is a universal which has major implications for the proper understanding of the leadership of groups.   The optimum satisfaction of each member of the group is achieved when each person can make fullest and most rewarding use of his mental and physical capabilities.   By *fullest* we mean that each person in the group can develop and use his capacities to the limit of their potential; by *most rewarding* we mean that the individual secures what he considers to be a fair and appropriate share of the total returns available to the group.   *Physical capabilities* refer to inborn physical aptitudes.   *Mental capabilities* are still largely unknown; they include intellectual qualities and those we ordinarily identify as moral and spiritual, which are a function of the mind as contrasted to the body.

WHAT CHARACTERIZES THE EVOLUTION OF GROUPS?

In studying the progressive changes that occur within groups, knowledge of two characteristics will help us better understand what is happening.

Incremental Nature

First, the evolutionary change of groups tends to be *incremental*. The group advances in terms of the way its individual members react, but the group as a whole can store the experience of its members and make this accumulated knowledge available to new members in the form of tradition, policy, and precedent.   The group literally creates its own culture.   It can build upon the accumulated knowledge and experience of the past, and, so long as it retains its integrity, can benefit from it.

Reversibility

The second characteristic in group evolution is its *reversibility*.   A group may reach a stage of stability and maturation and then, because of internal or external forces, it may regress and lose what it has accomplished.

The Martin Company, a leading aerospace corporation, well illustrates these points.   Started in 1909 by the pioneering Glenn L. Martin, the company specialized in military aircraft and its fortunes and personnel gyrated with widely fluctuating demand.   By the 1950s, Martin had shrunk substantially from its wartime peak.   A steady loss in personnel brought great stresses to the organization.   The pattern of evolutionary change was disrupted.   This instability spread to its top management and was corrected only with the introduction of a new, strong, and capable chief executive.

Almost literally, the Martin Company now started over as an organized group.   However, it had great resources of know-how, tradition, and experience to draw upon and, with perceptive leadership, was able to resume its progress and reach new levels of accomplishment.

Is this unique?   Again we point out that it is not.   Recently the same pattern has been graphically portrayed by, among others, Ampex Corp., General Dynamics Corp., Philco Corp., and Chrysler Corp.

WHAT FORCES INFLUENCE GROUP CHANGES?

As we study the way a business enterprise or any organized endeavor grows, we find that a number of forces are operative in bringing about changes in the needs of the group, and particularly in its requirements with respect to leadership.   A basic point is that changes will occur within the group as its members discover that they cannot have perfect freedom and still operate effectively as members of the group. As human beings we tend to want perfect liberty for ourselves, but perfect liberty does not exist in organized endeavors.

THE CONCEPT[2] OF LIMITS OF FREEDOM

When a normal group begins to operate, we know that each member tends to be concerned primarily with accomplishing what *he* wants, in doing things *his* way, in satisfying *his* physical and emotional hungers. *Each* wants complete personal freedom.   But each cannot have complete freedom without overstepping the rights of others and thus lessening *their* freedom.

The more license the individual assumes to overstep the boundaries of another's freedom of choice or action, the less the freedom that exists for all.   Since those who assume greater freedom tend to be numerically fewer than those whose freedom is infringed, their positions are in jeopardy.   Inevitably, countervailing forces build up.   Others seize the freedom they want, and, again, at the expense of the whole.   This disequilibrium will exist without end unless a means is found to secure an acceptable balance of freedom for the individual within the limits of subordination necessary to secure the greatest freedom for each member of the group.   The conclusion is plain: *to have the most freedom, we must lose some of it.*   But each individual has a deep, organic need for personal freedom.   He will resist giving up any part of it *unless he sees*

---

[2] We have developed a group of *management ideas* which we feel cannot be regarded yet as universal or fundamental truths but which should be stated systematically so that they can be understood and taught in uniform terms.   We have introduced the term *management concept* to be used as the appropriate semantic label.   We define a management concept as *a general idea in management stated in a formalized manner so that it can be communicated in a standardized fashion.*

clearly that he stands to gain more by losing some part of his freedom than by retaining it.

What may we now conclude? That each of us must be limited in his freedom. We will accept these limits willingly and support the nominal subjugation to the extent that we feel emotionally and know logically that our partial servitude is to our own eventual benefit, that our concessions to the needs of the larger group ensure the greatest possible personal freedom. The question is not: Shall we be slave or shall we be free? Every man has his own slavery and his own freedom. Some limits he creates himself; some are thrust upon him. The real problem is: How can we learn to work most effectively with others to provide for both our material and emotional needs while yet preserving the *greatest degree* of personal freedom? This is the true dichotomy— the contradiction in our human estate. How shall we work collectively, yet preserve personal freedom? The answer, and how we arrive at it, also is critical. Give too much freedom and the group becomes a rabble; hold the reins too tightly and its members become restive, unhappy, and eventually rebellious.

Statement of the Concept of Limits of Freedom

Freedom of action needs to be limited to the extent that the liberty of the individual to act does not encroach upon the rights of others.

Freedom can continue only in the presence of restriction. Freedom does not simply exist; it must be created. It does not continue as a natural condition; it must be cultivated, pruned, and tended. The important requirement is not to want freedom; the wanting of it is as persistent as life itself; vital, rather, is to know how to discipline ourselves to enjoy it and to educate ourselves and others to share it.

Central as is this problem to the successful maturation of every group, it is surprising that so little attention has been devoted to it. Our common tendency is to bewail the lack of freedom as an arbitrary infringement of human rights and not to analyze it to see why it occurs and how it can be corrected. Finding the answer is part of the puzzle we shall attempt to put together.

THE CONCEPT OF UNEQUAL SATISFACTIONS

We have seen that each individual wants the most of what he can get from the group effort, yet each must also accept limits to his freedom if he is to be an effective member of the group. If we postulate that a group will stabilize when each of its members enjoys optimum personal satisfaction, we can assume that group change, as is true of everything else, will tend to be continuous, for human satisfaction is the most transitory of things.

In general, the satisfactions people derive from membership in a group tend to vary widely and to change quickly. Two or more members will rarely find equal satisfaction from their participation. At any given time, when dissatisfactions prevail among the members of the group which are stronger than the level of satisfaction, dynamic disequilibrium will exist which will tend to stimulate change. The greater the level of dissatisfaction, the greater the pressure for change.

What forces tend to cause this imbalance or disequilibrium? We find that they may be internal, external, or a combination of both. When internal, a high level of general dissatisfaction may prevail because of competition among the members of the group to monopolize the inadequate sources of satisfaction that are available. For example, much good work may be done; only a few receive recognition, yet everybody wants it. This dissatisfaction arises also when the members see that most of the rewards, both psychological and material, go to the top leadership.

A high level of dissatisfaction may arise when the members of a group see that their peers in the same or other groups fare better. Dissatisfaction with compensation, for example, tends to become most acute when we know that somebody else is getting more than we are for doing the same work. If other people have a better house, a better automobile, or a more important title and yet occupy a similar group position, we tend to become dissatisfied.

For this reason we find that one of the most important causes of unrest in the world today is too-effective communication. In the undeveloped nations, particularly, people are learning quickly through radio, newspapers, and other media of the advantages enjoyed by the more advanced countries. People who think that everybody is hungry, diseased, and poorly housed may bewail their fate, but they tend to accept the condition as a necessary evil. Once they learn that good food, proper housing, and comfort are enjoyed by a segment of the world's population, the underprivileged become dissatisfied.

Statement of the Concept
of Unequal Satisfactions

The greater the difference in satisfactions derived by individuals from membership in a group, and the better the understanding of this disparity, the greater the tendency toward dissatisfaction with the existing condition.

From this it is clear that unequal satisfaction from group effort is a constant prod to changes in the group. We can conclude that pressure for change is a normal condition in any group. We can reasonably assume at all times that one or more of the members will want to change something to secure greater satisfaction. The problem is not how to eliminate this desire for change, for herein we have at the same time the greatest dynamic force for improvement. What we must do, rather, is learn how to integrate, guide, and channel this pressure so that the changes which inevitably will result contribute to the end purposes of the group as a whole. What we are saying is that changes are going to occur in any group; we must know how to make them constructive changes.

EVOLUTION—NATURAL OR CONSCIOUS?

Evolutionary change tends to be selective in character. Those organizational forms persist which best adapt to their environment. Those which cannot adapt successfully tend to be eliminated.

The forces that encourage the deterioration or dissolution of the group are many and varied. The existence of the group, then, obviously depends upon its ability to maintain both its identity and its integrity. Here we find that the ability of a group to survive and succeed in a competitive situation depends first upon its ability to develop internal cohesiveness so that it can act as a unified whole, second upon its ability to adapt to the environment more successfully than competing groups. Thus the first challenge is internal. To the extent that it is unified internally, the group is most successful in competition with external groups. The second challenge is external. To the extent that the group can adapt more successfully than competing organizational forms, it will tend to dominate and persist.

Selection of the organizational forms that persist may be by a predominant process of either natural selection or conscious selection. The process of natural selection is not consciously undertaken; selection is made by forces outside the command of the individual or of the group.

The brontosaurus, for example, evolved in response to the forces exerted upon it by its environment. Literally, it was commanded *by* its environment; it did not command its environment. To a substantial extent this has been true of human evolution. Men have reacted to the forces and challenges thrust upon them. Acting intuitively and naturally, human individuals and groups have survived because they adapted successfully to changing climate, to conquest, and to a host of other forces.

In surveying the tangled skeins of history, it is sometimes difficult to trace the pattern of evolutionary change. But as we understand the forces at work, we learn to identify the significant threads and to follow them through the conflicting welter of related events.

Up to the present we can see that most evolution has been natural;

that is, living forms and organized groups have become what their environment made of them.   Laws have been operative in commanding these changes which we do not yet fully understand.   An analogy would be the operation of the law of gravity in the physical world. For all of history men have watched things fall *down* and have been able to make them reverse their direction only by limited and intuitive reaction to the needs of their environment.   In terms of the long perspective of time, only yesterday have we learned to understand the forces at work and to command them because we understood them.   As a result, we can direct space vehicles to the moon and beyond to the realms of space.

But success lies in the hands of knowledge.   We have learned that a group can consciously command its environment when its members study, analyze, and identify the factors critical to both its own operation and the operation of competing groups and by selective emulation of those attributes which most largely contribute to competitive survival and success.   There is another kind of evolution which is *unnatural* and *unhuman* but in which lies the hope of the future for that animal who can think consciously—man.

THE PRINCIPLE OF CONSCIOUS SELECTION[3]

Those organizational forms will tend to dominate which can best select and adapt to their own use the most successful characteristics of their own and competing forms.

By this principle we identify conscious selection as a universal—a constant tendency which must be considered for all groups.   Survival need not be fortuitous; it may be conscious.   The process of conscious selection can be operative only in an organization whose members are *knowing* enough to be selective.   It is a sign of organizational maturity. A child is governed by its emotions and can command its own behavior only after it has learned to make a conscious choice from alternative paths of action.   This is true no matter how much the child knows. The precocious genius who has memorized the textbook still must learn to apply this knowledge.

Most adults react in the same emotional fashion as the child.   As we survey the growth, development, and evolution of the human being, we can see that, for all of us, relatively little of the *learning* and *willingness* to undertake self-discipline which are characteristic of true maturity have yet been accomplished.   We tend to look with great respect upon

---

[3] The Principle of Conscious Selection was first stated by the author in "A Unified Theory of Administration," a paper presented at an Interdisciplinary Seminar on Administrative Theory, The University of Texas, 1961.

the individual who has accomplished any substantial measure of self-discipline for himself.

Organizations face similar alternatives. Most organizations today are in the primary phase of evolution by natural selection. Virtually all of our prominent business enterprises and group undertakings of other types that have survived and grown successfully have, literally, blundered into maturity. Very few top executives can point with logic to the critical factors that have made for the continuing success of their own enterprises. Relatively few organizations have made a conscious choice of the characteristics of competing organizations superior to their own and thus have been enabled to progress upon the basis of a *continued conscious selection of superior evolutionary forms.*

In general, it would seem that the more direct and clearly understood the competitive challenge or threat, the greater the tendency to evolve organizational forms to meet it, provided there is the will and the ability to make the changes required. Also, the smaller the unit required to change, the faster the change occurs.

On every side we find organized groups that are, literally, ripe for maturity and, in some cases, that have all the essentials for continued dominance in their field. We can say with great confidence, however, that they will face a crisis because they cannot or will not change consciously to meet their internal and external needs for adaptation.

Typical is a leading small electronics firm. Founded by an outstanding engineer with great sales abilities, the company has competed fiercely and successfully in one of the most difficult of all industries. An innovator and inspiring leader of unique character, the president has built his company into a lengthened shadow of himself. Because he is outstanding, capable, and tremendously vigorous, so also is the monolithic organization he has arranged behind him.

Virtually all authority is vested in the president and literally flows from him to each person in the organization who makes decisions of any kind. When the top man wants action, he jumps as many organizational levels as necessary to get the job done. He encourages lower-level managers to maintain direct contact with him on the assignments that are thus set up.

Two days each week are plant visiting days, during which the top executive goes into every nook and cranny of the company's main plant, inspecting, correcting, advising, and chatting with the operating people, many of whom he has known since their earliest days with the company. He maintains the friendliest personal relationships with employees and they look forward to his visits with personal satisfaction. It gives them a direct line to the top executive and they get great emotional satisfaction from this.

In terms of our analysis, it is clear that the company has established a high degree of cohesion, primarily because of the unique abilities of its president.   Grown large, it hangs together and is effective because of the one man at the top.   Intermediate levels of managers become more frustrated and discouraged as the internal friction intensifies.   When the top man dies or the enterprise grows so large that he can no longer command all of its parts, the time of crisis will begin.

The example is merely illustrative.   We have thousands of enterprises in which the evolutionary process of group maturation is held up at the most critical point.

The reasons for this are clear.   Most important is the fact that, up to this writing, we have not known what is involved in organizational maturation, and the *leaders of immature groups have not known what their problem was or how to solve it.*   If we look to Woodrow Wilson, Henry Ford the elder, Thomas Watson, Sr., we see splendid, outstanding people who accomplished greatly but who did not know how to carry on beyond a certain point of achievement.   And this deficiency was a lack of understanding about the requirements of leadership.

To resume our analysis, we find that this process of evolution is operative in the case of individuals, societies, and organizational groups. The individual develops *naturally,* that is, by reaction to external and internal stimuli, until he adjusts internally to the point where he can select consciously improved characteristics developed by himself and others.   The individual who has not adjusted within himself finds it difficult to adjust to external forces.

These processes hold true for organizational groups within each society.   Both business enterprises and institutions tend to develop in terms of natural selection.   Companies grow fortuitously under the leadership of one or a few dominant individuals.   Maximum satisfaction is received by the smallest number.   The environment selects the businesses or institutions that will survive.   Here again the greater the internal cohesiveness, the stronger and better understood its objectives, the greater the chance of survival.

Eventually, one company learns how to make conscious selection of its own characteristics and those of competing companies which give best promise of enabling it to achieve its goals.   The company which consciously selects and adopts for its own use these superior characteristics inevitably forges ahead.

On our admittedly limited sample of business enterprises, a pattern of conscious selection has been shown in the transition of, among others, Ford Motor Company, Armco Steel Corporation, General Motors, E. I. du Pont de Nemours & Co., Standard Oil (N.J.), Shell Oil, A.T.&T., Standard Pressed Steel, International Business Machines, General Electric, and Cincinnati Milling Machine Company. We repeat that these companies are leaders because they selected, and consciously followed, those attributes necessary for dominance. We can prognosticate that they will remain at or near the top so long as success does not undermine and dissipate what has been so splendidly accomplished. Close study of the evolutionary development of these groups will provide many worthwhile lessons for any governmental body, institution, or business endeavor.

The Evolutionary Sequence

In our studies we have identified two stages of group evolution: (1) the *centric* stage—the immature stage or infancy of the group. This is followed by a transition to the next stage, (2) the *radic* stage—the stage of maturity.

There is a consistent pattern in this change, but it is easy to lose sight of the total outline because of the variability of the individuals comprising the group. Since individuals are different in background, education, training, and other qualities, they tend to react differently. Since each person has more or less freedom to leave the group, its make-up may alter, with further blurring of the evolutionary changes taking place. The younger the group, the greater the tendency toward this variability and the more difficult it is to identify the pattern of change.

We shall now examine the stages of group evolution in detail, noting in each case that there are logical reasons for each stage and logical need for change. We shall begin with the first stage—the group in its early years, the immature stage which we identify as the centric group.

SUMMARY

A group of people working together for some common purpose tends to assume a personality of its own. The group will change progressively or evolve to adapt better to the environment in which it functions. The primary purpose of group change is to enable each member of the group to get the most he can for himself from being a member of the group. Changes in groups are both incremental and reversible. Changes occur in response to the desire of each member to have as much freedom as possible for himself and the need to set limits to his freedom so that the individual will not encroach upon the rights of others. Group change can be natural or spontaneous, the historical pattern, or conscious and planned. The Principle of Conscious Selection is stated to show that "those organizational forms will tend to dominate which can best select and adapt to their own use the most successful characteristics of their own and competing forms."

CHAPTER 3

The Immature Stage—The Centric Group

> *Of the five vices, the vice of the mind is the worst. What is the vice of the mind? The vice of the mind is self-satisfaction.* CHUANG-TSE

AN EXAMPLE OF GROUP EVOLUTION

Let us begin by examining one of the most successful and best-matured group enterprises in the world, one that has grown through the trying periods of childhood and adolescence and now exhibits many of the characteristics of maturity—Standard Oil Co. (N.J.).

In Standard Oil (N.J.), one of the largest, most profitable, and most competitive of business enterprises, we can see much of the pattern of group development as it applies not only to business, but also to governmental, institutional, and other groups.

Standard Oil (N.J.) had its genesis in the 1860s in a tiny three-man firm consisting of Samuel Andrews, M. B. Clark, and John D. Rockefeller. Under the leadership of Rockefeller, the small firm prospered largely because of its ability to attend single-mindedly to its own interests. Concentrating on its own needs, the budding Standard Oil Company fought and overwhelmed its competitors. Rising rapidly to become the chief factor in the new oil industry, the company weathered boom and depression through the ability of its leaders to establish a hard, lean, and efficient organization.

Formally organized as The Standard Oil Company in 1870, the fledgling enterprise set out to conquer its particular world with as much confidence in its right to do so as inspired Alexander the Great, the Crusaders, or Mohammed II.

Succeeding through rigorous internal discipline and a hard, unrelenting, and calculated attack, The Standard Oil Company overwhelmed competitors as zealously as many of the religious bodies of the world

24

have ever sought to eliminate one another or nations to conquer others for fortune and glory.

Frequently held up to criticism because of its methods of attaining and holding its leadership, The Standard Oil Company simply did what all young, immature groups try to do as earnestly as they can. The primary reason this company has received particular censure is that its overwhelming success made it a conspicuous target.

In an attempt to understand and not to defend or condemn, we should establish that in the United States during the mid-1800s little restraining force was exercised and competition was both almost completely free and also completely unrestricted. As Charles H. Van Hise said, "Unrestrained competition as an economic principle is too destructive to be permitted to exist."[1]

In analyzing what occurred from a leadership standpoint, we find that the Principle of Leadership Force, which shall be introduced shortly, was operative. The United States as a nation needed as firm and effective controls over its constituent units as The Standard Oil Company exercised, as an individual enterprise, over its own internal operations. This disequilibrium, as we might anticipate, led to dissatisfaction on the part of the public at large. Controls were elaborated, not only against this one company, but as part of the overall effort of the nation to exercise the proper degree of leadership force. The United States government brought suit to dissolve The Standard Oil Company under the Sherman Act. The act was an implement that was developed for this type of internal control in the same fashion that a business enterprise develops internal policies.

In the final decision handed down by the Supreme Court in 1911, the court upheld that the Sherman Act was designed to prevent "undue restraints of every kind and nature" and that The Standard Oil Company had been able to "drive others from the field and exclude them from their right to trade . . ." primarily through its "genius for commercial development and organization." The Court ruled that the company in its existing form was to be dissolved.

Analogies here, in light of our concept of group evolution, are fascinating. In its early years, The Standard Oil Company is an excellent example of what we shall call a centric group. But here, also, is the father of the family exercising parental control over the children. Here also is the early Christian church disciplining its member units, the rebellion against leadership force, the schisms and separations. Here is the South in rebellion against the Federal Government of the United States, Britain against Imperial Rome, and a thousand other

[1] In his *Concentration and Control,* brochure, University of Wisconsin, Madison, 1912.

manifestations of groups in evolution.   Seen in the near perspective of
our own short life span, these events seem gigantic, sufficient to shape
the course of history in themselves.   Viewed against the long perspective of time, their relative importance in terms of this evolutionary process is no more significant than the incidental rebellion of the child
against parental authority as it grows from infancy to maturity.

If written records survive, the more perceptive and matured human
beings that people the earth in another hundred thousand years will see
these cataclysms in their true proportion and will wonder that we in the
twentieth century who are so forward in our technical wisdom should be
so unknowing in our understanding of how to live together peacefully
and productively.

As you read this, you perhaps may say: but this has far broader
application than to business alone.   It refers to me and to my family,
to education and government, to religion and society and any other kind
of organized endeavor.   True enough.   As we have developed these
conclusions, provocative indeed have been their implications.   We shall
investigate some of these shortly.

This somewhat philosophical digression did seem necessary at this
point.   Now that we have made it, let us examine groups made up of
human beings when these groups are in their young, immature stage of
growth.   We shall make our analysis primarily in terms of business
enterprises, and in so doing we shall find that companies tend to begin
as centric groups and evolve, through a transition, to become radic
groups.

THE CENTRIC GROUP

During the early, formative growth period of the group the concern
of its individual members centers primarily in their own personal interests and requirements, with the needs of other members of the group
as a whole subordinated.   Hence our derivation of the term *centric,*
which connotes the tendency of the members of the group to center their
concern in themselves.

We define a centric group as *a group in which the general level of
personal concern tends to be greater than the general level of group
concern.*   By *personal concern* here we mean concern with needs and
interests centered in ourselves; by *group concern* we mean a concern
which takes into consideration the needs and interests of all, or almost
all, of the other members of the group and of the group as a whole.

IMMATURITY THE TYPICAL CONDITION

From this definition it will be obvious that centric groups are most
prevalent.   The centric group is the *natural* group; this is the way peo-

ple working together tend to behave when they react primarily in terms of their innate, intuitive reactions to working with other people. To adopt the alternative of thinking first of the group as a whole, and then of ourselves, is, in a real sense, as contrary to our instinctive tendencies as turning the other cheek, or regarding our neighbors with as much consideration as we regard ourselves. This latter must be *learned*. It requires self-discipline.

CHARACTERISTICS OF THE CENTRIC GROUP

The most important characteristic of the centric group is that which we have already noted: the primacy of personal concern. We shall examine this more closely and also several other significant features found during this early stage of development of the group.

Primacy of Personal Concern

As we have noted, during the early stage of immaturity, the members of a young, newly formed group, whatever their education, experience, or background, *tend to put their personal and private interests ahead of those of the group*. This may be modified by internal motivation, outside pressures, or the ability of the leader, but the tendency is present and must be anticipated.

The reason this happens, we believe, is because of the natural and human inclination of individuals, and groups made up of individuals, to think *emotionally* rather than *logically*. This emotional reaction is spontaneous and intuitive. Both the individual and the group must learn to understand and put the needs of the group ahead of their own. The first stage in group evolution *tends to be by natural, not conscious, selection*.

As we study the centric group, we find that people in leadership positions tend to be self-centered. They reserve most authority and are primarily concerned with doing what they like. Rarely do they attempt to share with others on their team their knowledge of larger affairs to which only they are privy, or of their understanding of over-all problems or accomplishments. At this early stage, individuals and units in a staff relationship to one another are commonly regarded with suspicion, are dealt with at arm's length, and are often fought down in a series of running skirmishes.

Effect of Primacy of Personal Interests. What happens within the group because of this primacy of personal interests? We can see, first, a *lack of accountability*. One individual in the entire business enterprise, for example, is accountable for total end results—the chief executive. At lower levels, there is a failure in accountability because the chief executive cannot delegate the authority necessary to make accountability effective.

This lack of accountability tends to result in *lack of control*.   In the small, young business enterprise, people in leadership positions below the top tend to commandeer whatever authority they exercise.   Because there is little certainty as to who should make a specific decision, there is little possibility of holding one person accountable for mistakes and deficiencies.

Another result of this primacy of personal interests is *lack of coordination*.   The company is not a smooth, unified, functioning whole; rather, it is a centralized brain with rather haphazardly grown appendages, many of which do not operate with consistency or coordination so far as the needs of the whole are concerned.

In a manufacturing enterprise, we discover, this lack of coordination most often shows in failure to match sales demand with production volume, and in continuing and serious shortages and overages of finished goods inventory.   In service establishments, the most common symptom is failure to make enough trained people available to handle increased volume as business expands; if business falls off, lack of coordination shows in the abrupt decimation of employee ranks.

A further symptom is *lack of satisfaction*.   During this immature stage, the largest satisfactions and rewards go to a few at the top. There are rarely enough psychological rewards left to generate real interest and a sense of accomplishment at lower levels.

The dissatisfaction that arises is generally shown first at middle levels of the organization.   Frustrated and unhappy in their attempts to find a meaningful place for themselves and thwarted by the consolidation of authority at the top, some of the best leaders in subordinate positions tend to leave the group.

These symptoms of unrest generally mark a terminal point in the immature stage of the group.   The psychological dissatisfaction tends to increase because of the operation of the Principle of Resistance to Change[2] at the very top.   No longer in understanding contact with the realities of the operating levels and emotionally bound to the accomplishments of the past, there is a human tendency for the top-level leadership to combat with vigor all attempts to alter the eminently satisfying *status quo*.   Large conformance and small liberty are the rule at this stage.

When we look at larger groups acting within the framework of a still larger entity, we find that the same characteristic tends to hold true. A business enterprise, an organized church, a club, school, or hospital, while it is still young and immature as a group, will tend to be self-

[2] See page 103 of Chapter 9, Management Planning.

centered. It is primarily concerned with its own problems, needs, and interests. It pays little heed to the legitimate requirements of other enterprises and only as much attention to their rights as it is required to pay. We have found that it tends to have little sense of community obligation. Any agency which threatens to limit its freedom of action is regarded as a natural enemy and is fought bitterly.

Incompatibility of Objectives

In the young, newly formed group, whatever its size, there tends to be little agreement as to objectives and, in fact, the objectives of the individual members will have some tendency to be in opposition or even contradictory to one another. Each member has joined the group for his personal reasons and each has his own perception of what the group is trying to accomplish and what he can hope to secure from its efforts for himself. Usually two alternatives appear: The individual may change his perceptions to agree with the reality of what he finds in the group, or, possibly he will be able to influence the group enough to change its way of thinking to fit his more closely. Generally there is some of both, with the individual required to make the most change. If the individual cannot change, the group tends to reject him; if the group cannot be won to his way of thinking, the individual tends to leave. Disequilibrium here leads to continued agitation for change and may endanger the existence of the group.

Resistance to Authority

The members of the young, immature group tend to resist authority. They do not want to be dominated and they have not learned yet that each member must be willing to submit to a limitation of his personal freedom if the group as a whole is to function effectively.

This is natural and to be expected for, fundamentally, each person wants to make his own decisions in his own way. Unfortunately, in the immature group *the conditions have not been created which make it feasible for people to make their own decisions.* The members of the group tend to have little understanding of the needs of others in the group and there is a consequent lack of cooperation.

What is required is sufficient close interaction to establish a common acceptance of the need for, and submission to, the authority exercised by a leader. Basically, however, this innate resistance continues. Each individual has his own authority needs, and at some point he must get some satisfaction of these needs or resistance becomes overt and the disequilibrium innate to the situation intensifies.

An alternative is to break or subdue the resistance of the individual by external force, by indoctrination, or by other means. When made general, however, this suppression at the same time kills the vitality of the group and it remains effective only to the limits of the personal capabilities of its leader or leaders.

Lack of Uniformity

There is a lack of uniformity in the way the work is performed in the immature group.　Each member of the group will tend to do his part of the total task in the way he prefers.　Often his method will be in conflict with the methods others adopt.　Not only does he want to do his work in his own way, but each individual member also tends to concentrate upon those activities he thinks are most important.

Although the members of the newly organized group may have adequate skills, most often these are not developed in terms of the special requirements of the group, and generally they need to be altered or modified to better fit these new requirements.

What is needed is enough strength and ability on the part of the group or its leader to establish *necessary uniformity* in standardization of work and no more.　If the required uniformity exceeds the logical limits of human tolerance, there will be resistance and agitation, subtle or overt, for change.　The limits of tolerance can be extended by education and indoctrination.

Minimum of Personal Freedom

It is noteworthy here also that lack of personal liberty is a prevalent characteristic for all but the top leadership in the centric, immature group.　Because the top leader, of necessity, must make most of the important decisions himself, there is little opportunity for others to make their own decisions.　And because, literally, the members of the team have not learned to run in harness, are restive at any controls, and want more liberty than can be safely granted them at this stage, the agitation for change tends to be strong, emotional, and persistent.

The paradox is this: the more freedom that is given the individual members of the group at this stage, the more unstable the group becomes and the greater the organic need for strong, centralized leadership that will have the strength to deprive the members of the group of their freedom long enough to force upon the group the strictures and limits necessary to the granting of relative liberty to each member in the degree he can safely exercise.

LEADERSHIP NEEDS OF THE CENTRIC GROUP

We have seen that the centric group has innate characteristics which tend to result in lack of internal coordination as well as divisiveness in thinking and action, and that it has not yet developed the internal means of remedying these deficiencies. It must have leadership of a certain kind at this stage of evolution, or the group as a whole will fail. In our studies, we have been much perplexed at the seeming logic of what is required, for it tends to run counter to much of current thinking. This perplexity has been intensified by the difficulty of finding enough groups in which maturation has proceeded far enough to see this type of leadership in actual operation. Let us follow through the train of thinking required.

We begin with the assumption that if the centric group is to survive and grow successfully, it will not do so by itself; a leader must arise who will compensate for or override the deficiencies we see in the group itself. To this point in history, most leaders seem to have appeared in response to the forces and pressures generated by the group or the environment. The *way* these leaders can get results will be dictated, to a large extent, by the characteristics of the group. The most important problem the leader of the group has to solve at this stage is how to hold the members of the group together long enough to get them to subordinate their personal interests so that the group can work together as a cohesive team. This problem has baffled and finally led to the failure of some of the finest, most altruistic, and potentially most outstanding leadership material we have seen.

The Concept of Leadership Force

Much as we would like to be able to suggest that patience, humility, and tolerance will win the day, a candid recognition of the current stage of human development and a logical assessment of the characteristics typical of all of us who are normally human force us to another conclusion.

When the members of a group must be held together, the first answer is *force*. The human individual does not turn the other cheek naturally. He must *learn* to do this, and the circumstances of his learning are lengthy and frustrating. Until he learns he must be forced. The human individual does not submit to authority as a consequence of his natural make-up. He does not gain lasting satisfaction as a natural outgrowth of what he is and does. All of these things must be learned. Until the agencies of education are effective enough and the leadership sufficiently perceptive, the first step is force.

People can be forced to act as a group through authority, coercion, *internal* threat, and the fear this engenders. They can be forced through *external* threat and the even greater cohesiveness of the fear this generates. They can be forced by other pressures, overt, subtle, and varied beyond the present telling. This force can be effective—for a period.   At first it is the logical need and must be employed.   But because the emotional, seemingly unpredictable human being responds to a basic logic that is as immutable as the relationship of two hydrogen atoms to one of oxygen in water, eventually this force becomes ineffective.

The Principle of Leadership Force

The greater the divergence of the individual objectives of the members of the group from those of the group as a whole, the greater the leadership force required to cause the group to act as a cohesive unit.

We identify and anticipate the universal requirement for leadership force in the leadership of immature groups by stating this principle that describes its prevalent characteristics.   The situation now has these two features:

1. The immature group as a whole has not formulated its objectives.   As a group, literally, it doesn't know precisely why it exists. It will not discover this until there is mutual recognition of identical goals by the members of the group, an unlikely occurrence indeed, or the development of goals by the leaders which are either sufficiently close to the real and logical needs of the members of the group as to gain acceptance, or which the group is required to accept through force.

People are willing to accept leadership force so long as it gives them the satisfactions they want or offers believable promises of future satisfaction of those needs.   As the group works toward the ends which promise satisfaction of individual needs, the members who identify this promise of personal satisfaction with what they want will stay with, support, and assist the group.   Those who do not believe, or who cannot reconcile these promises with what *they want individually,* will tend to leave the group.

2. The overriding consideration is that, at first, each member of the group joins the group for what he can get out of it personally and stays with it willingly only to the extent he knows or believes it will give him personal satisfaction.

Recognizing that the needs of the individual change as he learns to know himself and learns how to gain enduring satisfactions for himself, and also that the needs of the group as a whole change correspondingly, it is clear that a viable group is dynamic; it changes continually, and its leadership must also be dynamic, in the sense that the leadership must be able to change quickly enough to satisfy the needs of the people being led.

We should stress here that the natural tendency of the leader at this period is to gather as much authority as possible to himself and to exercise it, for this is the prime implement by which he maintains leadership force. Again we point out, however, that the net result is to deprive the individual members of the group of personal freedom. The more they are deprived without acceptable compensation and the more knowing they are of it, the greater the agitation against the leadership. Even if the leadership changes, however, precisely the same degree of group immaturity will prevail and the cycle can only repeat itself until the forces of education and indoctrination set the stage for greater group maturation and a style of leadership that will make greater personal freedom a possibility.

We can now conclude that the characteristics of the centric group *dictate* the style of leadership required. Great demands are made upon the leader if he is to be successful at this unstable and unpredictable stage of the group's existence. He must be able to weld the individual members of the group into an integrated team.

The leader must see to it that formal or informal procedures, policies, and relationships are developed, and he must take steps to reconcile conflicting objectives, viewpoints, and needs. If the leader is successful, eventually the group accepts common goals, develops its own culture, and becomes an integrated entity. This will be attended by a period of attrition during which members who cannot adjust will tend to leave the group. Since the environment will select for survival the most efficient adaptive forms, the young, immature, organized endeavor that cannot produce the strong leadership required will tend to be eliminated during this period.

HOW LONG DOES THE GROUP REMAIN IMMATURE?

The duration of the centric stage may be long or short, depending upon three factors.

1. The make-up of the individuals within the group. If they are knowledgeable, experienced in group activity, and properly motivated, they will become cohesive quickly.

2. The make-up of the group itself. The general level of education, the vitality, and the previous history of the total membership of the group will determine how quickly it reacts as an entity.

3. The environment. Outside pressures, threats, and opportunities will strongly influence the ability of the members to learn to work together and to act as a unified whole. Environmental factors will also

affect the ability of the members of the group to develop loyalty to one another.

Before we go on to discuss the matured, or radic group, it might be helpful to review the first few pages of this chapter. The early history of The Standard Oil Company now becomes much more meaningful, as does that of Sweden and Switzerland, Ghana and Indonesia, the United States and Russia, China and Japan.

With this done, we should proceed to our study of the organized enterprise as it leaves behind the childish and immature days of its infancy and begins to mature. We should note here that in speaking of groups, their infancy and immaturity, we are not necessarily referring to the individuals who make up those groups. As a thought to chew on mentally, many an immature *group* is made up of matured *individuals*.

SUMMARY

Groups tend to evolve in a predictable sequence from immaturity to maturity. The immature group is identified as the centric group, in which the general level of personal concern tends to be greater than the general level of group concern. The centric group is characterized by the primacy of personal concern, incompatibility of personal objectives with those of the group, resistance to authority, lack of uniformity of methods and action, and a minimum of personal freedom. The centric group needs strong, authoritarian, adaptive leadership to hold its members together. The Principle of Leadership Force tells us that "the greater the divergence of the individual objectives of the members of the group from those of the group as a whole, the greater the leadership force required to cause the group to act as a cohesive whole."

CHAPTER 4

The Time of Maturity—The Radic Group

> *Were there a people of gods, their government would be democratic.* ROUSSEAU

As the members of a group continue to work together, they will tend to become more unified and to act as a cohesive whole. Now the group tends to change and evolve to meet the needs of its members and of the environment. Just as an individual evolves through adolescence to adulthood, the *centric group* evolves through its transitional period to a *radic stage* which marks group maturity.

THE RADIC GROUP

In the radic stage the concern of the members of the group *radiates out* (hence radic) to encompass the needs and interests of other members and of the group as a whole. We define a radic group as *a group in which the general level of group concern of the members of the group tends to be greater than the general level of personal concern.*

CHARACTERISTICS OF THE RADIC GROUP

The radic group will have characteristics which are largely *learned* and not natural or intuitive. We can identify the most important of these characteristics as follows:

Conscious Altruism

The individual member of the group will have learned to put the needs of the group as a whole ahead of his own personal needs and desires. He will do this in the knowledge that, over the long term, he will gain most as an individual from this altruism. If this seems unlikely to come about, it but marks the remoteness of our time of maturation.

Perceptive Teamwork

The members of the group will have learned how to work together effectively as a group. This will require that each individual has the means of planning and organizing his own work so that he can co-ordinate his efforts with those of others; that he can establish coopera-tive working relationships with others; that he can control his own actions; that he be able to communicate effectively; and that he know how to motivate others so that they want to work with him and do the things that have to be accomplished.

Nuclear Growth

The nucleus of maturation will tend to begin with the smallest ele-ments of any complex group. The family will be the matured module upon which the community matures; the business enterprise will shape the character of the economy, and so forth. The reason is that change and cohesiveness both are facilitated in smaller groups: the whole may be greater than its parts, but the unity of the whole can be no greater than the unity of its parts.

Concern Not Conformity

It is characteristic of the radic group that its members have learned to develop and support their own point of view and their own inde-pendent ideas in the face of opposition of other members of the group. They do this knowingly in the realization that independence in thought and imagination is mandatory if the group is to remain a dynamic entity.

We find that the members of the radic group are conscious of this requirement and that they encourage the expression of ideas that do not conform to the general body of thought of the group as a whole. We should note that this encouragement and support of nonconformity is as *unhuman* and *unnatural* as is the maturation of the radic group in its other aspects.

Also characteristic of the radic group is the fact that after a de-cision has been made that applies to the group as a whole, each member will support it as if it were his own decision and will speak for it in the same way. However, just as any wise and prudent manager would continue to examine and question his own decisions when they are to remain in effect over a period of time, so also we find that the indi-vidual members of the radic group and the group as a whole will continue to examine and question, in a constructive manner, the decisions that continue to be enforced.

Crawford H. Greenewalt, speaking as president of E. I. du Pont de Nemours & Co., made this point when he said:

Conformity in behavior is a necessity; conformity in patterns of thought a danger. Unfortunately, people have come in modern times to mistake one for the other. . . . In our organization we put the highest possible premium on ideas; fresh and original ideas that are important to the extent that they do not mirror traditional thinking. We are not conscious of any inhibiting restrictions. I have yet to see a man make his way to the upper levels by conforming to any precast or prefabricated mold. I have seen many fail by following such a course. And I have seen far more fail by pursuing conventional approaches than I have ever seen fail by ignoring them.

We see in Du Pont concrete application of this philosophy. Large, stable, and successful as it is, Du Pont has every good reason to be complacent and conforming; in fact, it is bold and enterprising beyond most others. Du Pont seeks out and encourages the man who has good manners enough to work harmoniously with others but who refuses to follow the crowd blindly in his thinking.

Du Pont has so far developed its encouragement of originality and initiative that it has an award for nonconformity built into its incentive system which provides special recognition to the person who achieves a goal "in the face of opposition from within or without."

In one case, for example, a Du Pont new products committee had turned down a proposal sponsored by an outstanding young engineer. Undaunted, the young man requested a *personal audience* and made a two-hour presentation at the next meeting of the group. He was turned down again. Still he persevered and finally was asked to present his idea to the executive committee. He was turned down again.

The important question now is: how was this energetic pushing of a creative idea received? In most large and stabilized organizations it would meet with resistance, antagonism, and a positive rebuff. In Du Pont, however, the young man received a special citation and an extra bonus payment for his nonconformity. To put it in Greenewalt's words again: "Original thinking has never found a ready made acceptance, but the corporation must find a way to encourage the risk-taker, the man who will fight for his ideas."

WHY DO GROUPS MATURE?

Now that we have identified the radic group, we must ask ourselves: Why does this maturation occur? There must be logical reasons if

we are to accept this proposition of evolutionary growth. While undoubtedly there are more reasons, we have concluded that the following
are important.

The Group Offers More Than
the Individual Can Provide

The members of the group will develop more concern with the welfare of others and of the group as a whole because they confirm, in
their emotions and their minds, something which, so far, they had assumed or hoped for; that is, they discover that they can get more from
the productivity of the group than they can from going it alone. The
more the individual sees that he can benefit personally thereby, either
psychologically or materially, the more loyalty he will tend to develop
toward the group and the more willing he will be to make concessions in
favor of the group.

It is most significant that there is a process leading to this development of loyalty to the group and willingness to make concessions in
favor of the group because the individual member realizes that, in this
way, he benefits most personally. Knowledge of this, and our ability
to facilitate it, *will enable us to make conscious selection of those
factors that lead to group maturation.*

The Individual Becomes More Competent
as a Member of the Group

The individual members of the group, as they work with the group,
become more competent in their performance and make a greater contribution to the group's output. They recognize that they have potential for greater accomplishment, both psychological and material.
As its members become more capable, the productivity of the group
improves; the more the total output increases and the members of the
group realize it, the more they want to share in the increase. The
greater the potential reward, the more willing they are to subordinate
their personal interests to the needs of the group because they see that
in this way they get more out of it for themselves. Here is the staging
ground for true maturation of the group. A beneficial cycle of
improvement has been set into motion; it is incremental and, properly
facilitated, may become exponential in its tendency toward increased
improvement. But here again we find that our human inadequacies
stand in the way. What happens now depends most largely upon the
leader. And the leader, being first a human being and secondly a
leader, will probably become the barrier toward further evolution.

WHAT IS NEEDED FOR GROUP MATURATION?

If maturation is to proceed, two things must happen. First, we must have some means of extending the limits of freedom, and secondly, there must be a relaxation of leadership force. Actually, the two are closely related and the one cannot be accomplished without the other. Let us now examine the possibilities of enabling each individual to become *a relatively independent, highly competent, appropriately rewarded, and thoroughly satisfied member of the group.* As a side comment, we should note that in this statement we have summarized what is probably the true end product of the matured group.

Extending the Limits of Freedom

Each member of the group can be given maximum freedom of personal action only if he knows the limits within which he can act without infringing upon, or jeopardizing, the freedom of others, or prejudicing the success of the group as a whole. *This cannot be accomplished in a natural, spontaneous fashion;* it requires the application of skills that must be *learned.*

If limits of personal freedom are to be extended, there must be established an overall purpose which each member of the group understands and accepts as his personal objective.

Very importantly, if these limits are to be kept as broad as possible, a means must be developed of mastering the future to some extent. If the endeavor is completely subject to the caprice of fortune and fate, if it must make sudden and violent changes in its direction on little notice, if it is continually beset by unanticipated emergencies of substantial magnitude, the reins will have to be held tightly at the top so that the whole team can be swung quickly and with some effectiveness to meet each unanticipated demand, and to avoid the barriers and pitfalls that suddenly appear.

Mastery of the Future. If a group is to mature, there must be a continual scouting ahead by the top leaders, a probing and investigation of the probable shape of the future, and careful analysis and study of the past, for in the past lie the seeds of the future. Within this framework, there must be established standing decisions that will help to identify for each member of the group the basic approaches the endeavor will take in its progress.

Each member of the group must be working systematically to accomplish specific activities which are necessary to and a part of the total task of the endeavor. He must time what he does so that it can be accomplished in coordination with other related activities carried out by other members of the group.

For limits to be effective, there must be some means of allocating the total resources of the endeavor so that each individual will know what he can safely spend, in monetary terms, to carry out his part of the whole. Since certain types of work must be carried out in a uniform fashion wherever they are done, there must be a means of establishing standardized methods of accomplishing this specific work.

Logical Allocation of Work. Each person can have maximum freedom in doing his work only if everybody knows what work he should be doing, and what is to be carried out by others. There must be a means of seeing to it that each person can make as many decisions as possible bearing on the work he does. The rules for effective teamwork must be understood and accepted, so that there will be little quarreling over authority and so that good working relationships can be maintained by each person with other members of the team.

A Means of Checking Up. Freedom requires a means of checking up to make sure that the important things are being done the way they should, within the limits of action that have been set. Checking can be done by the leader inspecting everything himself. But this will limit what is done to what he can inspect, and it will require that everything be done his way. Necessary as this is during the immaturity of the group, it is something we must learn to avoid if maturation is to take place. This checking up can take place without the leader's personal inspection if there is some means of differentiating between acceptable and unacceptable methods and results, if everybody concerned is kept constantly informed of what is going wrong, and if we have a systematic means of seeing to it that these deficiencies are corrected as closely as possible to the point where they occur.

Relaxing Leadership Force

The pressure at the top that is necessary to hold the group together must be decreased gradually, but it can be relaxed only so fast as the individual members of the group are capable of acting positively and effectively in carrying out their part of the total task. Each individual requires an understanding, first, of what the group is trying to accomplish, and second, of his part in it. Only if he understands can he accept and support effectively what the whole team is trying to do. Each member of the group must be encouraged and impelled to act in terms of the interests of the group as a whole, so that he will work as hard as he can and will apply his greatest abilities in his contribution toward the group results.

Leadership force can be relaxed when people are educated to the degree that they have the knowledge and skills necessary to do their work with maximum effectiveness and can be self-sufficient in carrying out their own part in the overall job.

These are difficult things to accomplish. To date, we know very little about how best to do them. But, at some point, we must begin to learn how to do these things as well as we have learned to operate machines, to fly through the air, and to see clearly what lies at the point of a needle. What we have said is that personal freedom depends most largely upon effective *management* of group effort.

OBSTACLES TO GROUP MATURATION

The primary requirements of the members of the matured group derive logically from the growth pattern we have traced. Now the members have both the desire and need to share the material advantages that come with increased productivity, and also to secure enhanced ego satisfaction from their participation in the group effort. It is to be repeated again that, up to this point in the history of the group's maturation, these advantages have been enjoyed largely by the top leadership. However, with successful growth there is more of both material and psychological satisfactions to be shared, and this can be accomplished with greater individual return both to the top leadership and to the members of the organization.

Again we come to the fact that this evolution and maturation is unnatural in the sense that it is at variance with the ordinary course of nature. The top leadership does not want to give up; the rank and file cannot understand their reasons for not so doing. All too frequently, revolution of one kind or another takes place as the underprivileged majority tries to secure a larger share of what the total group produces. This necessitates, of course, an apparent or actual *taking something away* from the minority that has enjoyed the largest share of the group output.

Note, here, that this is, first and foremost, a *human* situation, not political or economic. Reverse the roles, put the underprivileged where the privileged are now, and disequilibrium will result. When the leadership reacts to the symptoms, as it almost invariably does, the causative factors most often are not identified, and long-term corrective action does not take place.

The basic desire on the part of the normal members of the group is to make the greatest use of their personal abilities so that they can enjoy the greatest returns for themselves. In the immature group, this resulted in divisiveness and tended to pull the group apart because these personal desires were expressed at random and often were in conflict with one another. During transition, however, there is sufficient stability to make for an orderly and systematic presentation of these demands.

Now the leaders may change in an intuitive response to these needs, or they may respond favorably to the requests of their followers. If they do, the evolutionary process is permitted to proceed and the organization becomes more unified, stronger in all of its parts, and even more productive as a result.

More often than not, as we shall see later, the leader does not change. The maturing group then moves ahead of its leader and the disequilibrium poses a growing threat to survival.

THE MAINTENANCE OF LEADERSHIP FORCE

We know that the maintenance of leadership force is necessary until those conditions can be established that are conductive to the individual members of the group learning to become cohesive. As this cohesiveness is accomplished during the period of transition, the leader must change with it. In the past, such change has been fortuitous and in response to the environment. Very rarely has it been conscious or premeditated because there has been very little understanding of the causative factors involved.

We can say now, however, that the leader must do one of several things if he wishes to prolong the period of transition in the evolution of the group he leads.

1. He may intensify leadership force. Stalin, and most dictators of history, have done this.

2. He may offer further glowing promises of future rewards. To the extent that he can convince his followers, he will forestall their rejection of him. Castro has done this consistently.

3. He may indoctrinate his followers to believe that their deprivation of material and psychological satisfactions is a contribution to something greater than themselves. This is closely related to (2). Mao Tse-tung has done this.

4. He may weaken and enfeeble them physically and psychologically, or imprison them so that they cannot rebel.

Whatever the recourse of the leader, if the group retains its integrity and vitality, sooner or later it will (1) rebel, (2) generate sufficient internal force to require the leader to make the necessary changes, or (3) strive to achieve these changes through its own efforts.

SYMPTOMS OF MATURATION

Group maturation is not a permanent condition. Groups have the instabilities characteristic of their human members. However, in a group these instabilities are more prevalent because the group is a whole made up of differing units, while the individual is at least a monolithic unit. Once matured, the group will still be subject to the vicissitudes of the environment, acts of chance, and the inconsistencies both of its membership and its leadership.

We have had to draw upon logical deduction in establishing the characteristics of the matured group, for the simple reason that we have not been able to find an example of a fully matured group. Let us see if we can visualize a fully matured group.

At some time in the future, the typical member of the United States Congress will give consistent priority to the needs and interests of the United States first, and then to his own state, district, and himself, in that order. When we can normally expect this type of thinking we can anticipate that the United States, as a national group, will have matured.

Again, at some time in the future, the typical property owner in the average city of the United States will give first priority to the interests and needs of the city as a whole and second priority to his own property rights. Remote as they may seem, these characteristics will mark the maturation of the individual citizen in the United States.

As we have seen, these things will have to be learned. They are not natural, any more than goodness, humility, and virtue, as defined in human terms, are natural. The end product of self-discipline and education, such unnatural accomplishments will be the overt sign that our civilization has matured.

Maturation requires changes in the relationship between leaders and followers. The task of the leaders now is to educate, indoctrinate, and orient the members of the organization so that, with logic and intelligence, they can make most of the decisions involving their own activities, and can perform, as fully and completely as possible, their own logical part of the over-all work of the enterprise. The greatest potential for maximum material and psychological satisfaction by each member of the group is secured *when the leadership can enable each person to attain, as fully as possible, that which he is capable of becoming.*

SUMMARY

The radic group is the matured group. At this stage of evolution of the group, the general level of group concern tends to be greater than the general level of personal concern. The radic group is characterized by conscious altruism, perceptive teamwork, nuclear growth with the prevalence of concern but not conformity. Groups tend to mature because the members realize that the group offers more than the individual can provide and because the individual becomes more competent and better able to earn a larger share of the group productivity. If group maturation is to occur, the limits of freedom for the individual must be extended and broadened. This is accomplished by a leadership that knows how to command the future and not be commanded by it, that can make logical allocation of the work to be done so that overlap and personal friction are minimized, and that can check methods and results effectively enough to give each person maximum authority and freedom in the way he gets his work done.

CHAPTER 5   *The Evolution of Leadership*

The question "who ought to be boss?" is like asking "who ought to be tenor in the quartet?"   Obviously, the man who can sing tenor.   HENRY FORD

What work a leader does and *how* he does it are vastly important to the success of a business, a government, a church, an army, a baseball team, or an orchestra.   Most often we take the leader's role for granted; rarely do we stop to analyse it.   If we are to understand leadership and how it can be practiced most effectively, we must first examine the logical reasons why we need leaders and what work we expect a leader to do.

DEFINING LEADERSHIP

We readily accept the proposition that leaders are necessary in order *to attain identified ends.*   We have come to recognize that his role requires a leader to *do* and *be* those things that will facilitate the group, of which he is a member as well as the leader, to work effectively together toward accomplishing their purposes.   People *can* work together without a leader; however, at our current stage of human development, people work most effectively together under a leader.

The two key requirements we make of a leader are: (1) he must have followers, and (2) he must cause his followers to act with him or for him as a group toward common end results.

WHY DO WE NEED LEADERS?

We readily accept the proposition that leaders are necessary for effective human effort, but is this need logical?   Why cannot people work together effectively without a leader?

The Needs of the Group

Leaders are necessary because the people they lead need them. Let us examine a group of people (Figure 5-1) and see what happens if they do not have a leader. Here we have a group of six competent, self-sufficient, adequate individuals. This group finds it necessary to come to conclusions with respect to certain questions: What shall we try to accomplish? What shall we do? How shall we do it? When shall we begin? How much shall each person be paid? Great and small, these questions arise in unending succession.

Each person wants the answer that will best satisfy him, but his answer probably will not perfectly satisfy his teammates. Unless acceptable answers to these and a thousand other questions are found, however, the group cannot work effectively together. At this point we

FIG. 5-1. A group without a leader.

have two primary alternatives in getting answers to questions and problems that are of direct concern to the team as a whole: we can resort to a group agreement, or we can find a leader.

The Possibilities of Group Agreement

Theoretically the members of the group, acting together, could determine the goals, methods, and timing most acceptable to all, agree to carry out this course of action, and implement it.

It is true that every group of people has resources that should be drawn upon as fully as possible in determining the action to be undertaken. However, the members of the group, for both logical and practical reasons, are capable of making only a limited number of the decisions that affect the group as a whole.

Some decisions can be made by the group; included are the decisions that demand a maximum of acceptance, those that are largely within the province of the group to carry out for itself, and those that require little integration with the requirements and decisions of other groups.

This, of course, is contrary to a commonly held belief that group decision making is to be preferred whenever possible. The theory of pure group dynamics has enamored many. According to its advocates, "Let all who are involved in a group decision share equally in making it" is the greatest democracy. However, put to the test, the group approach has shown many practical disadvantages. Day-to-day decisions made by the group, at best, will be a compromise. The new, original, and unusually creative contribution will tend to be rejected or argued down to the level of the less imaginative. Those who do not secure acceptance of their views will tend to become impatient or dissatisfied and leave the group.

What conditions are necessary for group decision making and how likely are we to satisfy those conditions? If group decision making is to be successful, a high degree of maturity is required of each member. Each needs to consider other members as much as himself. He must be willing to compromise for the greater good of the whole and wholeheartedly accept compromise. Understanding, patience, and tolerance are essential.

Not only are all these unusual personal attributes necessary, but there is also the question of competition. Decisions made by the group itself generally are not fast or positive enough for success in a competitive situation. If other groups are working toward the same goals, the group that can act most quickly and most effectively will forge ahead. Except in certain unique instances, in a competitive situation the direction and guidance available from group decision making tend to be too slow and cumbersome. This leadership may have more acquiescence from the group as a whole, but it tends to lack speed, vigor, and originality.

The conclusion: group decision making has its advantages and its proper place. However, it is not a practical approach for enabling groups of people to work effectively together in demanding and competitive situations. Great as is its potential, the group approach to leadership must wait for a later century to find the large numbers of wise, intelligent, patient, and humble people who can implement it successfully.

The Logical Solution

We find that the logical solution is to adopt our second alternative, that of creating a leadership position. This is illustrated in Figure 5-2.

The leader may be elected or appointed; he may seize his position by force or inherit it. He may assume leadership for reasons of personal power, prestige, or as a duty. By whatever means he secures command,

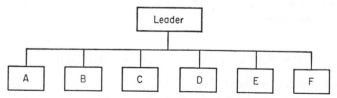

FIG. 5-2. The leadership position.

however, we now have a leader. *The way the leader leads will have a great deal to do with the effectiveness of the group, its survival, and the satisfaction each member derives from being a member of the group.*

NATURAL LEADERS AND MANAGEMENT LEADERS

Leadership is much like other skills, such as those necessary to the practice of medicine or surgery, of engineering or teaching, or the playing of golf or the violin.   As we study the way leaders lead, we find significant similarities to these other disciplines.   For example, the untrained musician or golfer tends to be clumsy and ineffective; so also is the untrained leader.   In the same way that some untrained persons who play golf have natural, intuitive coordination and learn to play well in a short time because of their physical endowment, so also some leaders lead well in an intuitive fashion.

To complete the parallel, there is a trained, disciplined, and more competent way of designing a bridge, performing surgery, or playing golf, but the individual who wishes to rise above his natural endowment must have access to the necessary knowledge and must discipline himself to master these more demanding and rigorous techniques.

To illustrate, Gene Littler, one of golfing's great and an outstanding money winner of all time, won tournament after tournament over several years.   Then his game fell off.   He seemed to have reached a plateau and lost out to improving competition.

Finally Littler, in 1958, went to Paul Runyon, the professional at La Jolla, California.   Runyon studied Littler's game and found that he was a great natural golfer.   He played golf almost as if by instinct.   But he had never studied the game logically.   He drove and putted and chipped without knowing why he played as he did.   Runyon helped Littler study his game, analyze what he was doing and why he was doing it, and finally helped him to put his game together again.   From there Littler forged on to new heights.   He had become a real professional in golf.

In following through with our analogy, we should keep in mind that a leader can get people to follow him both because of what he *is*—his personality characteristics, appearance, and manner—and because of what he *does*—the kind of physical and mental effort he puts forth in his leadership position.

THE EVOLUTIONARY SEQUENCE OF LEADERSHIP

In our studies we have found that there is a definite evolutionary sequence in the way leaders learn to lead.   If a leader is to continue to be successful over a long period of time, he must evolve; that is, he must accomplish a continuing adaptation to his environment by some internal, and hopefully identifiable, mechanism. The environment of leadership is largely shaped by the needs of the followers who are being led. The leader who does not change will be outmoded and become incapable of effective leadership as surely as the brontosaurus that failed to adapt became extinct.

We have established that there are two different types of leaders, *natural leaders* and *management leaders.* Every leader tends to begin his career as a natural leader; he *learns* to become a management leader.

THE NATURAL LEADER

We have natural musicians, golfers, and even engineers and preachers. The term designates a person who has unusual innate abilities to do a prescribed kind of work and who is effective primarily because of his natural endowment. In the same sense we have natural leaders. The natural leader is *a person in a leadership position who enables people to work together for identified ends primarily by using his own innate, natural aptitudes and personality characteristics.*[1]

The natural leader must rely upon his innate capabilities because he has not developed conscious techniques of leadership. He leads instinctively and not through skills which he has identified and systematically developed to enable him to secure most effective results in working with others. The natural leader is the untrained leader who can be effective primarily because of what he *is,* not because of what he has learned to do in order to lead effectively.

PREVALENCE OF NATURAL LEADERS

In our studies, we have discovered a most significant fact: the overwhelming majority of people in leadership positions today are natural leaders. To make the point even more emphatic, throughout history virtually all leaders have secured their leadership results intuitively and not through conscious mastery of the physical and mental effort necessary to get people to work effectively together.

This puts leadership today in the primitive stage of music when tunes were beat out intuitively on hollow logs by our savage forebears, or of rocketry when the Chinese in medieval times exploded gunpowder

[1] This evolutionary pattern was first identified by the author in his *Management and Organization,* McGraw-Hill Book Company, New York, 1958, as the change from *personal* leadership to management leadership. The term *natural* leadership is substituted for *personal* leadership to help avoid certain confusing implications that have appeared in use.

under a figure to lift it dramatically into the air in celebration of a feast.

Think a moment: to say that most leaders are and have been natural leaders is to establish a situation similar to that which would prevail if most engineers were talented mechanics without rigorous training in engineering disciplines, or if most swimmers were well-coordinated individuals who were untrained in performance of the work necessary to swim most effectively.

We repeat that virtually every organized enterprise of any importance has been founded by natural leaders. Almost all of the major business enterprises, governments, institutions, and religious groups of the world are led today by individuals who have not had rigorous, disciplined training in the skills necessary to enable people to work effectively together. In fact, our knowledge of these skills is meager and primitive indeed, compared to our understanding of biology, inertial guidance, or atomic physics. We have only to examine the wasted effort, friction, and dissatisfaction that everywhere prevail in group undertakings to confirm the validity of this conclusion.

In order to understand better the natural leader and the effects of this kind of leadership, we have attempted to identify universal characteristics that tend to be found in the effective natural leader.

CHARACTERISTICS OF THE NATURAL LEADER

We find that the natural leader tends to be authoritarian. He will do much of the work of his people for them; he makes most of the decisions; and he will control by personal inspection. We can anticipate these characteristics with as much confidence as that the untrained singer will find it difficult to hold a note or that the untrained golfer will have a clumsy, uncoordinated swing. The singer may have read all the books on singing, and the golfer may have memorized the manual on "How to Play Golf in 10 Hours." However, each will have to learn how to convert this knowledge to the requisite skills. In the same manner, a leader may have an advanced degree in management or in business administration, but he still needs to convert his knowledge to management skills. In each case, of course, the more knowledge the individual has, the more quickly he can develop the level of skill required, provided the arrogance of knowledge does not hamper the process.

The Natural Leader Tends to Be Authoritarian

When first put into a leadership position, a person with energy, good abilities, and adequate intelligence will assume that his proper role is to make decisions. One reason for this is that his followers will be forced to ask him to decide matters that involve the group as a whole. Unable to discriminate between decisions he must make and those he should not, the untrained leader generally ends up making most of them. He feels this gives him firmest command; it ensures that everything will be done the way he wants; and it makes command relatively simple. Happily, at first this is precisely what the immature group requires; if the untrained leader is firm and decisive by nature and if his judgments are reasonably sound, he will probably enjoy substantial success.

International Business Machines, a top company in electronics and computers, provides an excellent example of an enterprise which secured its first momentum because of the outstanding abilities and the authoritarian characteristics of a great natural leader.

During its early years, IBM was the lengthened shadow of Thomas J. Watson, Sr. When he became president, IBM, then known as the Computing-Tabulating-Recording Company, seemed to have little prospects of surviving. Watson borrowed $40,000, most of which was spent to set up an engineering laboratory. Under his strong guidance, the company grew to its first stature. The key to its success was Thomas J. Watson's policy of providing first for the customer, who, he insisted, must receive good value for his money; second, for the employees, who must receive proper compensation; and third, for the stockholders of the corporation, who must receive return on their investments.

During the Great Depression when most United States business was declining, IBM, led by Thomas J. Watson, Sr., undertook an expansion program. Instead of resorting to mass factory layoffs, the company kept people employed producing parts for inventory. At the same time, Watson continued to hire salesmen.

Thomas J. Watson, Sr., was a strong natural leader. His hand was unmistakably on the helm as IBM weathered its early years. He made most decisions of any real significance; but because he had faith and confidence in his people, Watson let them handle routine in their own way. If a man could think through and develop a new idea, he would find a great deal of encouragement in putting it into effect.

This heavy emphasis on people helping themselves actually facilitated the progress of the company toward maturation. A strong guiding hand at the helm during the early years, balanced by a real feeling for people, developed a highly loyal and stable employee group.

Functional Orientation

The strong natural leader tends to be expert in some of the work that is important to the success of the group. Frequently, this is the reason he is elected or appointed leader. Thomas J. Watson, Sr., for example, was often known as the "world's greatest salesman." Typical, also, is the fact that Herbert Dow, the strong natural leader who founded the Dow Chemical Company, was an excellent chemist; Walter P. Chrysler, who founded the Chrysler Corporation, was a skilled machinist.

Because of this functional orientation, the spontaneous tendency of the natural leader is to busy himself with the work of the people he leads. He tends to concentrate upon the work of selling, machining, bookkeeping, purchasing, or other specialized functional tasks and not upon the work of *leading,* which is his proper concern. There are many reasons for this. He may not trust his people. Perhaps he does not know how to train them. Most often he does not know how to differentiate between the work he should be doing and that which he should get others to do for him.

The net result of this tendency is that the natural leader rapidly becomes overburdened. He tends to work overtime and to take a full brief case home with him on week ends. Since the boss does the most difficult parts of their work for them, his subordinates have little or no opportunity to master this work themselves. The long-term results are to overwhelm the boss with responsibility and gradually to weaken and discourage the very people who should be assuming the major part of the load for him. The most capable members of the group tend to become dissatisfied and to drift away. At the top level of the enterprise, this pattern of the leader's early performance will often stamp the future of the company and, in terms of his personal abilities, paradoxically enough, it may ensure the momentum necessary to place it in the van of its industry.

The National Cash Register Company is an excellent example. The company's origin goes back to James Ritty, a Dayton, Ohio, restaurant owner who invented the first cash register in 1879 as a device to keep track of the daily cash transactions of his business. Under its first owners, Ritty and his brother and two successive proprietors, the company barely stayed alive. In 1884 John H. Patterson, owner of a general store, bought the controlling interest for $6,500.

A great natural promotor, Patterson literally sold his new company to success and established its leadership in terms of his own remarkable personal skills. He conducted sales meetings and conventions, and was among the first to use role playing, motion pictures, and slides. Prominent among all these activities was John H. Patterson, who took a leading role in everything himself. Because of what *he* could do, National Cash Register was able to take the lead in its industry. Under succeeding leaders, National Cash Register has worked out the pattern established by Patterson; today many of its outstanding characteristics, which make it a leader in its field, can be traced back to him.

Expedient Action

It is typical of the strong natural leader that he tends to move quickly to adapt to any situation that comes up. He can do this primarily because he rarely commits himself to a predetermined course of action. For this reason, what becomes a liability in the matured organization serves as a definite asset in the early, immature stage of growth.

Because the newly organized group has, as yet, no history and no experience upon which to base its expectations of the future, the group itself must stand ready to act quickly, to shift course with little or no warning, and to pounce upon fortuitous opportunities as they occur. Such concerted, highly focused action is vitally important to the undertaking while it is new, small, and young. Lacking momentum and the self-perpetuation which continued stability affords, it requires a leader who can move quickly himself and can carry the entire undertaking with him to meet a challenge or threat or to take advantage of a fortuitous opportunity.

The effective but untrained natural leader tends to have these needed characteristics. His actions are largely unplanned because he rarely stops to think things through. Having no route to follow, he can create his own path as he goes. He tends to take action in terms of fortuitous occurrences. His opportunities are created by events; he does not anticipate events and create his own opportunities. When the natural leader is an outstanding individual, this type of fast, highly flexible action can be most advantageous. However, because it does not take into consideration long-term alternatives, inevitably it tends to commit the endeavor to activities which may be profitable immediately but which, over the long term, limit its range of action to a dangerous degree.

The Goodyear Tire & Rubber Company illustrates this point. Goodyear was established in the early 1900s by Frank and Charles Seiberling on a borrowed $13,000. Primarily concerned with sales, the Seiberlings strongly pursued every marketing opportunity that presented itself. Although sales received every attention, other essential elements were left to chance and circumstances. In October, 1919, beset by the need for an adequate supply of natural rubber, the Seiberlings contracted for a huge inventory at the going rate, which, at war's end, was abnormally high. They failed to plan, to establish alternatives which they could follow if the market broke. Six months later, the same rubber was available at one-fifth the price. The company was in desperate financial circumstances, and the strong personal leaders were forced to sell out. The management that succeeded them carried the company successfully through its transition to become the largest rubber products manufacturer in the world.

Exercise of Personal Control

As work goes on and results are achieved, it is necessary to check to make sure that all is in good order. How can this be accomplished? At first there are no established criteria for differentiating between good work and poor, the reporting system is embryonic, and few people have a clear idea of what is to be accomplished or how it can best be done. These conditions are more or less inherent in the situation. If he is to check up on how the work is done and the results secured, the leader has only one logical recourse: at first he must do it in person. He makes personal inspection and this serves as his basis for control.

The untrained natural leader tends to check results by personal observation because this is the natural way and because he knows no other. He observes *what* is being done, *how* it is being done, and the *results* accomplished. However, since he has no other criterion, his standard tends to be: if the work is being done the way I would do it myself, and if these are the results *I* would expect to secure, all is well; if not, there is probably something wrong.

The natural leader reviews most operating detail and makes spontaneous decisions to settle even detail matters for managers far down the line. His usual pattern is to visit the operating units and plants to make sure that they are run the way he would do it himself. Because his ability is outstanding and his touch is sure, his contribution is sound. However, the company will inevitably outgrow this type of leadership. Soon it will be at a point where it will be forced to change.

In endless examples, we find that the control of the natural leader can be extremely effective so long as the man at the top has the time and the strength to check every detail, to do the most important part of everything himself. But in the growing enterprise everything cannot continue to be done the way the boss would do it himself. Peremptory demands for change because "I would do it differently" and repeated discouragement of independent creativity eventually take their toll.

THE PERSONALITY OF NATURAL LEADERS

A natural leader will tend to have a certain type of personality for the reason that people follow him as much because of *the kind of person he is* as because of what he *does* to lead. We naturally gravitate to the forceful, emphatic, decisive, and persuasive person who knows what he wants to do and can make us feel that it is important to us to help him do it. We do not want to minimize the importance of personality, but we must recognize that, while a leader can get people to follow him willingly and even enthusiastically because of his personal characteristics, personality alone is not enough.   A good leadership personality by itself will not enable a leader to continue to satisfy the basic requirements of leadership: to enable people to work most effectively together to attain ends they hold in common.

The early years of General Motors, one of the largest and most successful manufacturing enterprises in the world, provide an illustration. In the early 1920's, General Motors was, literally, an extension of the personal genius, the likes and dislikes, the strengths and weaknesses, of one man—William C. Durant.   Durant was a salesman of insurance and patent medicines who became interested in the burgeoning automobile industry.   A man of great enthusiasm and tremendous vigor, he built a series of enterprises around himself.

A dynamic personality, Durant put together General Motors in 1908 and brought into it a segment of the leading automobile manufacturers of the day.   He negotiated to buy Ford Motor Company but could not quite scrape up the necessary $8 million.

William C. Durant was both an autocrat and a genius.   Kindly in disposition, nevertheless he was indefatigable in his drive and aggressiveness.   He kept the affairs of a corporation of almost $100 million in his head and made virtually every decision himself that had any important bearing on those affairs.   Because his intuition was sharp and his brain keen, many of those decisions were brilliant.   He talked a few minutes to a French automobile racer named Champion, who had invented a way to make spark plugs using a porcelain casing, and, on little more basis than that conversation, founded what eventually became the AC Spark Plug Company.   A friend brought to his attention a newly developed "electric icebox."   Durant organized a company, gave the inventor a stock interest, put him on the payroll, and from this sprang Frigidaire.

To cite again the most persistent theme in the history of organized undertakings, the enterprise outgrew its early leader.   Durant was a dictator, and so long as he could continue to provide good answers to most of the important questions that arose, he remained successful. Outstanding as a salesman and promoter, a great innovator, Durant displayed most of the characteristics of the strong natural leader but never rose above them.

Although Durant was a kindly man who showed a consistent and innate consideration for the people who worked for him, he acted unilaterally in most of his undertakings and rarely bothered to tell his executives what he was doing.   He maintained personal accountability and personal control.   There was no consistent policy, no sound budgetary control, and, in short, the company was unorganized and the individual units largely out of control.[2]

General Motors was in serious difficulty twice, in 1910 and 1920. By 1921 it had a deficit of $38 million.

During this period one of Durant's two assistants, Alfred P. Sloan, Jr., had given much study to the deterioration of the enterprise. He thought through a new plan of organization which, he felt, would provide the management base the company surely needed. When Sloan presented his idea in 1920, however, Durant rejected it. Here we have, in facsimile, a small drama, a crisis and a chance for survival that are repeated frequently in organized endeavors at this stage of growth.

As the General Motors crisis deepened, E. I. du Pont de Nemours & Co., which had a large financial interest, moved to protect its investment. Pierre S. du Pont became chief executive of the company but relinquished the position in 1923 to Alfred P. Sloan, who had rapidly demonstrated his competence as a management leader.

THE WORK OF NATURAL LEADERS

The mental and physical effort or *work* a person performs largely determines his effectiveness and the character of his accomplishment. So also with leadership; in the final analysis, what the leader can accomplish will depend most largely not upon his personality, but upon the mental and physical effort he puts forth.

Natural leaders tend to do the work they best like to do; most often this is not the work they should be doing. Here, as we shall see, is the crux of the matter. We know, for example, that the teacher who tries to write essays for his students, the swimming coach who spends most of his time competing with his swimmers, the sales manager who spends most of his time selling, the company president who immerses himself in his research laboratory, may all have the personality attributes necessary for effective leadership, but none of these will continue to be an effective teacher or coach or leader because he is not doing the work necessary to fulfill his primary role effectively.

Simple and logical as it is, this salient point has been overlooked consistently in the development of leadership. If a swimming coach is to coach effectively he must do the work of the coach, not that of the person being coached; if a teacher is to teach he must do the work required of the teacher, not that of the student; if a leader is to lead he must do the work of leadership, not the work that should be done by

---

[2] From a statement by Harlow H. Curtice, President, General Motors, before the Subcommittee on Antitrust and Monopoly of the U.S. Senate Committee on the Judiciary, Dec. 2, 1955.

his followers.   Inevitably and for logical reasons, however, the natural leader, until he *learns* better, will tend to devote most of his thought and energy to work others should be doing for him.

Here some of the confusing gaps in the puzzle become obvious.   To what should the leader change?   How can he know what he *should* be doing?   If most leadership so far has been natural leadership and this has not been fully effective, why have many leaders been able to accomplish so greatly in all fields of human endeavor?   Before we go on to investigate these questions, we should pause to emphasize the importance of natural leaders, for fear that what we have said may belittle this type of leadership.

THE IMPORTANCE OF NATURAL LEADERS

At this stage of history, enterprises and organizations tend to be spawned by natural leaders.   We should stress that the strong natural leader may be extremely successful, particularly over the short term. Because a strong, capable person with outstanding abilities is doing much of the work, it tends to be well done; the decisions that carry the stamp of his genius most often are good decisions.

When we find that competing groups are under the direction of strong personal leaders, the match tends to be between the personal qualities of the leaders.   If an organization can be maintained as a monolithic extension of its leader and can reflect his capabilities directly, if the leader excels, the organization will tend to excel so long as this primordial arrangement remains successful.

Our research shows that this strong leadership, centered in one or a few people, is mandatory for the young enterprise.   The primary reason is that the young, new company tends to be unstable; its members have not had time or opportunity to develop full competence in their work. They are not skilled or confident enough to make many of their own decisions.

The first task of the successful leader is to develop cohesiveness so that his followers can act cooperatively together as a unit and not as independent individuals.   The force necessary to hold the group together during this early, formative stage of growth, we find, is provided through strong, authoritarian, personal, and highly centralized leadership.   The greater the tendency toward individual divergencies from group objectives, the greater the personal force that must be exercised by the leader to hold the group together.

Since the environment will select for survival the most efficient adaptive forms, it follows that the young, formative enterprise, if it is in a competitive environment, will tend to be eliminated unless it has the strong personal leadership necessary to enable it to act in a unified and effective manner.

WHY NATURAL LEADERSHIP BECOMES INADEQUATE

There are logical reasons why natural leadership tends to become inadequate to the needs of a growing, diversifying, and maturing group endeavor.   Obvious is the sheer inability of the leader himself to do everything and be everything for the group he leads.   Eventually the job becomes larger than one man can possibly accomplish.   At this point the leader must learn how to concentrate on the work that only he can do and get other people to help him with everything else.   To do this requires knowledge, self-discipline, and the mastery of skills which will be new to the natural leader.

The Desire for Firm Guidance

There is also the fact that, at first, the members of the group are insecure enough in their roles to *want* the firm, positive guidance provided by this kind of leadership.   They develop loyalty, in part, because of the promise of future satisfactions.   They will get these satisfactions, they feel, from a larger share of the material wealth produced through group effort or greater ego enhancement as a result of group participation.

The Desire for Freedom

So long as one or a few leaders can exert enough force, give immediate rewards, or hold out a promise of future satisfaction sufficient to satisfy the personal goals of most of its members, the group will tend to hold together.   But people want freedom to do their own work, to make their own decisions, and to receive an equitable part of the group output. They resist coercion, force, and the personal type of control which insists that the work be done the way the boss would do it himself.   As these dissatisfactions become operative, they exert increasing pressure upon the leader.

As the company expands, diversifies, and becomes more complex, the burden upon the leader and his immediate group increases; decision making multiplies; controls proliferate; communications slow down.   At each step, dissatisfaction mounts.

The need for change is imperative.   If change does not take place, the leader most often imposes new discipline in an attempt to subdue the unrest.   As individuals and nations, subjugated against their will, have shown throughout history, this force, in itself, is self-defeating.   Action commanded by force is at best reluctant; it is rarely most efficient; it can be maintained only by a continuation of ever-increasing force.

Resistance to Change

We have found that a further reason the evolution of leadership does not proceed is that the successful natural leader tends to be very resistant to change. Resting on a platform of success generated by his own efforts and ability, he refuses to believe that his organization has outgrown him. Supported by a profitable past, complacent in his regard of the future, and shielded from the pressures of operations by intervening levels of complaisant subordinates he often maintains his place until he is forcibly replaced.

At this writing we have identified seven major enterprises in the United States caught in the iron grip of a strong natural leadership that is outmoded. Some enjoy a strong patent or proprietary position; others have forged to the front under the inventive genius of their founder; still others command unique sources of raw materials that almost guarantee profitability. In each, the entire organization stands and marks time, waiting impatiently for the strong leader to retire gracefully or to die. In these companies, many of the strongest and most independent subordinate executives have already left; those who remain generate constantly increasing pressure for change.

We still must ask ourselves: Why is this pattern of leadership so stubbornly maintained by strong natural leaders? The most obvious answer, of course, is that until the findings of these studies are known to him, he will not be aware of what is occurring. He will not know to what to change. When we consider the primitive state of our knowledge of leadership, it is quite clear that there is not yet much of this knowledge sorted and labeled.

Another reason is the arrogance of success. The leader who has seen most of his actions turn out successfully becomes imbued with the feeling that he possesses some inherent capability that places him above other men. Call him a "genius" and he accepts it easily and naturally.

This very success inevitably leads to a derogation of the ideas and efforts of others. As one company president said, "This company has turned a profit every one of twenty-three years and I just don't know what anybody can tell me about managing a business that I don't already know." The president belittled continued suggestions from his department heads for modernization and streamlining of the growing business. Finally, profits began to erode. He was voted out by the board of directors, forced to retire, and spent the seven remaining months of his life in bitter denunciation of some nebulous "raiders" who supposedly had maneuvered his downfall.

One of the very real dangers of this arrogance of success is an accompanying lack of desire to change and improve. Many a company, for example, has maintained continued profitability because of ownership of patents or a unique endowment of natural resources and raw materials. The enterprise that literally sits on top of a gold mine, or a rich source of oil, copper, diamonds, uranium, or iron ore, can be inefficient, expensive, and yet resist change for a surprisingly long time. Lack of competition breeds the same circumstances. When markets are guaranteed through cartels and other arrangements, or when competition is forced out or absorbed, the arrogance of success becomes the prevalent pattern, the urge to improve diminishes, and the skids are greased for the downhill slide.

In the future we can assume that more top leaders will identify the pattern of change and will look ahead to the need for transition to a different style of leadership. If the strong natural leader can understand the forces at work and consciously school himself to change, we have the best prognosis for continuing success of the endeavor.

SUMMARY

Leaders are necessary to enable people to work most effectively together. The way a leader leads has a great deal to do with the effectiveness of his followers. There is an evolutionary development of leadership from natural leadership to management leadership. The natural leader is able to secure results because of his own innate, natural aptitudes and personality characteristics. He tends to be authoritarian and to be most expert in the work done by his followers. He takes fast, spontaneous action and controls by personal inspection. Because of these characteristics he is limited to the scope of his own personal skills and aptitudes and has minimum opportunity to multiply himself through his followers.

CHAPTER 6   *The Management Leader*

*If the trumpet give an uncertain sound, who shall prepare
himself to the battle?*   I CORINTHIANS

We find that natural leaders are most effective for young companies
and that, in fact, their style of leadership is required by these immature
groups.   This largely explains why many strong, capable natural
leaders have succeeded so greatly while their organizations were young.

AGENCIES OF MANAGEMENT EVOLUTION

There are identifiable agencies which are operative and which
provide much of the impetus for the leadership changes that occur.
Let us examine the dynamics involved.

The Dynamics of Improvement

The underlying dynamic force which is present and operative in
every competitive situation is the drive for improvement.   In human
beings there is a basic psychological need which prompts the individual to establish his sense of personal importance and recognition by
excelling others.   This becomes a hunger for progress and advancement—a real *need* to improve.   Members of groups attempt to improve
their personal participation in the group effort and this leads to group
changes.   When the members of groups become satisfied, this evolutionary process tends to slow down.   This is also true of leaders who
strive to improve their personal psychological and material rewards.
Leaders tend to secure the greatest rewards first and, as a result,
will tend to become satisfied and to cease their evolutionary efforts
earliest.   The greatest handicap to most groups in their evolutionary

61

progress eventually becomes their leader, who cannot or will not change to meet the changing group demands.

The Logic of Progress

We have seen that improvement and progress are first the result of natural and spontaneous reaction to the environment in an attempt to survive. But this instinctive progress is least efficient, requires most effort, and is extremely wasteful both of resources and energy. Far better is *logical, conscious improvement,* deliberately undertaken to achieve predetermined ends. This is scientific improvement and is the pattern which has led to phenomenal advances in science, medicine, and engineering. If leadership is to become truly effective and is to overcome its backwardness, it must become scientific in the same sense that biology, physics, anthropology, and chemistry are scientific. This scientific leadership we have identified as *management leadership.*

When transition to a different style of leadership is indicated, we must find the logical thread involved so that we will know what change is necessary and can identify the logical reasons why the change will work. We must now ask ourselves: What should the natural leader change *to?* We can best arrive at the answer if we determine what work we expect a leader to perform if he is to get people to work most effectively together.

WHAT WORK SHOULD LEADERS PERFORM?

We found that we could not determine what leaders should do by studying leaders and tabulating the things they happened to be doing. Because virtually all leadership is still spontaneous, intuitive, and often illogical as a result, we discovered that most people we have found in leadership positions had little logical basis for the work they happened to be doing.

We then sought some means of analyzing leadership positions so that we could determine, in conclusive and inescapable terms, the logical reasons why leaders must do certain work if they are to secure most effective results through and with others. We assumed that if we could develop such a theory, it should be practical enough that any reasonable and knowledgeable leader could apply this logic to his own position.

In our analysis of management positions, we have found that there are logical bases for identifying the proper work of the leader. We can do this by studying the relationship of the leader to the group he leads and determining the requirements of the unique organizational position in which he finds himself. We can also look at the multiple role of the leader and from it make certain deductions as to what is required of him.

The Unique Organizational Position of the Leader

If we study the leader in his relationship to his group, we find that he is the only one who can have objectivity, perspective, and true understanding of the needs of the group as a whole. Let us look at our group again, now with a leader added (Figure 6-1).

Here we have six people under a leader working toward one common objective. The leader here is in a unique organizational position. He is a member of the group yet need not involve himself in the work and interests of any one member to the extent that he

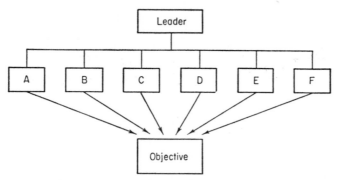

FIG. 6-1. The unique organizational position of the leader.

loses perspective and understanding of the needs and demands of the others.

Because of this organizational position, the leader is able *to do work for the group that the individual members cannot do effectively for themselves.* As an example, assume that we have enough money to give only one member of the group a raise in pay. We can hardly expect an unbiased assessment of his own contribution by any one member. He will be inclined to be prejudiced in his own favor. Who is best placed to make an impartial decision? This is work for the leader to perform.

Who is to check up to make sure that the work done by each member of the group is satisfactory, that it meets the standards set? The individual members, being human, will have a tendency to rationalize their own mistakes and to excuse their deficiencies. To reach a true evaluation of what has been accomplished, we need to create the unique organizational position of the leader and to put in that position a human being who knows how to do the work of leadership effectively.

The Multiple Role of the Leader

A leader in an organized endeavor generally is a member of several different groups. In each he plays a different role and bears varying and often conflicting responsibilities.

In Figure 6-2 the leader is shown in his relation to a group next above and to people with whom he works on his own level.   In one

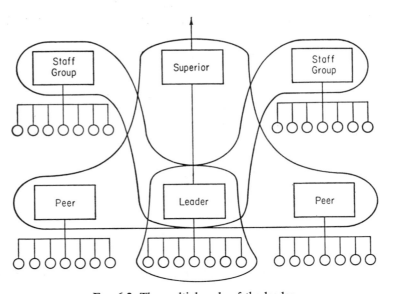

FIG. 6-2. The multiple role of the leader.

role he is leader of his own group.   To work effectively in this role, he must show loyalty to his own people, understand what they require to get satisfaction from the work they do, and help them to act as effective team members.   In this *leadership* role, the leader guides and directs the efforts of his team.   This requires him to make decisions in the best interests of his group, to serve as a communication channel, and to represent the interests of his group to his superiors.

But now observe that the leader is a *follower* on a second team, that which is made up of himself and the other people reporting to his superior.   In this followership role, he owes his loyalty to the man for whom he works.   However, if he sides with his boss against his subordinates, his followers will be alienated, and morale and productivity will suffer. On the other hand, if he stands up too positively for the needs of his followers, his boss will tend to look upon him with disfavor and may withhold opportunity for reward or advancement.

In his *peer* role, a third relationship, the leader is a member of one or more groups made up of his peers. Here he must side with his associates or he will tend to lose favor in their eyes and they will withhold cooperation and support. Since his personal effectiveness depends in some measure upon his ability to work with others at his own level, this lack of mutual support can be detrimental in many ways.

In his fourth role, that of *outside relationships,* the leader must act as a member of groups which may be only indirectly related to his own position and which may be organizationally removed from it. He must work with groups in a staff relationship to him, in committees, task forces, and informal groups made up of members of staff agencies and other departments or divisions. He works with outside groups containing representatives from government, other companies, and associations. In this role, the leader must conform to the purposes and policies of the sometimes alien groups and support their activities sufficiently to be considered a contributing member. Otherwise, he will not be able to fulfill the requirements of his primary leadership role as effectively as he should.

The leader must reconcile the requirements of all of his roles. If there are conflicts he must resolve them or he loses effectiveness. In each case, he is subjected to the varying pressures of people who have their own specialized interests and objectives. He is caught in an emotional tug of war that accounts in substantial part for much of the psychological stress that accompanies the practice of leadership.

The best way the leader can satisfy the requirements of his role and perform with maximum effectiveness as an individual is to identify that work which only he can perform effectively, because of his unique organizational position and his multiple role, and then to concentrate upon it. If he learns to do this work competently and if he practices it consistently, he will be doing everything within his capacity to secure most effective results through and with the people he leads. Once he learns how to do this work effectively, the difference in *what* he does, *how* he does it, and the *results* he obtains are as significant as the difference between a barber performing an operation for appendicitis and the work of a trained professional surgeon. We identify a leader who has become competent in the work of leadership as a *manager.* A manager specializes in the functions, or the work, of management.

What is probably one of the first attempts to identify and classify the work of management was undertaken by Henri Fayol some fifty years ago. Fayol described the following:

1. Technical activities
2. Commercial activities
3. Financial activities
4. Security activities
5. Managerial (administrative) activities

Fayol divided managerial activities into planning, organization, command, coordination, and control.[1] His pioneering work has been the basis for much of the thinking that has since developed.

THE UNIFIED CONCEPT OF MANAGEMENT

We have attempted to proceed from the basic thinking established by Fayol and have developed what we have called the Unified Concept of Management.[2] This has five characteristics which differ or add to Fayol's approach.

1. *Management is a special kind of work.* We identify management as a kind of *work* a manager performs to enable people to work most effectively together. A manager does not perform technical, commercial, financial, security, accounting, and managerial activities as Fayol had it, but rather, he *manages* technical, commercial, and other specialized functions of the business.

2. *Management work can be classified.* We have analyzed and classified management work and have been able to group it into four management functions and nineteen management activities, each of which is a separable and identifiable kind of work.

3. *Management must be learned.* Managing is not instinctive or intuitive; in fact, it is often directly opposed to the spontaneous, natural mode of action. We do not manage naturally. Managing involves skills that must be learned in terms of logical, verifiable concepts, principles, and techniques as must medicine, engineering, and law.

4. *Management work is measurable.* We can determine how much of this work should be performed in any given position and whether the predetermined amount is being carried out effectively. This is an important consideration. If a manager can measure his work, he can also control it. Furthermore, he can tell where he is strong and where

[1] Henri Fayol's *General and Industrial Management* was first published in Paris in 1916. The English translation was published by Sir Isaac Pitman & Sons, Ltd., London, 1949.

[2] A first statement of the Unified Concept of Management, which is further elaborated here, was made by the author in his *Management and Organization*, McGraw-Hill Company, New York, 1958, pp. 24–48.

he is weak in his performance, and what steps he should take to improve himself.

5. *Management skills are transferable.* A manager who masters the skills involved in leading, planning, organizing, and controlling can apply these skills effectively in the management of different kinds of specialized functions. Provided he has the proper background of functional knowledge in each case, with appropriate preparation, he can transfer his managing skills to management of manufacturing, engineering, marketing, finance, research, or other functions. The more expert a manager is in management skills and the higher his organizational position, the more easily he can do this.

Statement of the Unified Concept of Management

Management is best understood as a unified group of functions made up of specialized activities which are measurable and transferable, can be classified, and must be learned like other skills.

THE ALLEN CLASSIFICATION OF MANAGEMENT FUNCTIONS

In our classification of the work of management, we have analyzed the work managers must perform in terms of the logical criteria we have discussed. We have isolated and identified those parts which are separable from the whole, but logically related, and have classified those parts by assigning each kind of work to a category distinguished by the logic of the related characteristics of the mental and physical effort involved.

Management Functions

We have defined a management function as *a group of related kinds of management work, made up of activities which are closely related to one another and which have characteristics in common derived from the essential nature of the work done.* Each function can be defined so as to separate it logically from other functions.

Management Activities

A function is made up of a group of related activities. The activity is *the basic category of management work;* each activity has an essential sameness which distinguishes it from all other activities.

We have identified the functions and activities of management by first analyzing and identifying the work managers must do to enable people to work most effectively together, then logically grouping these different kinds of work into the proper functions and activities. We have attempted to retain semantic labels commonly in use to identify the functions and activities, but the definitions we have provided will, in many cases, differ from those which have become accepted through precedent.

THE FUNCTIONS AND ACTIVITIES OF MANAGEMENT

Function: Management Planning

ACTIVITIES: Forecasting
Establishing objectives
Programming
Scheduling
Budgeting
Establishing procedures
Developing policies

Function: Management Organizing

ACTIVITIES: Developing organization structure
Delegating
Establishing relationships

Function: Management Leading

ACTIVITIES: Decision making
Communicating
Motivating
Selecting people
Developing people

Function: Management controlling

ACTIVITIES: Establishing performance standards
Performance measuring
Performance evaluating
Performance correcting

A more detailed description of these functions and activities, as developed from our analysis of the work managers perform in managing, is outlined below:

THE FUNCTION OF MANAGEMENT PLANNING

A manager does a certain kind of work that enables him to command the future and not be commanded by it. We define management planning as *the work a manager performs to predetermine a course of action.*

The Activities of Planning

Forecasting. The manager continually looks ahead as far as he can to anticipate the conditions, problems, and opportunities that will probably confront him at future periods of time. *Forecasting* is the work a manager performs to estimate the future.

Establishing Objectives. We must know what we are trying to accomplish before we can expect to achieve it. In spite of this common sense, individuals, companies, and nations without limit have wasted their resources and strength without knowing what end results they wanted from the effort they put forth. *Establishing objectives* is the work a manager performs to determine the end results to be accomplished.

Programming. There are many paths to follow in reaching most goals; some are roundabout and wasteful, others more direct and efficient. Instead of finding his way haphazardly or by trial and error, the manager consciously thinks through the specific activities he will follow to reach his objective. *Programming* is the work a manager performs to establish the sequence and priority of action steps to be followed in reaching objectives.

Scheduling. Timing is always an important element of effective action. To harness time, the manager schedules. *Scheduling* is the work a manager performs to establish a time sequence for program steps.

Budgeting. Cost is a decisive factor. Rather than spending money haphazardly, the manager thinks through in advance how best to use the funds he has available. *Budgeting* is the work a manager performs to allocate resources necessary to accomplish objectives.

Establishing Procedures. Certain work must be performed in precisely the same way wherever it is carried out if we are to attain uniform or predictable results. *Establishing procedures* is the work a manager performs to develop and apply standardized methods of performing specified work.

Developing Policies. When important questions and problems arise repeatedly in the organization, it is generally best to provide standing answers that will anticipate and provide for the action that will be in the interests of the organization as a whole. *Developing policies* is the work a manager performs to interpret standing decisions that apply to repetitive questions and problems of significance to the enterprise as a whole.

THE FUNCTION OF MANAGEMENT ORGANIZING

People in a group undertaking will always find work to do. The important requirement is that they perform work that will contribute to objectives and not the work they happen to want to do. We define management organizing as *the work a manager performs to arrange and relate the work to be done so that it can be performed most effectively by people.*

The Activities of Organizing

Developing Organization Structure. Knowing what work must be done and seeing to it that the proper people do it are a basic requirement for efficient performance. *Developing organization structure* is the work a manager does to identify and group the work to be performed.

Delegating. The manager can do everything himself and make most of the decisions or he can assign as much as possible to his people, reserving for himself only that which others cannot do effectively for him. *Delegating* is the work a manager performs to entrust responsibility and authority to others and to create accountability for results.

Establishing Relationships. Teamwork is primary to effective group effort; it can come about through friction and attrition or by design. *Establishing relationships* is the work a manager performs to create the conditions necessary for mutually cooperative efforts of people.

THE FUNCTION OF MANAGEMENT LEADING

People are the energizing element in any organized group. Good people can get results even without planning and organization; backed by sound plans and organization, good people become outstanding. Providing for the needs of people is one of the important functions of management. We define management leading as *the work a manager performs to cause people to take effective action.*

The Activities of Management Leading

Decision Making. The kind of decisions a manager makes and how he makes them has everything to do with the results he can accomplish. Making sound decisions involves an identifiable kind of work. *Decision making* is the work a manager performs to arrive at conclusions and judgments.

Communicating. What people will do and how well they do it is influenced largely by what they understand. The most effective understanding rarely occurs fortuitously; it is accomplished through work. *Communicating* is the work a manager performs to create understanding.

Motivating. Knowing how to get people to do things because they want to and not because they are forced to is a skill every effective manager must master. *Motivating* is the work a manager performs to inspire, encourage, and impel people to take required action.

Selecting People. The future depends upon the people who create it. Finding the proper people is a critical part of the manager's job. To do this effectively requires performance of a difficult type of work, that of selecting people. *Selecting people* is the work a manager performs to choose people for positions in the organization.

Developing People. Few of us use any substantial part of our potential abilities. It is part of the manager's job to see to it that his people make greatest use of their capabilities. *Developing people* is the work a manager performs to help people improve their knowledge, attitudes, and skills.

THE FUNCTION OF MANAGEMENT CONTROLLING

A continuing need of every manager is to check up to make sure that plans are carried out effectively, that the organization is sound, and that leading is effective. The manager can check up by observing everything himself, or he can perform a group of activities that will enable him to concentrate on exceptional matters without becoming mired in routine and detail. Management controlling is *the work a manager performs to assess and regulate work in progress and completed.*

The Activities of Controlling

Establishing Performance Standards. The ability to differentiate between good work and poor work, acceptable and unacceptable results is a vital requirement. *Establishing performance standards* is the work a manager performs to establish the criteria by which methods and results will be evaluated.

Performance Measuring. Keeping accurate record of what is done and the results secured and transmitting this information to those concerned are at the heart of the control process. *Performance measuring* is the work a manager performs to record and report work in progress and completed.

Performance Evaluating. The manager determines the significance of what is done and the results secured by conscious performance of the work of evaluating. *Performance evaluating* is the work a manager does to appraise work in progress and results secured.

Performance Correcting. The final requirement of control is that variances be corrected. This is accomplished through corrective action. *Performance correcting* is the work a manager performs to regulate and improve methods and results.

FUNCTIONS BOTH INDEPENDENT AND INTERRELATED

So far as we have been able to determine, the functions we have outlined are the separate and disparate activities that go to make up the whole of the management process. A continuation of this logical analysis will probably enable us to identify further components of the management job. For convenience, we have placed the functions into familiar families or categories. While it would be quite feasible to invent new names to describe these families, it would seem far more practical to utilize terms already in common use. First undertaken in 1957, this classification has been continued and revised to the present publication.

Each of the twenty-three management functions and activities is identifiable as a separate kind of work. For each we can identify concepts, principles, and techniques. However, we should keep in mind that each function is also interrelated with all the others. This is the same as saying that pathology, surgery, and urology are all interrelated in medicine but are not the whole of medicine in themselves and can be defined as separate entities.

Each practicing manager is conscious of the close interrelationship of these functions. For example, we make decisions with respect to all of the management functions. We must measure all of the work that we have done. All aspects of the process must be planned. We cannot organize effectively without considering the needs of the people involved.

As we have already noted, no one of these management functions is necessarily first in order of time or importance. First priority is given to whichever kind of work is needed at a specified point in time. If a new job is to be undertaken, planning may come first. If the work is already under way, leading or controlling may be needed. If effort is being improperly applied, organization may have first order of importance.

The process of management as a whole is more important than its parts. But each of the parts is vital to a successful whole.

DEFINITION OF MANAGEMENT LEADERSHIP

In terms of this analysis, we can now define management leadership as *the work of planning, organizing, leading, and controlling performed by a person in a leadership position to enable people to work most effectively together to attain identified ends.*

We specify that this work must be performed by a person in a leadership position with full recognition that it will also be performed by individual contributors and persons concerned with self-improvement. The work of management is purposeful; therefore, it must lead to accomplishment of identified ends. The performance of management work by the leader enables people to work most effectively together in the sense that it is a significant contribution to the group effort.

THE PRINCIPLE OF MANAGEMENT RESULTS

A leader tends to secure most effective results through others by performing the management work of planning, organizing, leading, and controlling.

To manage, every manager at every level must perform the work of planning, organizing, leading, and controlling, *as it applies to his position.* Only when he performs the management work which must be performed *in his position* can he be said to be managing. Furthermore, the manager must carry out these *functions in such a way that their performance constitutes a systematic whole.*

In performing this management work, the scientific manager uses the leadership style required by the group he leads and the environment in which he operates. He can vary, consciously, from an authoritarian to a more democratic approach; he may be concerned primarily with the functional work he manages or the management content of his own job, as the situation requires. He knows how to control by personal inspection and by exception, and he can utilize the proper blend of both.

Wherever he is located in the organization, a manager multiplies himself and the results he can accomplish by the number of people for whom he can plan, organize, lead, and control. In management terms, the chief difference between the president and the first-line supervisor is that the first-line supervisor knows how to get only a few people to work effectively under his direction, while the president has the ability to obtain results through a team made up of all the people in the organization and can reconcile the interests of his team, that is, the company as a whole, and those of stockholders and of the public at large.

SUMMARY

The management leader is a person in a leadership position who specializes in the work which only he has the perspective, objectivity, and balance to do for his followers and for others with whom he has relationships. Management work is classified into the four functions of planning, organizing, leading, and controlling, and nineteen activities. Taken together, these constitute the specialized area of competence of the manager.

CHAPTER 7

Managing and Operating

> *Work is of two kinds: first, altering the position of matter at or near the earth's surface relative to other such matter; second, telling other people to do so. The first kind is unpleasant and ill paid; the second is pleasant and highly paid.* BERTRAND RUSSELL

Much as a manager might want to do so, he finds it difficult if not impossible to concern himself exclusively with management work. To do so, his people would have to be perfectly competent, he would have to act in a highly stabilized situation, and his own skills would need to be nearly perfect. So long as managers are human, they will probably continue to do nonmanagement tasks in the performance of their responsibilities.

OPERATING WORK

All managers do a certain amount of nonmanagement or operating work. Operating work is *the work a manager performs other than the planning, organizing, leading, and controlling work that logically belong in his position.* Although the relative proportions vary, we show these two categories of responsibilities in a management position in Figure 7-1.

The kind of operating work a manager performs will vary. The president of the company, for example, may call upon an important customer to complete a sale. This is not managing; it is the functional work of selling. The vice president of research may be a first-class inventor. Perhaps he develops a new design of great value to the company. However, when he is doing such research, he is not managing.

In some companies the first-line foreman, in an emergency, may step in and operate a crane because the crane operator is in the dispensary. He may write up an order because the clerk is having coffee. In each case, he is not managing but is performing operating work.

The logical approach to identifying operating work is to isolate that work which the manager must do because of his unique organizational position and his multidimensional role. This is his *management* work.

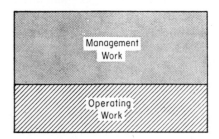

FIG. 7-1. Management and operating work.

All the other work that he does can be characterized as operating work. We can generally identify three categories of operating work.

1. *Execution of Plans and Instructions*

The manager may carry out, himself, some of the plans that have been established or the instructions he has given to others. He may do some of the more difficult or complex parts of their work for others on his team. If new assignments are made to his group, the manager may do the work himself the first time and then train others to do it for him. For example, the engineer may try out and run the first samples with the new electronic microscope his department has acquired. The personnel manager may administer the new psychological tests himself until he gets the "feel" of them and then assign the testing to his testing specialists. In each of these cases, the manager is performing operating work for others.

2. *Management Work Others Could Help Him Perform*

The second category of operating work is part of the manager's planning, organizing, leading, and controlling work that could be performed just as effectively, or even better, by staff units or by the manager's own people. In budgeting, he can obtain accounting help; in selecting people, the personnel department is available to assist him. In our discussion of delegation, we shall define the limits beyond which the manager cannot safely delegate parts of his management work. In general, he must always himself *initiate* and *make final decisions* with respect to each of the management activities assigned to his management position. However, he can frequently secure advice and service from others in carrying out other work involved in these activities.

Throughout Southern Counties Gas Company of California, for example, the department manager develops objectives for his major activities. However, he secures a great deal of help from the section heads who report to him, from staff departments, and from his own superior. This minimizes the detail the manager handles and enables him to concentrate upon the important elements of managing.

When he performs the detail and routine parts of his management work that could be performed just as effectively or better by others, the manager is actually performing work that is operating work to him.

3. *Management Work He Performs for Others*

In surveying his operating work, the manager will find he frequently performs management work that should be carried out in other positions. This becomes operating work to him. For example, the manager may develop objectives or he may prepare a program and budget for one of his people. Should that person be able to do the work within the limits set by his unique organizational position and his multiple role? If so, the manager is probably doing operating work.

THE IMPORTANCE OF OPERATING WORK

A manager's legitimate operating work *is just as important as his management work*. The danger lies in the manager's doing more operating work than he should; as we shall see, there is every tendency for him to do this. Since the time available and the capacities of managers are always limited, it follows that the primary concern of every manager should be the performance of the management work assigned to his position. To the extent that he concentrates on this kind of work, the manager can enable the members of his group to accomplish over-all objectives and, in the process, satisfy their own personal goals. He can also coordinate and integrate the efforts of the group he manages with those of other groups doing related work.

By concentrating upon planning, organizing, leading, and controlling for his group, the manager can multiply its total effectiveness. What is more, by confining himself as largely as possible to the work he *should* be doing, he avoids the temptation to perform for them the work of other members of the team. As a result, each person has an opportunity to carry out the most important and challenging responsibility and authority that can be assigned to his position, and his efforts are not relegated to mere detail and routine. This, in itself, is one of the most potent sources of deep and enduring job satisfaction. In spite of the importance of management work, our research shows that there is a very human tendency for managers to prefer to operate. Validated now in almost every industrialized country of the world, this has become known as Allen's First Principle, or as we originally called it, The Principle of Operating Priority.

ALLEN'S FIRST PRINCIPLE: THE PRINCIPLE OF OPERATING PRIORITY

When called upon to perform both management work and operating work during the same time period, a manager will tend to give first priority to operating work.

Almost invariably, managers put too little time on management work, too much time on operating work. The reasons for this can be readily discerned. Management work tends to be more difficult and demanding than operating work. It is largely mental; it requires concentration and the application of logical thinking. Most people prefer to do things or operate rather than to think about them, and thinking is the essence of management.

Management involves getting other people to do things; operating means that we accomplish the end result ourselves. When we operate, we may appear to get desired results faster. Actually, however, it usually means that we are carrying out work other people should be doing for us.

Operating through Familiarity

The manager may operate because he is most familiar with the operating work. Quite likely, he came to the top through a functional channel. Before he became a manager, he probably was an expert in sales, production, finance, engineering, or some other specialized function. Probably he was good at his work; he liked it. Given the opportunity, he will still tend to perform as much of it as he can. In contrast, the management part of his job seems nebulous. He often refers to it as "paper work." The principles and techniques he should use may be unknown to him. He finds the problems intangible. Even after he makes a decision, it generally is carried out by somebody else, and he rarely sees the end results firsthand. It is therefore little wonder that he prefers to operate.

Operating Because of Lack of Confidence

The manager may concentrate on operating work because he lacks confidence in his subordinates. He assumes that nobody else can do the work as well as he can. By this, he probably means that nobody else would do it exactly the same way as he would. As a result, he tends to keep the most important jobs for himself. Often, however, he will get into unimportant detail because he is convinced he still knows how to do it best. The president of a $1 billion company, for example, who started out as a stock boy, inadvertently received a customer letter complaining of nondelivery of an order. The executive personally spent six days in the company's stock rooms, showing the inventory clerks how to do their jobs properly. In the chain of command, six other people were also held accountable for the same work and were being paid to see that it was done.

Operating through Example

The boss's boss is often an important factor in forcing the manager to concentrate upon operating work. If the top man insists that his subordinate managers know everything about matters all the way down the line, he will literally force his subordinates into operating work. The production superintendent, for example, in a large metal-goods manufacturing plant near London, England, spent the first hour every morning touring each department in the plant. Asked why he spent so much time checking his supervisors, he replied: "If a production line falls behind, or rejects start piling up, the plant manager calls me and expects me to know all about it. If I have to check back in the production centers, he makes it clear he doesn't think I am doing my job. I am an operator in self-defense."

It is clear that the amount of time and effort a manager devotes to management work, in part, depends upon the standards and the personal example set by his own superiors. If the superior appraises his subordinate's performance in terms of management results, management will receive emphasis. If operating proficiency is a basis for performance evaluation, nonmanagement work will receive first attention.

THE PRINCIPLE OF ORGANIZATION LEVELS

The lower his organization level, the more operating work a manager tends to perform.

We have established this principle as a result of our studies of the relative amounts of management work managers at different levels are required to perform. This principle enables us to anticipate that lower-level managers will tend to devote more of their time and effort to nonmanagement work than will those at upper levels. There are several reasons for this, including proximity to the line of operations, opportunity to delegate, and familiarity with the work.

Proximity to the Line of Operations

Foremen and other managers at the first level supervise people who are assigned only operating work. Any task the operators cannot perform for themselves most easily falls to the lot of the supervisor. If there is an overload or an emergency, instead of calling in somebody from another department or from the outside, the supervisor will probably help if he can. If a man is injured or becomes sick, the supervisor will fill in until a substitute can be found. If a new job is taken on which his men cannot handle by themselves, the supervisor will probably lend his assistance until he can train his people to do the work.

When an executive higher in the organization becomes irate or begins to ring the alarm bell because of a breakdown or stoppage, the supervisor is most easily and conveniently thrown into the fray.

Opportunity to Delegate

At upper levels of the organization, managers are concerned primarily with managing other managers. When the next man in line is competent in doing the work of management, it is much easier to delegate the details of management work to him. At lower levels, the people being supervised are largely unfamiliar with management work, and there is little opportunity to delegate this kind of work to them. In most companies, staff advice and service become increasingly available at higher levels of the organization. As a result, managers have more access to specialists in budgeting, forecasting, organization, and controls who can help them to do a more complete management job.

Familiarity with the Work

As we have seen, it is very human for people to prefer to do those things with which they are most familiar. The closer he is to the function in which he specialized before he came into the management ranks, the greater the tendency of the manager to prefer to do this kind of work.

RATIO OF MANAGING AND OPERATING WORK

Our studies have shown that the ratio of management to operating work tends to decrease as we go down the organization. At the top levels of the company, managers have maximum opportunity to delegate and can concentrate most fully upon management work. At lower levels, managers are called upon more and more to assume operating responsibilities.   At the first supervisory level, the management content of the work is least.

If we look at an organization of, let us say, eight levels, we discover some interesting facts about the relative proportions of management and operating work.

At the first level of management, it is clear that managers are concerned with planning, organizing, leading, and controlling the efforts of others who are engaged primarily in operating work. At the second level of management, we find managers who are managing other managers.   This process continues with each added level of management organization, with more managers managing more managers.

Obviously, a great deal of management work is being performed. The blunt truth of the matter is that, in most companies, a great deal of this work is overlap, duplication, or unnecessary effort. In many instances, managers at upper levels reserve to their positions parts of the operating work they want to perform themselves.   Unless his own boss intervenes, there is nobody to refuse this assumption of responsibility by the accountable manager.   As a result, in most organizations, we find a great deal of unnecessary operating work being done at all levels.   This means that managers at lower levels are deprived of the opportunity to do the more difficult and demanding management tasks and to learn to master this work.

A direct outgrowth of this pattern is the tendency to generate excessively high management costs.   These generally show as overhead or administrative expense.   Because they must be allocated to every unit of product sold, they inevitably tend to raise both the cost and the price.

In most companies, if managers would concentrate upon the work they should be doing in their positions and if they would delegate as fully and completely as possible, fewer managers would be needed. What is even more important, the interesting and significant tasks could be delegated closer to the line of operations where they could be exercised most effectively.

In our analysis of the proportions of management and operating work performed at various levels, we have been able to establish a typical pattern that seems to hold true for most companies.   If we look at the ratio of management and operating work from a *theoretical* standpoint, we find that, at the top level of the company, the chief executive position, in theory at least, should be able to devote about 90 per cent of his time and effort to managing, 10 per cent to operating. At successively lower levels, the proportion of management decreases and that of operating increases.   At the first line of management—the foreman level—we find that, again in theory, the foreman can, at best, devote 50 per cent of his time to managing, 50 per cent to operating.

In actual fact, if we examine the management and operating content of these positions by means of time diaries and ratio delay studies, we find that the general tendency for the top executive is to devote about 50 per cent of his time to managing and 50 per cent to operating. At successively lower levels, the percentage of operating emphasis increases until, at the lowest level, we tend to find the foreman

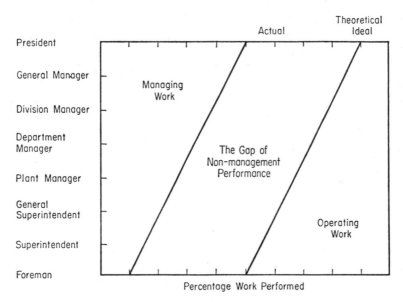

FIG. 7-2. Proportions of management and operating work.

devoting roughly 10 per cent of his time to managing and 90 per cent to operating. Charted out, this gives us the picture shown in Figure 7-2.

THE DEVELOPMENT OF MANAGEMENT LEADERSHIP

There is no panacea for accomplishing the transition from natural to management leadership. It requires the mastery of the work of management at all levels of the company. The *managed* organization grows and progresses under the conscious and systematic planning, organizing, leading, and controlling work performed by its managers at all levels. It studies and analyzes its own activities and those of competing organizations and consciously adopts those attributes which will contribute to its own advancement and enrichment.

Litton Industries is a case in point. Specializing in highly diversified advanced electronics, the company has systematically built its business through carefully planned acquisitions. Through foresight, it has managed to avoid most of the pitfalls other leading diversifiers have fallen into and in seven years is in a position to compete effectively with much larger companies.

Beginning in 1946 as a producer of precision glassworking lathes, the company grew slowly under Charles V. Litton, a highly capable engineer. It established real momentum in 1953 when Charles B. Thornton first assumed command. Since then, it has grown, under Thornton and Roy L. Ash, through carefully planned acquisitions to a leading position in its industry.

Management leadership enables the organization to develop to the limits of its innate capacity. It provides guidance and direction that will ensure greatest personal satisfaction for each of its members and, in consequence, greatest success for the organization.

It organizes for continued growth so that autonomy of its parts can be maintained without jeopardizing the integrity of the whole. It establishes the controls necessary for stability and security while yet permitting its members freedom to pursue their goals and satisfactions.

MANAGEMENT AND AUTOMATION

Far-reaching changes in management are under way based upon use of the computer and electronic data processing. Important now, these new developments will be of even greater significance during the next few years. Much uninformed speculation usually attends the advent of developments of such far-reaching significance, and this has been markedly true of the computer. It is well, from the beginning, to clarify what we can reasonably expect to happen.

WHAT IS AUTOMATION?

To understand what automation is, we must review briefly the basic elements of human productive effort. To produce real wealth, useful to society, we must have people who will put forth mental and physical effort to convert raw or component materials into products or services.[1]

The great multiplier in this process has been the use of machines and

---

[1] For an excellent, straightforward discussion of these basic considerations, see Fred G. Clark and Richard Stanton Rimanoczy, *How We Live,* D. Van Nostrand Company, Inc., Princeton, N.J., 1944.

tools. From the first wheel invented by Neolithic man, through the steam engine, cotton gin, adding machine, and nuclear energy, tools have added an exponential factor to our production of goods and services.

The primary use of a tool is to multiply human mental and physical effort. Two thousand men with shovels, baskets, mauls, and tampers might build a mile of modern highway in a year. Twenty men with machines can do the job faster and more efficiently in a small fraction of the time.

People use both their brains and their muscles to do work. Until the recent past, machines have been used most largely to replace and supplement *muscle power*. This has had a prodigious effect upon expanding our capacity to produce, increasing the share available to each person who benefits from machine utilization, and making more time available for cultural and recreational purposes. If we keep in mind that the pooled physical effort of the more than three billions of human beings in the world would not begin to equal the machine power available in the United States alone, it will be obvious that this multiplier is potent indeed.

Machines can also be used to supplement and replace mental skills. The adding machine does work for a person that would otherwise have to be performed largely by his own brain. One machine can do a million or more times as much adding and subtracting as a human brain—and do it faster, more accurately, and without tiring.

For certain types of mental work, machines are far superior to the human brain. Happily enough, these are repetitive, noncreative kinds of work that provide least challenge and satisfaction to humans.

MECHANIZATION AND AUTOMATION

We have identified two separate but closely interrelated developments: the replacement of *human muscle power* by machines and the enhancement of *human brain power* through machines. *Mechanization* we define as the process of using machine power primarily to multiply human physical skills. *Automation* is the process of using machine power primarily to augment human mental skills. The two, of course, go together just as do the hand and the brain, the airplane and the mind that guides it. Semantically, however, it is useful to differentiate between the muscle and brain components.

The most significant characteristic of our age is the invention of new and more powerful tools of both kinds. Nuclear energy is greater than steam or electric energy; the jet engine is more powerful than the gas engine. Just as these extend and amplify muscle power, we now have mental tools that increase and expedite our mental processes. Chief of these, at present, is the computer.

WHAT IS THE COMPUTER?

A characteristic of the human brain is its ability to take in information, retain it, and while it is in storage, perform operations upon it that change its nature, content, and meaning. The brain can then put out this new or altered information through the agencies of speech, writing, and other means. The computer is a machine designed to do similar operations. It has a means of accepting *inputs,* a memory or *storage* mechanism, a *calculating* unit for performing logical operations such as multiplying, dividing, adding, and subtracting, and an *output* unit for giving out the information.

Since it is an inanimate machine, in a real sense the computer can do only what it is directed to do by a human mind. The process of "telling the machine" what to do is called *programming.* Use of this term is important for it recognizes that the machine must be given instructions in the form of a logical sequence of action steps before it can be used effectively.

CHANGES AND REQUIREMENTS

Far-reaching changes in management are already occurring through use of the computer. Utilized to collect, analyze, and report information, the new machines can take in and give out routine, clerical-type information several thousand times as fast as the human brain; they can perform simple calculations with a million or more times the speed and accuracy we could expect of a human being, with other marvels of speed and computational dexterity to match. Because of this lightning speed and the accuracy that accompanies it, the computer is being used extensively to replace human brain power. Factories which already have been highly *mechanized,* with most manual work replaced by machine power, are now being *automated,* with the programming, scheduling, operation, and control of machines taken over by other machines. These changes are rapidly occurring also in office and clerical applications. Within ten years there probably will be more talking done between machines in business and industry than there will be between persons.

The pattern of change which mechanization brought about is being duplicated with automation. We have developed a means for vastly increasing our output of goods and services of all kinds. To use automation we need much greater capital investment; we need a higher level of management and operating skills on the part of the people who will work with the automated tools and controls; and we need to develop methods of integrating the people displaced so that they can continue to share in the new productivity.

USES OF AUTOMATION IN MANAGEMENT

Because management work is primarily *mental,* we find that the computer is having a profound impact upon planning, control, decision making, and communication.[2] It is making new demands upon our organizations and putting our ability to motivate at a premium. We shall investigate a few of these new applications in the chapters to follow.

SUMMARY

All managers perform both management work and nonmanagement or operating work. The Principle of Operating Priority establishes that when a manager is called upon to perform both management work and operating work during the same time period, he will tend to give first priority to operating work. This tendency leads to redundancy in management positions, duplication and overlap of work, and substantial waste and inefficiency. Managers at different levels of the organization are required to perform different proportions of management and operating work. In general, the higher his organization level, the more management work a manager is required to perform. The converse is stated as the Principle of Organization Levels, to the effect that the lower his organization level, the more operating work a manager tends to perform.

[2] Useful summaries of some of the more recent practical applications of the computer in management will be found in Donald G. Malcolm and Alan J. Rowe (eds.), *Management Control Systems,* John Wiley & Sons, Inc., New York, 1960, and James O. Gallagher, *Management Information Systems and the Computer,* American Management Association, New York, 1961.

CHAPTER 8   *Management—Art, Science, or Profession?*

One of the great differences between the amateur and the professional is that the latter has the capacity to progress. W. SOMERSET MAUGHAM

In analyzing management, we should examine the confusion that has arisen in attempts to determine whether it is an art, a science, or a profession. Perhaps the important significance of making this distinction is to help us to think more clearly about management and what is required to improve it. Dictionaries show a substantial overlap in meaning; therefore, we have been rather arbitrary in our attempt to establish clear-cut definitions.

MANAGEMENT AS AN ART

We define an art as *a skill exercised in terms of the individual personality of the practitioner.* In these terms, leadership can certainly be regarded as an art; to a substantial extent, so also can management. We find that most leaders have developed their own bundle of skills to fit their own personalities. This natural leadership may be strong and positive. It has great flexibility. Probably there will always be an art, or personal practice of management, just as there is art as well as science in medicine and engineering. If we deal with management exclusively as an art, however, we will find it difficult to formalize and systematize our knowledge of leadership and to teach it to others. We need more than artistic practice of leadership.

MANAGEMENT AS A SCIENCE

Can we consider management as a true science? We define a science as *a unified and systematically arranged body of knowledge dealing with facts or truths and showing the operation of general laws or principles.*

Clearly, management is not now a science. In fact, the specialized kind of work we identify as management is practiced largely by natural leaders who do, spontaneously and intuitively, what is necessary to get results from the people they lead. Frederick Winslow Taylor postulated a science of management. He systematized and advanced our thinking. He had not yet made management truly scientific, but his work was a great contribution to this end. In time, we will accept a true science of leadership, but this can be brought about only through systematic, orderly, and conscious work toward the development, validation, and classification of the additional knowledge we need.

This new science of management will need to draw upon such other sciences as psychology, sociology, anthropology, and mathematics, but we already have evidence that we will be able to satisfy the requirements of a science of management leadership as fully as we are able to satisfy the requirements of psychology, sociology, and anthropology as sciences today.[1]

THE PROFESSION OF MANAGEMENT

We define a profession as *a specialized kind of work practiced through the use of classified knowledge, a common vocabulary, and requiring standards of practice and a code of ethics established by a recognized body.* A profession is a vocation. It draws upon the sciences and other fields of knowledge but has its own sources of information logically sorted out and labeled. A professional can utilize the experience of others by applying recognized principles in the performance of his work. He belongs to a homogeneous group, the members of which are characterized by their adherence to accepted ethical standards, their understanding of a common language, and the competent performance of the work of their profession.

Practitioners of a science or of an art may form a profession, depending upon whether or not they utilize classified knowledge, subscribe to recognized standards of competence, use a common vocabulary, and adhere to a code of ethics. A profession is an organized group in that the practitioners recognize a professional body that establishes and enforces standards of conduct and practice.

The important requirement for management now is that it becomes a profession. Certainly this movement would help to standardize, formalize, and advance much of our scientific knowledge. We should emphasize that this will not be a profession limited to *business*. It will

[1] We use the terms "scientific leadership," "management leadership," "scientific management," and "management" interchangeably to identify this future science of management because common usage has not yet crystallized to a point that any one term is dominant.

be practiced by leaders in government, the military, education, and all other types of organized endeavors.   Confronted with this opportunity, there is little point now in quarreling about the labels; far better to devote our energies to analysis, test, and verification of the knowledge and principles we are just now beginning to crystallize.   Wherever it is necessary to improve the ability of people to work more effectively together, we need both a science and a profession of management.   This, assuredly, is the end to which our efforts should be directed.

Some Requirements of a Profession of Management

Substantial progress has been made toward creation of a profession of management.   If this is to be brought to completion, three steps have yet to be taken.

1. *The Creation of a Professional Association.*   An association, national in scope, should be organized to provide impartial, objective leadership in the development of the scientific and professional aspects of management.   Such an association must be fully subsidized; it can have nothing to sell, in a commercial sense.   It must offer its services as a right of professional membership, not market them as a product.

2. *Increase in Knowledge.*   There should be a great acceleration in the tempo of study and research in scientific management.   This probably will have to be stimulated by business enterprise since no other agency has yet shown the initiative or the ability to think along such fresh and creative lines as has already been demonstrated by some of our leading companies.   Some of the foundations might study the true needs in this area and subsidize creative effort.   A more positive contribution is greatly needed.

3. *Improved Education of Managers.*   There is need for better education of young and aspiring leaders in the difficult and complex requirements of scientific and professional management.   Education is our greatest need, and here creative leadership is urgently required.   A form of internship and residency is probably mandatory and should be available also to teachers and professors of management at the beginning of their teaching careers.

CHARACTERISTICS OF A PROFESSIONAL MANAGER

As management has become more highly formalized and professional, we find that the practitioners whom we can most confidently label as the forerunners of this new leadership tend to exhibit certain characteristics.

The Professional Manager Is a Specialist

The professional manager, contrary to the general assumption, does not regard himself as a generalist.   He is a specialist in a demanding, difficult, and often frustrating kind of work. He does not look upon himself primarily as an expert in sales, production, engineering, or finance, but as master of the work of management.

Much of this is contrary to the solidification of past mistakes which we often label as "tradition." Not long ago we selected people for leadership positions because of their personalities; we promoted them because of their expertness in selling, engineering, research, or production. We paid people for their "experience," "responsibility," and the work they happened to be doing. The question of whether it was important work, or even necessary, seldom arose. One result is that management positions are now filled with natural leaders who are expert in the work of the people they supervise. Because these managers concentrate on the day-to-day operating problems their people are paid to handle, they seldom have time, and rarely develop the ability, to master the unfamiliar and more difficult management work they are paid to do.

The results are expensive. Count the number of managers and operators in a typical business, governmental, or institutional unit, and you will frequently find a proportion of 1 to 4 or 1 to 5. Furthermore, this manager, working feverishly to manage one or two people, is often surrounded by a corps of assistants, buttressed by the efforts of six or seven committees, and supported by several staff people. All are busy. The total expense is heavy. The sad fact is much of the work done is unnecessary or repetitious. When we require managers to specialize in their proper responsibilities, the ratios improve perceptibly and costs decrease with gratifying promptness.

Managers should specialize in management work. More and more, we are coming to realize that selection and promotion of people to management positions should be on the basis of their potential and their ability to perform this specialized work. The performance of people in management positions should be appraised largely in these terms. Managers should be compensated for their demonstrated competence in managing. People educated for management should be helped to develop the broad background, the understanding, and the specific skills necessary to become professional practitioners in the work of management.

The Professional Manager Utilizes Valid Principles

There is a widely held belief that principles of management cannot be stated, that managers of each generation must, through trial and error, develop anew their personal approaches to the supposedly unique problems that confront them. So far, we have discovered few immutable laws which govern business results. However, in our studies, we have been able to isolate and state fundamental truths as principles which apply to management wherever it is practiced.   A principle is *a means of capitalizing upon the accumulated experience of the past.*   It predicts, accurately, what will *tend* to happen in many problem situations.   Sound principles can serve as basic tools to guide managers in their decisions and actions.   Those stated in this volume have now been validated thoroughly by operating managers throughout the world, and have been soundly tested in practice.

The Professional Manager Utilizes a Common Vocabulary

Confusion and misunderstanding of management concepts arise as much from lack of common definition of management terms as from any other source.   If we are to communicate effectively and to continue to advance and improve our methods of management, it is important for all managers to speak the same language.   Managers, everywhere, who are attempting to become professionals in their work recognize this.   To assist in the process, the management terms used in this book have been carefully selected to describe the things that actually happen when managers perform the work of managing.   We have attempted to make the definitions logical and precise, and to ensure that they are consistent with the pattern of sound management.   The definitions of management terms provided in this book already have earned wide acceptance in the United States and Canada, Europe, Australia, the Orient, and Africa.

The Professional Manager Develops Transferable Skills

A manager who masters the skills involved in the work of management can apply these skills effectively in the management of different kinds of specialized functions.   *In each case, it is imperative that he have the proper background and knowledge of the functions he is managing.*   With this preparation, he can transfer his managing skills to management of manufacturing, engineering, marketing, finance, research, or other functions.   *The more expert a manager is in management skills and the higher his organizational position, the more easily he can do this.*

Professional Managers Have Many Personalities

There is a widely held belief that a manager should have a certain kind of personality.   We have not been able to discover an "ideal" personality for managers.   Because the people *being led* vary so widely in their personality characteristics, we have discovered that effective managers may also have greatly varying personalities.   We have found that the successful manager does not necessarily conform to the personality pattern predicated upon the behavior studies of conventional leaders. He may be friendly or reserved, modest or brilliant, cautious or bold. His educational background may run the gamut from liberal arts to nuclear physics, from accounting to law. Just as successful doctors, engineers, and scientists come in all shapes and sizes, professional managers have different characteristics. Their uniqueness is not in their personalities but in the work they do.

The Professional Manager Has an Exacting Philosophy

The professional manager tends to have a practical philosophy, oriented to the real needs of people. He tends to avoid the extremes and the empty panaceas—the cult of "personality," the shallow manipulations of "human relations," and the powerless philosophy of "group think group do." He rarely subscribes to the proposition that people are unhappy because their jobs do not make them worthwhile. He emphasizes that people make jobs; jobs do not make people. The professional manager stresses that happiness is *in* people, and that almost any job can be important and rewarding if leaders learn how to make it significant and if people can be motivated to work effectively at it.

The professional manager has few cure-alls in his approach to leadership. He does not offer comfort and happiness to all. Rather, his leadership emphasizes that accomplishment is the result of logically applied effort. This pragmatic viewpoint helps to highlight, in cold relief, the shirker and the nonperformer, and it provides blunt encouragement for greater attainment. To some extent, this philosophy is perhaps a reaction to the soft and palliative approach advocated by the dreamers and theorists who dwell mentally in the millennium and rarely experience the harsh brambles of the present.

In his philosophy, the manager is dedicated to the proposition that *personal fulfillment can be realized best through personal effort.* By helping people to find satisfaction within themselves, the manager is accomplishing something of enduring significance. He is translating to the demands of a new age and a changed environment the philosophy upon which all great human accomplishment has been founded. He is demonstrating that this stern, demanding, and ultimately most satisfying credo can be discovered again by each of us.

The Professional Manager Encourages Personal Freedom

The paradox of organizational growth is the need to preserve individual freedom within the limits of conformity necessary to maintain organizational integrity. The competent leader recognizes this and knows how to encourage the greatest possible liberty of expression and of action for each person without jeopardizing the liberty of others or of the group as a whole.

To create and maintain individual liberty within the necessary limits requires skill and understanding. The tendency of the leader is to demand more conformity than he requires, and of followers to want more liberty than they need. Since the leader already has a measure of liberty relative to that of his followers, his tendency is to preserve it by requiring his followers to conform. Followers, of their condition being required to conform, tend to want to remove the restrictions placed upon them.

The leader of a group wants conformity also because he needs it for emotional support; he is eternally insecure in his authority and to permit disagreement seems to threaten his power. Followers want perfect liberty because any restriction of freedom seems to deprive them of something which is rightfully theirs. Since disequilibrium tends to exist continually, striking a proper balance at any given time is difficult. To find and hold the path that lies between the sterility of absolute conformance and the chaos of perfect freedom is an accomplishment worthy of a real professional in management.

The Professional Manager Sponsors a Managerial Code of Ethics

While an accepted code of ethics for managers does not yet exist, there is an increasing belief that basic standards of right conduct are a necessary part of this new profession. Certainly, successful results are best ensured over the long term if managers can conduct themselves in terms of clearly defined, ethical standards. We find that many managers have formulated and already adopted their own personal code of ethics. So, also, have many companies. With time, we can anticipate that this movement will spread gradually. There is common agreement that every manager who is concerned with the recognition of management as a science and a profession has an obligation to conduct his personal activities so as to reflect the highest standards of professional conduct.

SUMMARY

Management is identified as an art, a science, and a profession. Already an art in that it is a skill exercised in terms of the individual personality of the practitioner, management has not yet become a science because it cannot yet be characterized as a unified and systematically arranged body of knowledge dealing with facts or truths and showing the operation of general laws or principles. Management should become a profession as rapidly as possible. This will require that we advance our knowledge of management until it becomes a specialized kind of work practiced through the use of classified knowledge and a common vocabulary. It will require standards of practice and a code of ethics established by a recognized body.

When the professional manager emerges within the next ten or twelve years he will be a specialist. He will utilize principles of management to capitalize upon the accumulated experience of the past. He will speak a vocabulary understandable to other professional managers and will employ skills that can be transferred from one kind of functional work to another. The professional manager will have a vigorous and exacting personal philosophy that will stress the encouragement of personal freedom within the limits of professional discipline.

PART TWO

Management Planning

CHAPTER 9

Management Planning

> *Whatever failures I have known, whatever errors I have committed, whatever follies I have witnessed in private and public life have been the consequence of action without thought.* BERNARD BARUCH

DEFINITIONS

The Function of Planning

The work a manager performs to predetermine a course of action.

The Activities of Planning

Forecasting: the work a manager performs to estimate the future.

Establishing Objectives: the work a manager performs to determine the end results to be accomplished.

Programming: the work a manager performs to establish the sequence and priority of action steps to be followed in reaching objectives.

Scheduling: the work a manager performs to establish a time sequence for program steps.

Budgeting: the work a manager performs to allocate resources necessary to accomplish objectives.

Establishing Procedures: the work a manager performs to develop and apply standardized methods of performing specified work.

Developing Policies: the work a manager performs to develop and interpret standing decisions that apply to repetitive questions and problems of significance to the enterprise as a whole.

THE APPROACH

In our discussion of planning we shall try to establish a logical framework within which planning can be carried out most effectively. We

97

shall establish those principles of planning which we have been able to develop and validate up to this time. Where helpful, we shall cite illustrations to clarify some of the issues involved. Since this volume is not intended to be a work book, we shall not attempt to develop the specific techniques to be used in planning nor shall we delve into the detail steps which, while interesting in themselves, might detract from the sharp outlines of the over-all picture.

THE LOGIC OF PLANNING

In our analysis of management, we found that one of the vital kinds of work required of a manager, because of his unique organizational position and his dual role, is that of doing everything within his command to help his followers and himself to create the kind of future they want. This work we identified as the function of planning, and we grouped as its activities all of those identifiable kinds of work necessary to predetermine a course of action.

To visualize properly what planning entails, we should establish that if results are to be accomplished, action must be taken. There are two basic ways of getting things done. The first is to plunge ahead, doing the things that appear to be necessary, handling problems as they come up, and taking advantage of opportunities as they occur. This approach may be successful, but it generally requires an extremely capable individual who will be able to mastermind everything that must be done. If he can be alert to the needs of everyone and make the decisions required to keep the whole enterprise moving, his leadership will be effective. Even if we were to find such an individual, however, we would discover that the work and the problems eventually would become too large and too complex for any one man. It is here that the alternative becomes important. This involves thinking through, in advance, both what we want to accomplish and how it might best be accomplished. Essentially, a plan is a mental picture of future accomplishment.

Planning in American Telephone and Telegraph Company

To illustrate the cumulative effect of sound and consistent planning, let us examine the American Telephone and Telegraph Company. Alexander Graham Bell, who invented the telephone, visualized a universal network of telephones as early as 1878. Shortly after the first commercial telephone exchange was opened, Bell wrote that "telephone wires could be laid underground, uniting private dwellings, counting houses, shops, and manufactories with a central office, establishing direct communication between any two places." Further, he wrote, "in the future, wires will unite the head offices of the Telephone Company in different cities, and a man in one part of the country may communicate by word of mouth with another in a different place."

Though later many a dubious bassoon was to be sounded, Bell foresaw the need to direct every activity to the accomplishment of this end. "I impress upon you all the advisability of keeping this end in view," he said, "that all arrangements of the telephone may be eventually realized in this grand system."

Today, at almost any second of any day, more than seven thousand Americans talk to one another over this "direct communication" system. More complex than most other business activities, this system is at the same time one of the most efficient. Most of the 80 million telephones in service handle their complement of two calls per day by each member of the family with attention only once every three and one-half years. Intricate and infinitely complex, the system is the result of continued planning.

CHARACTERISTICS OF PLANNING

Planning is the basis for successful management action. A plan is a trap laid to capture the future. It is the process a manager follows in thinking through beforehand what he wants to accomplish and how he will do it. Neither the individual nor the enterprise need be at the back and call of chance. We are beginning to discover that, to a surprising degree, we can master the future. We can *make* happen what we *want* to happen.

When we plan, we take time to reflect and analyze, to consider alternatives, to make sound, considered decisions about the future. We decide in advance what we are going to do, how we will do it, under what conditions we will carry it out, how we will accomplish it, and what we will require to get the results we want. Because we think ahead, we avoid the tendency to make hasty judgments and to take haphazard action.

THE ADVANTAGES OF PLANNING

Proper planning greatly simplifies the task of a manager. It makes integrated and coordinated effort possible. If we know where we are going, we are much more likely to get there. Once we have the whole picture in mind, it is easier to make the parts fit together and to ensure that the action that follows is timed so it will take place in the proper sequence.

Planning enables us to make most effective and economical use of manpower, equipment, facilities, and money. If we identify in advance our needs for people, we can develop individuals inside the organization so that they will be ready when the opportunity for promotion appears. Planning makes it possible to let subordinates know what is required of them and to give them an opportunity to participate in the decisions that are made. This keeps interest and enthusiasm at a high level and enables the manager to incorporate into his plans the best thinking of those closest to the point where the action will be carried out.

The importance of planning is highlighted by the emphasis well-managed companies put upon it. Industry leaders, convinced that their future success depends as much upon the thought their managers give to planning as to process and technology, expect managers at all levels, from first-line supervisor to top executive, to devote a substantial portion of their time to planning before taking action.

BARRIERS TO PLANNING

The greatest source of long-term failure for organized endeavors undoubtedly is the failure to plan. In substance, this amounts to failure of the leaders of the enterprise to think consistently ahead and, as importantly, to get all others in management positions to think *with* and *for* them. This failure most often is due to identifiable barriers, which can be anticipated and overcome.

One barrier is the fact that many of us tend to put first emphasis on operations and to push our planning work to the background. The more time we spend fighting fires, the less we have to make plans that would prevent the fires. Thus, we fall into a vicious circle which forces us to put continuing emphasis on operations. It can be broken only by taking a firm stand and making a positive attack on the planning work that must be done.

We may fail to plan because of the uncertainty of the future. Looking ahead, we may conclude that anticipating future events has a strong resemblance to looking into a crystal ball. Since we cannot know precisely what is going to happen at future periods, it may even seem pointless to take present action to deal with these future imponderables. The fact is, of course, that the plans we make today are the best way we know to command the future and not to be commanded by it.

Planning often falls by the wayside because it is difficult and sometimes frustrating work which demands careful, analytical thought. Planning is mostly intangible and must be carried out in the mind, where it will prosper only to the extent that imagination and intelligence are brought to bear upon it. Since the manager develops plans for others to carry out, he rarely has the satisfaction of tangible accomplishment from his planning work but must content himself vicariously with what others have been able to achieve with his ideas.

The inadequacy of our knowledge is another barrier. We have few principles or effective techniques of planning and there is little common agreement about what we *do* know. Semantic ambiguities are commonplace and it is sometimes difficult to know what another person *means* when he talks about budgets, forecasts, and programs.

Real as these barriers are, if we recognize them and work to overcome them, we can make of planning a more precise and useful tool. Certainly a manager must learn to plan effectively if he makes any pretense of professional practice.

The untrained leader who has not learned that an ounce of logical thought is worth more than a ton of activity typically plunges ahead into the uncharted sea of the future, never stopping to set his course or even to determine his destination. The endeavor he commands may be successful through good fortune, but its long-term survival is at best uncertain.

The case of Yuba Consolidated Industries well illustrates the point. Highly successful and profitable in its basic business of gold mining, in 1958 Yuba felt it necessary to use part of its close to $2 million yearly profit on diversification. Looking around for opportunities, the company spotted a welding company and quickly bought it up. Almost as fast as it could spend the money, it acquired a steel mill, a petrochemical manufacturing firm, a firm building industrial cranes, another manufacturer of power tools, and a conglomerate of steel plate and boiler equipment units.

Within three years the company skyrocketed sales from $22 million to $330 million and had seventeen operating divisions. But the precipitate and largely unplanned growth quickly got out of hand. Within another year the company was in debt almost as much as its assets were worth, and the enterprise found itself in severe difficulty.

Compare to this the planned progress of Harris-Intertype Corporation, a leader in the manufacture of printing equipment. The company grew slowly to a sales volume of $20 million in 1949. Then, under the strong direction of its top management, the company began to plan systematically for growth. It improved and expanded its basic product line, increased product development, and brought its marketing to a sharper focus. A series of five-year plans was instituted and carried out, with the net result that the company was able to double and redouble its volume. It has diversified successfully into electronics and has strengthened its position in its basic markets. Its planning has been so effective that only once in fifteen years has the company missed its annual corporate objective by more than 10 per cent.

As another case in point, North American Aviation, Inc., at the end of World War II, was working at top capacity to deliver orders for 8,000 aircraft. The company had 90,000 employees and great sums invested in design, manufacturing, and test facilities.

Within a period of three months at War's end, orders had shrunk to twenty-four planes and the company had about 85,000 too many people. Abruptly the company's excellent financial results deteriorated and resulted in a small loss.

Faced with the supreme challenge of its career, the company planned a careful but rapid diversification. Quickly it moved into electronics, electromechanics, and atomics. With great foresight, it prepared itself to become a major factor in aeronautics, astronautics, and rocket propulsion. As space became a new theater of operations, North American was among the first to master the new technologies, and within a few years it had converted its loss to one of the best financial results in its industry. Since 1947 it has posted a steadily increasing sales and net profit.

THE ALLEN PRINCIPLES OF PLANNING

Several principles apply to all aspects of planning. Properly utilized, these principles can help guide us in selecting planning alternatives.

Principle of Present Choices

Current decisions tend to limit future action.

The plans and decisions we make today restrict our potential in the future. Often we overlook this. However, it is clear that the quality and type of people we select today will largely determine the kind of company we will have in the future. The product plans we make now determine the markets we can enter next year. Because the planning decisions we make have such long-range implications, it is important that they be made in context. Before we decide what action we will carry out tomorrow, we must determine whether that action will help or hinder our progress toward a goal we want to reach a month or a year from now.

To illustrate, in 1946 one of the large electrical manufacturers had to make a critical decision. Should it put greater emphasis on appliances and consumer goods or on heavy apparatus? Largely oriented toward electrical equipment and heavy apparatus, the company decided to commit its major resources to this field. A large competitor noted the opportunity and moved solidly into the consumer field. By the time the manufacturer had broadened its focus, the competitor had established a dominant position in the consumer market.

Principle of Planning Stability

The stability of a plan tends to vary inversely with its extension.

The further ahead we project current decisions, the less certain we are that future events will occur as we anticipate. Therefore, the further ahead we project our plans, the more flexible and generalized they should be. There is not much point in deciding now, to the last small move, what we will do five years from now. It is enough to block out the large moves so that we can foresee clearly our general progress.

Again, it is not good strategy to settle immovably upon one course of action for long-term implementation. Planning in a dynamic situation requires that we anticipate the probable movement of future events, including the actions of competitors. We develop logical alternatives to meet or counter each possible movement. These alternatives should be completed in the detail warranted by the probability and imminence of the action to be taken. As we move closer to the point of action, more data become available to help us decide which alternative course of action is preferable. Our short-term plan then narrows to selection of the best alternative and commitment to carry out the necessary course of action.

Principle of Resistance to Change

The greater the departure of planned changes from accepted ways, the greater the potential resistance by the people involved.

This principle tells us that we must build into our plans provision for overcoming the resistance of people. The broader the plans, the more profound the changes, the more we know people will fear and oppose them. Ordinarily we devote 98 per cent of our planning effort to technical perfection and 2 per cent to anticipating the needs of people. We would probably accomplish much more if we devoted as much time to the people factor as we do to techniques.

Why People Resist Change. When change is in the air, people affected tend to sniff in suspicion and throw up the bulwarks of opposition. There are many reasons for this. Fear is a large factor. We are afraid of the unknown. We fear a loss in position, a change in our social status. Inertia looms large. In human psychology as well as in physics, a body in motion tends to remain in motion, a body at rest tends to remain at rest. The rut of habit is comfortable and people tend to resist being forced out of it.

Resistance may occur because of lack of confidence in the planners. If past proposals have proved unsound or have failed, new propositions are dubiously received. Sometimes plans carry the obvious habit of the ivory tower: they are clothed in large generalities; they fall short in their assessment of the current situation; they are out at the elbow on logic. These plans are usually met with attitudes of distrust and resistance.

How to Overcome Resistance. The key words in overcoming resistance are *participation* and *communication.* The more opportunity people have to suggest and recommend ideas and to see their ideas incorporated in the planning, the more they will develop a feeling of ownership in what is being done and swing to acceptance and support.

The manager should avoid handing down plans, newly minted and as yet not understood, as a personal edict. The attitude "ours not to reason why, ours but to do and die" may be appropriate in warfare, but it has little application in business affairs. If he wants wholehearted and enthusiastic compliance in carrying out his plans, the manager will ask his subordinates to help formulate those plans.

Showing the benefits of change will help overcome resistance. If the manager can illustrate that the individual will benefit and his over-all opportunities will be enhanced, he will enlist support more quickly. A success story helps. If the first move in the change meets with approval, the subsequent steps will encounter decreasing resistance. It usually pays to bring up the heavy artillery and to marshal the resources the manager needs to help guarantee that the first move will be an unqualified success.

Timing is important. Earthquakes should be avoided. People should be given enough time to understand and implement the plan. When they can clearly see its inner workings and have an opportunity to visualize the end results, this familiarity will act as a potent self-persuader and will encourage them to go along with the plan.

Whenever possible, the manager should make the new plan a continuation of something that is already being done. He should start where people now are, then carry them forward to the new aspects of the plan. If the change seems radical and sweeping in scope, people will tend to generate resistance to about the same extent that their settled ideas and habits are jerked out of place.

LONG- AND SHORT-TERM PLANNING

The action we take now greatly restricts our potential range of action in the future. To ensure that we have the latitude we require for future action, it is important that we recognize the difference between long- and short-term planning.

Long-term Planning

Long-term planning involves looking ahead as far as we can and building a picture of the end results we want to accomplish. Once we know where we are going, the process of charting the immediate steps is greatly simplified. If we want to make the best decisions today, we first must fix in our minds the purpose of those decisions.

How far ahead should we project our long-range plans? This will differ with the type of business. Some companies can look ahead fifteen to twenty years; others find that their sight blurs at a range of five to seven years. A useful rule here is that when the cost of carrying out a plan is justified by an anticipated economic return, spread over a period of time, the decision involving that expenditure should be projected at least as far ahead as the period required to secure that return. For example, if a company buys a new machine, it will be necessary to use that machine over a substantial number of years to justify the investment. In planning for the machine, it is therefore necessary to consider the full period involved. If the machine is likely to be outmoded when it is only half paid for, we had better give added thought to shortening the payout period or devising some other means of securing adequate return on our investment.

Consideration of long-term implications often puts a different perspective on short-term decisions. It is quite conceivable that we might be able to save money immediately and yet satisfy our customers if we get along on the smallest possible investment in equipment and facilities. But if we look ahead to the pattern for five or ten years, we may see clearly that this short-run saving will cost dearly over the long term. This same reasoning applies to research, personnel development, and decisions. We may save money by skimping on research or training now but find ourselves in difficulty in a few years because of an inadequate product line or poor management performance.

Short-term Planning

Short-term planning is concerned with determining the short-range activities necessary to accomplish long-term results. As we have seen, there is a direct relationship because today's decision markedly affects the opportunities that will be available to us and the conditions under which we will operate five, ten, or even more years in the future.

Transition between Short- and Long-term Plans

Today has a habit of moving on and engulfing tomorrow. Short-term planning tends to eat up the long-term unless we make special provision for advancing our long-term plans as rapidly as our short terms are accomplished, and for effecting a transition between the two.

We accomplish this by planning on a sliding basis. Long-range plans are reviewed periodically, at least once or twice annually. At each review, the long-range plan is extended for the length of the review period. If five-year plans are reviewed annually, for example, each year the forecasts, objectives, programs, and budgets are projected an additional year, while the short-term plans are also moved ahead one year. This results in sliding coverage and ensures smooth transition from one planning phase to the next.

THE STRUCTURE OF PLANNING

An integrated structure of planning should be developed for the company as a whole. This requires that each level of management must do the planning work which only it can perform. The factors outlined below will help to highlight the nature of planning responsibilities at various levels.

The Higher the Level, the Broader the Scope

Top levels of management, including the board of directors and chief executive, are so placed organizationally that they have best perspective and objectivity with respect to the needs of the company over-all. We look to top managers with their staff agencies to consider the total needs of all organization components and future opportunities for the entire organization.

Top-level plans require integration of the viewpoints of the company as a whole, the stockholders, and the public at large. If they are to be realistic, they should be based upon the capabilities and requirements of lower operating levels. This means that company planning best proceeds if top managers constantly have before them the tentative plans of lower levels, if they reconcile and integrate these with the needs of shareholders and the public, and finally if they authorize the course of action best designed to satisfy all three groups and give purposeful guidance to the company as a whole.

The Higher the Level, the Further the Projection

Because of its advantage in perspective, we look to top management to devote most of its planning effort to long-range forecasts, objectives, programs, budgets, and policies. Lower levels are more concerned with shorter-range objectives, programs, schedules, procedures, and budgets.

PLANNING AND THE COMPUTER

Because planning involves a great deal of mental activity, much of it routine, we are finding that the computer can be an effective tool for the manager who understands and can use it effectively. A prime recognition here is that sound decision making is at the heart of good planning. In effect, a plan is a series of decisions we make *now* to determine what we will try to accomplish in the future, how best to do it, how much it will cost, and under what conditions it can best be carried out.

Basis for Effective Use of the Computer

The computer can be most valuable in helping us to make these planning decisions if we keep in mind three things. First, the foundation of a sound decision has already been laid in the past. The past is factual and the computer is fast and accurate in dealing with established facts. Second, the creative aspects of planning lie in our identification and utilization of the lessons we learn from the past. Here judgment and intuition are both necessary; it is here that the human brain must provide the creative effort that we cannot expect from the computer. Our third point is that the making of a decision is a separate and distinct activity in itself. A decision is part of a plan, but it is not the plan itself. A multipurpose tool, a decision can be used in the same way that a knife can be used to slice ham, butter toast, or chop onions without becoming ham, toast, or onions. The decision may be an ingredient—an integral part of something larger. Here it bears the same relationship to the whole as flour does to the bread of which it is a part.

Decisions make plans and plans provide the basis for sound controls. We can see, therefore, that effective utilization of the computer can speed immeasurably the whole process of making things happen the way we want, and of checking up to see to it that accomplishment matches plan.

The Planning and Control Loop

Looking at any plan—an objective, program, budget, or policy—we can best relate it to computer utilization by visualizing the plan as part of a planning and control loop in the total management system. This is shown in Figure 9-1.

Each level of management, in effect, forms a planning and control loop in the total management system. The decisions guiding each level are the plans authorized at the next higher level; the controls ensuring accomplishment of plan are the feedback to each decision point.

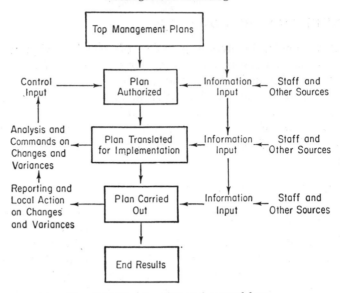

FIG. 9-1. The planning and control loop.

THE DEMANDS OF AUTOMATION

As the routine and detail of planning become more automated, we can anticipate a growing demand for three seemingly inconsistent qualities in professional managers: (1) the mastery of logical planning skills, the willingness to conform to a strict rationale of planning; (2) the ability to think, creatively, to innovate and develop nonconforming approaches; and (3) the ability to think of people first, the machine second.

Logical Planning Skills

Managers will be required to plan logically because it is only in a rational context that the computer can be used effectively. Fuzzy ideas and uncertain goals will result inevitably in poor and incomplete computer applications. We are finding that one benefit of automation has been to force managers to *think before acting,* to identify *real* problems instead of *apparent* problems, and to spend time weighing and assessing alternatives before committing themselves to a course of action.

Creative Thinking

Automation will demand of professional managers the ability to think creatively. Computers can perform the routine and detail of planning more quickly than the human mind. However, the computer will not be able to bridge the gap between the known and the unknown; the human mind will still have to provide the creative solution, the new insight not implicit in the data. This will be a challenge. If, as is even now a tendency, we rely exclusively upon the logical answer proposed by the computer, we will discover that the computer can make our planning and subsequent action sterile and self-limiting.

The Needs of People

The ability to give proper emphasis to people will be high among the essentials of using computers as an effective planning tool. It will become increasingly easy to think through and develop a logical plan with great internal validity by use of the machine alone and to overlook the requirements of the people concerned. But machines are made for people, not people for machines. So long as the basic module of organized effort remains the human individual, we shall find it necessary to adapt the more perfect symmetry of machine solutions to the peculiarities and asymmetry of the human personality.

The answer will lie in the principles of motivation. Increased attention must be given to consultation and participation to help validate the choices of the computer and to infuse the unprogrammed item. Human originality will become increasingly important; so far as we can visualize the future, this will continue to be unique to the human brain.

SUMMARY

Planning is the work a manager does to master the future. Planning requires that a manager think before acting. In the process of doing this, he will map out beforehand what he expects to accomplish, how he can best do it, and the limits of cost and other factors that are significant. The principles of planning stress the importance of current decisions in limiting our potential range of action in the future. They point out that the further we project a plan into the future, the more unstable and undependable it becomes. A key principle emphasizes the tendency of people to resist changes. The greater the departure of the change from accepted ways, the greater the potential resistance. Resistance to change can be overcome primarily by providing for participation and communication in the planning process. In planning, provision should be made for both long-term and short-term plans, and the gap between the two should be bridged by planning on a sliding basis. Plans are considered in terms of the specific activities of forecasting, establishing objectives, programming, scheduling, budgeting, and developing policies and procedures.

CHAPTER 10

Management Forecasting

> *An inventory of foresight produces a profit in hindsight.* J. WILSON NEWMAN

DEFINITIONS

Forecasting: the work a manager performs to estimate the future.

Mechanical Projection: a forecast made by assuming that future trends will assume precisely the same characteristics as those of the past.

Analytical Projection: a forecast made by determining why events have occurred in the past and transferring this reasoning to analysis of probable future occurrences.

THE LOGIC OF FORECASTING

Stripped to its essentials, business is the development of a strategy based on the odds attending various alternatives. A manager engaged in making the decisions that will determine the action he will take needs to look ahead on a systematic, continuing basis to anticipate the opportunities and hazards of the future. He does this by forecasting.

In charting the course we shall follow, it is necessary, first, to take a long look ahead to determine the conditions that will probably prevail at a future time. If the economy is booming, the political picture stable, and the demand for our goods or services increasing, we can be much more optimistic in committing ourselves to projects and incurring expenses than if the general picture is gloomy or uncertain. In forecasting, we look ahead in order to anticipate these general conditions. We try to visualize what conditions will prevail so that we can better prepare ourselves for what lies ahead.

When a manager forecasts that a specific accomplishment is possible ten or fifteen years from now, he will probably begin to do the things *now* that will make that future a reality. Alexander Graham Bell had a dream eighty years ago of every person in the world being able to talk to every other person. His dream is now a reality. What does American Telephone and Telegraph forecast as the logical culmination of that dream?

Claude M. Blair, a vice president, describes it.

We can expect that the telephone in Century 21 will be a pretty versatile tool. You'll have a telephone with you wherever you go. With it you can reach almost anyone else on earth—and even out in space.

The telephone, or whatever it might be called in Century 21, will serve as a master control unit around the house. It will answer the door— you'll be able to see and talk to the caller from any part of the house. It will control appliances—enabling you to cook your food, cool and heat your house—from remote locations. You'll be able to shop by video phone. And you'll be able to take training courses, cultural courses and educational instructions—all by telephone. Instead of dialing, you'll use some form of pushbuttons. You possibly may even speak the number wanted into your telephone and the equipment will respond.

A tremendous amount of business information will be transmitted over the telephone lines. You'll do your banking by telephone. Machines will talk to machines. A computer with information to send will initiate a call, get a signal when the call has gone through, and then transmit its information to the machine at the other end. These things will be done more rapidly, accurately and economically than humans could ever hope to do them.

With tomorrow's communications, we can expect faster business procedures. The interval between the start of a business negotiation and the signing of a contract will be speeded up considerably. We will have greater mobility for ourselves since we can conduct our business from almost any spot on earth.

IMPORTANCE OF FORECASTING

Forecasting is important because it forces a manager to lift his sights from the hurly-burly of current operations and to scout and probe the future so that he can identify the economic climate, the social conditions, the market changes, and other major movements that are likely to influence his undertakings.

A systematic attempt to probe the future by inference from known facts helps integrate all management planning so that unified over-all plans can be developed into which division and departmental plans can be meshed. It enables a company to commit its resources with greatest assurance of profit over the long term.   By helping to identify future demand patterns, it facilitates development of new products.

First Step in Planning

Forecasting is not a separate and unique activity, carried out by planners far removed from consideration of everyday operating matters. Forecasting is useful only if it is made part of the company's day-to-day administration.   From a management viewpoint, a forecast should be regarded as one step in planning any activity.

Consider the management task of setting meaningful objectives. Professional managers are coming to realize that this can best be done within logical limits established by far-ranging forecasts covering such elements as the probable character of the future economy, population trends, and developments in education, technology, and human motivations.

For instance, Ford Motor Company, in forecasting the future, anticipates the possibility of radically different types of personal transportation.   "What kind of business will we have if automobiles cruise on a cushion of air, are controlled by transistorized computers and servomechanisms, and are powered by gas turbines?" Ford Motor's top executives ask themselves.   In the process of finding the answers, they are anticipating some possible characteristics of their business in 1975 and 1980.

Sound policy making depends upon accurate forecasting.   If the company can anticipate the future requirements of its customers, it can best cater to their needs.

Better Use of Resources

Forecasts can help adjust production, sales, purchasing, and financing to long-term trends.   This is particularly important if employment is to be stabilized and facilities are to be used at peak level.

For example, the seasonal nature of photographic activity has always been recognized in the photographic industry.   Because sunshine and leisure, commodities most plentiful in the summer, are necessary for picture making, summer and vacation time have tended to constitute the picture-making season.

As early as 1904, Eastman Kodak Company found that the demand for film was stimulated in the summer but that picture taking fell off with cold weather.   Because photosensitive films had a relatively short shelf life, it was necessary to produce film in volume in spring and early summer.   With the season's demand met, production slowed down and all but a core of skilled employees in the film departments had to be let go.   Then, in late winter, new people had to be trained.

Determined to correct this, Eastman studied its sales pattern and found that it could forecast with accuracy the number of rolls of film it would sell for at least one year ahead. It decided to invest in needed inventory and refrigerated storage facilities. But a problem appeared. Tests showed that the emulsion on the film would not keep in storage. Research turned up a more stable emulsion, and the company was able to manufacture at a constant volume, with assurance that peak demand would eat up accumulated inventory each summer.

The technique of forecasting has now improved to the point that companies can predict, with some accuracy, not only their sales, but also their profits and their capital outlays. On the basis of forecasts, they can also program machine and equipment commitments and the expansion of plant facilities.

A large Eastern electrical company, once subject to wide short-term fluctuations of demand for electronic and communications equipment, has developed means of forecasting economic and industry trends to the point that it can predict for five years in advance, with reasonable assurance, what and how much it will sell for each of its product lines and its cost for sales, research, engineering, and other administrative expenses.

These forecasts have a stabilizing influence on every aspect of the business. They enable the company to anticipate for years ahead the number of people it will need, the amount of floor space that will have to be added, what processes will need improvement, and what equipment will have to be bought, redesigned, and replaced.

New Products

Innovation is the lifeblood of business enterprise in a competitive economy. But developing and introducing new products are one of the costliest and most hazardous undertakings which management faces. For a firm like Westinghouse Electric Corp., for example, 60 per cent of the consumer products it sells now were not on the market ten years ago. Westinghouse spends many millions each year to research and develop these products. It has to be right a good part of the time in its choice of the new products it decides to market or its dollar loss will be staggering. While smaller companies do not spend as much in dollars on research and development, their investment is often even larger in proportion to their total assets.

Forecasting helps minimize mistakes by anticipating the kind of products people are likely to buy and the volume the demand will warrant. To illustrate, immediately after World War II, the Dow Chemical Co. took a careful look ahead at the probable demand for organic chemical derivatives made from benzene. The forecasts showed that coke, the existing source of supply, would fall far short of the future demand. Alerted to this probable market opportunity, Dow took several steps to capitalize on it. First, through research, it developed a process to make methylstyrene, a substitute material made from toluene instead of benzene. It then built a plant for volume production. Further, the company developed a means of recovering benzene from an ethylene plant by-product and lined up sources for importing benzene from Europe. As demand climbed, Dow was able to tap its new sources and earn a profit on its forecasting ability.

Forecasting can be of great value in alerting companies to *stay out* of new markets. For example, Pacific Finance Company was intrigued with the possibility of entering the credit card business. Before taking the step, however, the company forecast the probable effect on its existing markets. Primarily concerned with financing sales contracts, Pacific Finance found that credit cards would simply offer its customers an option of doing the same thing in a different way and would probably not add substantially to its customers or its business. Alerted by its careful forecasting, the company stayed out.

THE UNCERTAINTIES OF FORECASTING

With all of its importance, it is necessary to accept the fact that forecasting is not a science. We cannot foretell future events with certainty. However, since we must look ahead in order to plan at all, forecasting of some kind must take place. The question is not whether to forecast, but whether to move ahead haphazardly and fortuitously, or in terms of a logical and systematic assessment of the future.

We cannot forecast with precision. The best we can do is to estimate the range of possibilities of what will probably happen in the future. Forecasts *can* be wrong. It is well to remember this so that we can maintain an open mind and the flexibility to revise our forecasts as conditions change.

A classical example of the unpredictables is Ford Motor Company's experience with its Edsel model. The Edsel was introduced in 1957. The forecasting on which it was based was undertaken in 1954. Ford's studies in 1954 showed that family income was rising. By 1965 more than half of the families in the United States would be earning at least $5,000 a year. This promised further increase in the demand for medium-priced automobiles. The Edsel was designed to appeal to this growing middle-income buyer.

The trend in 1954 showed that this customer wanted a smart-looking, gadget-heavy automobile that was impressively large and powerful. Ford produced an automobile tailored in every detail to satisfy this need. In the two years it required to tool up and produce this new model, however, the tastes of middle-income customers had begun to change. The small, compact car had usurped the spotlight. When the Edsel was marketed, it was met by the first surge of this new demand. In spite of Ford's heroic efforts, the new model failed and was taken out of production in late 1959.

Every company, even the best, makes mistakes. The critical question is: What has it learned from its error? Ford, one of the best-managed companies in the world, profited from its mistake with the Edsel by refining its forecasting techniques until it became outstanding. When the company was ready to enter the compact car field, it forecast the market with such accuracy that Ford's Falcon captured a leading place.

IMPORTANCE OF THE SALES FORECAST

Forecasting can be a costly operation, which involves not only administrative expense but also time of the operating people asked to participate. There is no point in preparing a forecast unless there is promise of a direct dollar return. Since the continuity and profits of a business largely depend upon what products it makes and markets, it follows that the major forecasting effort should be spent in predicting sales and markets.

In planning for the future, we need some way to determine the limits within which we must work. The essential base is the actual dollars of income which can be expected from sales. When a properly prepared sales and market forecast has been made, it can be applied immediately to many other aspects of the business. Forecasts can be converted into production schedules. They can be used as a basis for planning production, purchasing, and flow of goods. They help in adjusting seasonable and economic changes in equipment and personnel. They can be used to determine the requirements of the company for short-term financing and to establish the probable level of dividend payments.

Used in this fashion by Johnson & Johnson, surgical goods manufacturer, for example, forecasts enable the company to maintain a smooth, level flow of finished goods. They also ensure full, economical use of machinery and equipment and help to level ups and downs in employment.

A company which specializes in the manufacture of a single product and which sells primarily to relatively few large customers has little difficulty in forecasting. They need only inquire from their company purchaser the number of units that will be needed in a given time. When Sears, Roebuck and Company orders goods from its small suppliers, for example, the order in itself provides the backbone of the demand forecast for the supplier.

For a larger and more diverse organization, with many products and widespread markets, the making of forecasts becomes complex. Kaiser Aluminum & Chemical Corporation, for example, must not only forecast sales to be produced directly for customers' specific requirements, but they must also maintain inventories of standard products in warehouses. These warehouse inventories must be maintained at levels sufficient to meet customer needs, yet not so high as to tie up too much money. This problem is complicated by seasonal fluctuations and demand, differing production capacities, plants, and similar factors. The warehouse manager can do a good job only by tying in his requirements with over-all company sales and production forecasts. This knowledge of over-all corporate volumes, prices, types, and sizes of products expected to be sold, and when and what fabricating plants will be available to meet this market demand, are essential to proper forecasting of inventories in warehouse operations.

Capitol Records, Inc., makes its sales forecast in dollars and converts it directly into a production forecast for the coming half year. The forecast is translated into units for each type of product after introducing the appropriate lead time factor. However, short-term planning for "hit" records at Capitol involves extremely difficult forecasting. Such a record, for example, may sell a half million copies within two weeks of its introduction. The company must be prepared with the materials, facilities, and personnel to provide the required production, distribution, and sales on short notice.

THE ALLEN PRINCIPLES OF FORECASTING

If we are to bring forecasting out of the realm of the crystal ball, we must establish basic principles that will enable us to anticipate the probable shape of the future with some accuracy. We have two such principles.

Principle of Cause and Effect

Future events tend to result from current and past occurrences.

This principle tells us that the future does not materialize full blown and without antecedent. The things that have happened in the past and that are happening now will give rise to future events. If we want to know what will happen in the future, we can best study what has happened in the past.

We should note that individual factors by themselves can rarely be identified as the causes that precipitate future occurrences. A number of forces shape most changes.   The relative importance of these various pressures differs from time to time.   They are most difficult to identify before the fact, but often irritatingly obvious when viewed in perspective.

One of the greatest difficulties in forecasting is the problem of distinguishing those factors which are basic causes and which contribute most to the developments of the future.   When properly identified, these key indicators can have great predictive value.   Sometimes complex, they can also be disarmingly simple.

Principle of Gradual Economic Change

Economic magnitudes tend to change slowly over the long term.

It often appears that an economic decline or an increase in demand occurs suddenly.   However, investigation will generally show that the forces at work have been apparent for quite a long time and can be identified if we know where to look.   Most often, we confuse the symptoms with the causes.   Thus, a stock-market break may seem to give rise to a recession when in fact it is a symptom of a deeper, underlying cause that may have been at work over a long period.

Short-term fluctuations which arise from temporary factors often greatly distort the picture.   In the United States, for example, if we looked only at the short-term variation of the gross national product, we might plunge from booming optimism to frantic retreat from one year to the next.   To cite two extremes, if we had been forecasting our 1951 business on the basis of what had happened between 1949 and 1950, we would be thinking in terms of an 8.5 per cent increase in gross national product.   Moving ahead a few years to a forecast for 1959 based on gross national product between 1957 and 1958, we would be thinking in terms of a minus 2.7 per cent level.   Over the long term, however, the total physical volume of goods and services in the United States has been growing at a rate of about 3 per cent per year and the real volume of goods and services has been doubling about every twenty-five years.

THE THREE DIMENSIONS OF FORECASTING

In looking to the future, we should have definite questions in mind that will enable us to place properly the movements that we expect to occur.   These questions stem from the three dimensions of forecasting—time, direction, and magnitude.

Time

A first question in forecasting is: How far ahead?   The kind of forecast we make and the accuracy of the conclusions we reach are directly related to the time element. For convenience, forecasts are often classified as long-term, mid-term, and short-term. The length of time for each varies with the industry. Long-term forecasts are often classified as those projected beyond five years. Mid-term applies to those from two to five years, and short-term up to two years. This classification is purely for convenience. If we think of forecasts as beginning and ending at arbitrary periods in time, we will be misled because time, of course, moves on like a stream and has no breaks.

Direction

The forecaster is very much concerned with the *direction* of the movements he is attempting to predict. Will the demand for a product move up, decline, or remain stationary? The *trend* may have considerable significance, for the Principle of Gradual Economic Change tells us that upward movements will tend to continue upward, and downward movements continue to decline until some new factor affects the direction.

Another phenomenon of direction is that of recurrent cycles. Certain economic movements show a cyclical nature; that is, they tend to reach a peak, to recede to a low, then to repeat the peak again over approximately the same time period. In identifying the linear or cyclic nature of trends, we are establishing an effective basis for sound forecasting.

Magnitude

A third dimension of forecasting is size. How large will the predicted movement be? Measurement may be in units, percentages, or other values. The units compared should be equivalent. It is misleading, for example, to compare building values of today with those of ten years ago. Where there has been a change in magnitude, a constant base should be selected and defined. For example, 1948 dollars represent a different measure from today's dollars.

METHODS OF FORECASTING

The principles we have noted are the basis for the two forecasting methods in most common use. Since these methods relate the future to the past and the present, they are properly called *projections*.

Mechanical Projection

In utilizing this type of forecast, the manager assumes that the future will be an uninterrupted continuation of the past and present. He develops a clear-cut picture of what has happened up to now, disregarding minor irregularities, and bodily lifts the past into the future, assuming that the same trend will continue unchanged. The process is mechanical because no attempt is made to get at the *causes* of what has happened. What is happening is accepted at its face value, and we assume that it will continue to happen in exactly the same fashion. For example, if we have had an average 6 per cent increase in sales volume for the past ten years, a mechanical projection would lead us to assume that we would also enjoy a 6 per cent increase on the average for each of the next ten years.

Mechanical projections may be fairly accurate over the short term because we know that economic changes tend to occur slowly. From an economic point of view, tomorrow will probably be much like today. However, when we begin to cast ahead, the probability of more radical changes increases. Blind reliance upon unchanged continuation of the past may lead us into unnecessary hazards. For this reason we find that mechanical projections are most useful over the short term, but even here, they must be regarded with caution. A better approach is to try to get at the causes of past events. If we know *why* things happened in the past, this is the best possible index to what will probably happen in the future. This calls for analytical projections.

Analytical Projection

Analytical projections enable us to make use of logical analysis in forecasting. Looking back, we can distill significant lessons from our past experience; we can determine *why* certain movements or events have taken place; then we can apply the same reasoning to what will happen in the future. Three types of analytical projections are commonly used—planning, psychological, and statistical.

1. *Planning Analysis*. In this method of forecasting, we project existing plans to their logical completion. For example, we know that if a business enterprise has approved its capital budgets, it has committed itself to spend certain sums of money at future periods. If construction contracts are let, a definite volume of purchases will follow.

Planning analysis is most useful if we have access to a reliable source of planning data. Since the task of gathering these planning data for a large number of companies is usually too great for one organization, we generally rely upon business associations and governmental agencies to provide this type of information.

The United States Steel Corporation, a company with outstanding long-term success, uses planning analysis in forecasting construction activity. Constant scrutiny of government policies in government-supported home loans gives an indication of the trend in large-scale home-building projects. Surveys of plans for plant and equipment expansion and of contracts awarded provides an index to industrial and commercial construction. Approved budgets for public construction, including highways, schools, hospitals, and recreation projects, give a useful indication of volume of demand in these areas.

2. *Psychological Analysis.* People are the great unpredictables in forecasting. However, if we know *why* people do what they do, we can predict their future actions with more confidence. Psychological analysis involves an investigation into the motivations of people.

This type of analysis is of growing importance. For example, if we know why people in one part of the country prefer red furniture polish to white, we have a much more meaningful basis for determining our probable sales in those regions. If we know that people do not buy tooth paste but rather buy beauty, health, and cleanliness, we can much better understand the factors that will determine increased sales of our tooth paste.

Many companies have marched with great vigor into bankruptcy because they did not stop to find out why people bought, or failed to buy, their product. On the other hand, entire industries have been revolutionized because somebody stopped to think through the real problem—the psychological wants of people.

As a case in point, Nationwide Insurance Company's research indicated that many people dislike dealing with different agents for different kinds of insurance; people find it inconvenient and confusing to keep track of payments due at several places at different times of the year. Moreover, the growing complexity of today's protection needs aggravates the situation.

Nationwide, which has offered all kinds of insurance for years, refined its operations to provide the modern "one-stop" service desired today. The company developed a program, called Family Securance Service, which enables an agent to give people professional advice on their total insurance needs, both present and future. In buying policies from the one agent, clients can lump their premiums for life, fire, health, and many other kinds of policies in a single account which can be paid for through a variety of convenient installment plans. To handle budget payments, Nationwide even organized a new subsidiary company. The program has resulted in increased service and greater policyholder satisfaction.

3. *Statistical Analysis.* We can make use of statistical relationships to help determine why certain movements occur and to predict what will happen in the future. As a simple example, we can show statistically that there tends to be a relationship between the number of new babies born and the subsequent sale of diapers, nursing bottles, and bicycles, in that order. If we detect a sharp increase in the birth rate,

we can anticipate a sharp increase later in the sale of these products. Statistical analysis is often complex and highly technical, particularly when we use mathematical and econometric models of various kinds. Using these techniques, professional economists are learning to predict with growing assurance the general level of business activity and demand for specific products.

SUMMARY

In forecasting, a manager estimates the future. Here his concern is to look ahead to anticipate the problems and conditions that will probably confront him at future periods of time. Most important in forecasting is the need to recognize that what happens in the future will largely result from what has already occurred in the past; therefore, careful and analytical study of past occurrences is basic to sound forecasting. We can forecast mechanically by moving the past ahead into the future as if no change were to occur. Better is the use of analytical forecasts, in which we determine why changes occurred in the past and carry this reasoning forward into the future. The three most important types of analytical forecasts are planning analysis, psychological analysis, and statistical analysis.

CHAPTER 11

Management Objectives

> *I subscribe to the view that we can, within fairly narrow limits, control the fate of our companies if we plan properly. In spite of all the unknowns, uncertainties and imponderables, if we analyze the situation carefully we can arrive at a reasonable degree of rationalization. The end result is some course of action that has a good probability of being successful.* CLINTON F. ROBINSON, THE CARBORUNDUM COMPANY

DEFINITIONS

Objective: an end result.   Synonyms: goal, target, event.

General Objective: an over-all, long-term end result.   The general objective is the longest range and culminating end result, generally in a series of identified accomplishments.

Specific Objective: an intermediate, shorter-term end result leading to a general objective.

Establishing Management Objectives: the work a manager performs to determine the end results to be accomplished.

THE LOGIC OF OBJECTIVES

The manager who does not know where he is going will probably have difficulty getting there.   Even though he happens to arrive at a destination that is to his liking, in the process he will probably have wasted a great deal of time and effort.   If others are traveling with him and none knows the destination, it is almost certain that confusion, frustration, and waste will result.   In order to prevent this, the professional manager determines the goals he wants to accomplish before he commits money and time to the effort.

122

We must establish objectives if we expect to take logical action. A moment's thought will show that we cannot expect to make prudent and efficient use of materials, tools, and the time of people unless we first determine what we are trying to accomplish by use of these resources. To emphasize again, we cannot reach a destination unless we first determine what that destination is.

When we establish objectives we are thinking through in advance what we expect to accomplish. It is true that a human being may be capable and resourceful enough to improvise a destination as he moves along and to change and modify it while still continuing to move forward. But when hundreds and thousands of people are following that individual, frequent changes in the objective will inevitably lead to confusion and waste of time and resources. If the situation is competitive, the competitor who has thought through his destination most carefully and who holds to it most firmly will, in all probability, accomplish it first.

With the computer, it is imperative that we know in advance what we want to accomplish so that we can program the machine logically toward that end. A machine which operates on a systematic and orderly basis will question the common sense of its user if data are fed into it that are irrational and disorderly in terms of the end result it is expected to accomplish.

Logically, then, we develop and define objectives because we need to know what we expect to make happen before we set out to accomplish it. For example, the work of designing a relay system ends with the relay system designed. Evidence of this may be a set of blueprints, but the preparation of the blueprints is not the objective; rather, it is the activity that leads to the objective. The objective does not consume manpower or materials. It *does* occur at an identifiable moment in time, but, for practical purposes, it does not require time in itself.[1]

This distinction is not specious. It is vitally important if we are to use the computer to plan logically and effectively. Rational planning requires that we differentiate between a thousand units of goods sold and the work required to sell those units, or that we not confuse a bull's-eye with the work of shooting the gun that leads to a bull's-eye.

IMPORTANCE OF OBJECTIVES

Objectives serve all levels of the company. Top management must know what it wants to accomplish in each of the key aspects of the business if the company as a whole is to advance in a systematic and orderly fashion. But what is true in the president's office is true also

[1] This same point will be made in our later discussion of PERT or networking.

at each lower level of management. Within the framework set by over-all company objectives, each manager establishes the objectives which will guide the activities of his own unit.

Objectives serve as the unifying thread that ties together all other plans. Is this program necessary? Is that budget justified? We can best decide by determining the extent to which each contributes to the achievement of objectives. Suppose research is being carried on in two different divisions of the company. We must coordinate the two activities to minimize duplication and overlap. One way to do this is by screening all activities in unending committee meetings that consume a good deal of the time of managers of the two divisions. Careful definition of the research objectives of the two groups is more effective than development of separate but integrated programs designed to accomplish these goals.

Carefully stated objectives are the keystone of performance standards. If we want to know how well work is being done, the best way to find out is to assess our actual accomplishment against the objectives that we have set. If we do not know what we are trying to accomplish, it is unlikely that we will know whether we have achieved it.

Objectives serve an important purpose in helping to motivate people. Each of us has a *need* to achieve, to do work that is worthwhile. The person who feels his work lacks importance has no motive for continuing it.

Great attainment of any kind rarely occurs full blown. It is pieced together, slowly and patiently, from small accomplishments of each day. How effectively the pieces fit together, how promptly the omissions are repaired, how consistently the failures are overcome depend largely upon our ability to hold to a clear and positive picture of what we want to achieve in the end.

THE DIFFERENCE BETWEEN GENERAL AND SPECIFIC OBJECTIVES

If one were to travel from New York to Sydney, Australia, and also had business in San Francisco, Tokyo, and Manila, the objective would be to arrive in Sydney. However, leading to this relatively long-term, over-all end result would be the necessary accomplishment of intermediate, shorter-term end results, namely, to reach San Francisco, Tokyo, and Manila. In this sequence of events, we have a major objective, which we call the *general objective,* and subobjectives, which we call *specific objectives*.

General and specific objectives are used at all levels of the company. Planning a year ahead, the foreman has a general objective of 150,000 units of standard production. But if it is now January 1, he cannot plan effectively in terms of twelve months' production. He breaks his general objective down so that his specific objective for January is 11,000 for February, 12,600 units, and so forth.

At the over-all company level, assume that we establish a general objective of maintaining 40 per cent of the market for our primary product line. While this objective governs all of our thinking, it is too big to serve as an effective guide for next month. Again, we must break it down to a realizable interim goal in terms of a specific objective.

A *general objective* is an over-all, long-term end result. The general objective is the longest-range and culminating end result, generally in a series of identified accomplishments; the *specific objectives* are the intermediate, shorter-term end results leading to a general objective. Any failure to attain specific objectives or any change in them immediately alerts us to a need to review and reconsider the general objective. In terms of the structure of planning we have already developed, this gives us confidence in the development of concrete and relatively fixed short-term objectives because we know that our long-term goals are sufficiently flexible to enable us to move quickly to meet the unpredictables of future time.

GENERAL OBJECTIVES

The company that is most certain of success is the one that builds a clearly defined outline of itself and all of its parts. It projects this image as far ahead as it can reasonably visualize and then proceeds patiently, systematically, and with great determination to fill in the picture step by step.

Many companies fail to do this. They operate by taking advantage of opportunities as they occur. When this is the case, the future of the enterprise is continually in jeopardy. Its characteristics change from day to day and its survival is as unpredictable as fortune itself.

Often we think of general objectives as being important primarily for the large company. But they are even more significant for the small one because it is during its early formative years that the enterprise fashions the pattern which will determine its future.

What Type of General Objective?

For every endeavor there are critical areas of its operation in which consistent accomplishment is required for survival and success. A first requirement in establishing general objectives is to identify the end results the company will strive to accomplish in these areas with the understanding that, failing this, the company as a whole will not prosper, but if these are accomplished, the purposes of the company will be served.[2]

General objectives should be identified from the viewpoint of the owners or shareholders of the business, from that of the employees and of the public at large, if the enterprise is to justify its existence and merit its long-term continuance. The key characteristic of these general objectives is improvement in the sense that minimizing loss is as much improvement as maximization of profit.

For the typical business enterprise, general objectives will most often fall in the following areas:

1. Character of the company
2. Improvement of sales
3. Improvement of product
4. Efficiency of operations
5. Improvement of management
6. Contribution to public welfare
7. Profitability.

1. *Character of the Company.* General objectives help determine what kind of company we will have. The major decisions made at the top levels of the company today spell out the salient characteristics of the enterprise five and ten years from now. The more realistic and detailed this picture, the more broadly known and understood it is, the greater the probability it will be implemented.

WHITE MOTOR COMPANY. A good illustration is found in the case of the White Motor Company, a small producer of medium-sized trucks. By 1950 White found itself in danger of following the route to oblivion that some 1,800 other companies had taken in its industry. There seemed to be little future in the fiercely competitive medium- and small-sized truck markets.

Taking stock at this point, the company decided that it had to plan a more certain future for itself. Forecasting demand, White determined that heavy-duty trucks would have the major market appeal. The company established a clear-cut objective to move into the heavy-duty field and capture a substantial slice of it. Holding unswervingly to its goal, the company set specific objectives and programmed a series of acquisitions of smaller companies in this new field. By careful inte-

---

[2] An interesting study of the logical integration of general objectives in the total process of planning and control will be found in *Management Planning and Control, the H. J. Heinz Approach,* The Controllership Foundation, Inc., New York, 1957.

gration, it became a dominant factor in its industry within ten years, overtaking in the process some of its largest competitors.

THE STOUFFER CORPORATION.   There are thousands of restaurants, cafes, and eating establishments of all kinds in the United States.   Of this multitude only a few stand out.   One such is the Stouffer Corporation, a leader in its field.   To guide all parts of the corporation in achieving this leadership, Stouffer's top management has thought through, vividly and in detail, the kind of company they want.   What was this Stouffer Corporation to be like?   Its top management visualized restaurants in which appetizing, nutritious food would be found, of a quality that would be served proudly at home.   In their kitchens they saw proud cooks racking skillfully prepared, sweet-smelling fruit pies, and food handlers who strove for perfection in the smallest detail. When guests entered the restaurant, Stouffer management visualized the warm, sincere welcome extended by the greeters, hostesses, and receptionists to each person, and the attentive, gracious, and well-groomed Stouffer girl serving her guests proudly and efficiently.   Finally, the company management envisioned a trusted management supervisor tuned to the individual's thinking; a manager who cared enough to listen, to observe, to teach, and to communicate in an understanding, helpful way.

To help keep this picture clearly before all of its people, the Stouffer Corporation established a consistent set of general objectives—among these the objectives with respect to the important aspects of the business.   It stated the general character of its business as follows:

Scope.   To provide the public with high-quality, American-type food and related services through the conduct of a growing and profitable business; at home, in industry and institutions, and in our restaurants and inns.

THE CARBORUNDUM COMPANY.   A dominant factor in the abrasives field, the Carborundum Company has a clearly stated general objective that guides its over-all activities.   It is stated as follows:

To conduct throughout the world, under all economic and political conditions consistent with the corporate nature of the Company, a profitable, continuous, independent business in the manufacture and sale of

(1) silicon carbide, aluminum oxide, and similar and related basic materials,

(2) a complete line of abrasive products, a complete line of super refractories, metal additives, electric heating elements and resistors, and other products containing or produced from those basic materials,

(3) similar, related, and auxiliary products, and

(4) other products consistent with the general nature of the Company,

which can be undertaken successfully by the existing organization or an appropriate expansion thereof, with resulting growth in profits, financial stability, essential productive facilities, quality and quantity of products, reputation, and equitable benefits to the Company's stockholders, customers and employees.

2. *Improvement of Sales.* Effective marketing requires that the company know who its customers are and that it provide the kind of product they want, at the price and in the quality they demand, and under the conditions they are most willing to buy. Basic as this is, many companies have given little or no thought to these critical considerations. The best starting place is in the establishment of sound general objectives in this area.

A primary requirement is balance. All of the factors that enter into the sales effort should be clearly identified, their relative weight assessed, and their importance established in the objective as it is formulated. Only in this way can the company provide a sound basis for continuing market success. The danger is that if this basic determination is not made for the company as a whole, keeping in mind its total requirements, disproportionate emphasis will be brought to bear by a temporary operating difficulty or by an unusually strong and aggressive manager operating at a leverage point lower in the organization.

THE CARBORUNDUM COMPANY. The Carborundum Company has established these general objectives to serve as guides in the improvement of sales.

• To produce an unsurpassed quality of products in profitable quantity, at lowest costs consistent with that quality, to meet the needs of the Company's customers. As a corollary "sub standard" products generally have no place in the Company's line.
• To obtain for the Company the maximum possible participation in the available markets for its products. To foster and improve sound and mutually profitable relations with the Company's distributors. To conduct appropriate advertising campaigns to reach all profitable markets.
• To create new and enlarged markets through the introduction of new and improved products and new uses and tools and methods for existing products.
• To expand the sale of the profitable products of the Company. As a corollary to eliminate unprofitable items, except where otherwise justified for competitive and advertising purposes.

THE STOUFFER CORPORATION. Marketing a much different product, The Stouffer Corporation visualized the end results it expects to attain in catering to its customers and has stated this clearly in its objectives, as follows:

Service to the Consumer. To satisfy our consumers' tastes and fulfill their needs, through variety in our foods, menus, and product line, assortments and price lines, and through our services offered at fair prices in locations where Stouffer quality will be most desired and appreciated; and to serve our customers in an efficient and attentive manner:
• In an inviting, clean and friendly atmosphere in our restaurants and inns.
• Through factual, attractive and practical merchandising of our frozen cooked foods.
• Through bright and tasty presentation in industrial and institutional locations.

Research. To employ research techniques in all areas of our business to develop products, equipment, processes, and management methods which will enhance our products and services and contribute to the growth, quality and earnings of the company.

3. *Improvement of Product.* Products tend to become obsolete either through change in customer preferences or through competitive innovation. Unless the company is constantly alert and directs its efforts toward consistent upgrading of its products, it will probably find that it has been edged out of its primary markets and is concentrating upon products that have diminishing appeal and profitability.

The impetus for continuing product improvement should come from basic objectives established in three areas: (*a*) improvement of existing products, (*b*) introduction of new products, and (*c*) elimination of obsolete or unprofitable products.

Improvement of existing products is accomplished through product research and engineering. Improvement of existing products should be considered both from the viewpoint of the customer and of the company's capacity. Advances in engineering of the product, upgrading of quality, and changes in price should not be undertaken simply because they seem a good idea, but because known customer preferences dictate the moves.

New product introduction is at best a gamble. However, the odds can be improved if the company will study not only its potential customers but also the means of distribution it will use to get the product into the consumer's hands. In establishing product policy, it is necessary to think through basic strategy. Does the company intend to be first, or will it be content with a "me too" position? Both have their advantages and dangers. Will it price to take the cream off the market, to establish a continuing demand, or to make the market inhospitable to new competition?

Many companies turn over their entire product lines within twenty years and, in some cases, in ten years or less.   Where this is the case, early identification of product obsolescence is of vital importance.   A planned retirement over a period of time will provide an opportunity to develop new products to take up the slack.

THE CARBORUNDUM COMPANY.   This company considers these factors in its guiding objectives:

• To provide a satisfactory and continuous volume of products for sale with minimum productive cycles; to maintain inventories consistent with good customer service, sound practices, and manufacturing procedures; to develop firm long-term commitments to cover the requirements of major customers; so that a continuity of efficient plant operations and minimum labor turnover can be achieved.

4. *Efficiency of Operations.*   Much potential profit is frequently lost through operating inefficiencies.   To combat this, continuing effort on the part of each accountable manager is required.   Efficiency of production is imperative, but important also is continuing scrutiny of clerical and administrative activities to ensure that a minimum work force is getting out a maximum of production at least cost.

The best measure of the efficiency of any component of the company is obtained by study of its program and budget.   The *program* specifies the activities that it is carrying out, the *budget* indicates how much it costs to do this work.   When programs and budgets are not used wisely, improved efficiency and the corollary reduction in costs largely become a hit-or-miss proposition.

THE CARBORUNDUM COMPANY.   The objective stated to cover this requirement is as follows:

To increase the return from sales by greater efficiencies in manufacture, distribution and administration and through sound sales policies and practices.

5. *Improvement of Management.*   Every company can improve its methods of planning, organizing, leading, and controlling; in so doing, it can make the single greatest contribution to survival and success. As is true with other objectives, this end result must be clearly visualized at the top levels of the organization and the means of accomplishing it should be detailed before consistent improvement at lower levels can be expected.

Every manager, from chief executive to first-line supervisor, should develop and maintain objectives, programs, and budgets to guide his daily work.   When called upon at any given time, he should be able to point to a basis for his current activity in detailed plans that have been discussed, reconciled, and approved by his own superior.

Perhaps the greatest single cause of operational inefficiency is poor organization. When too many people are used, when overlap and duplication exist, and when there is no clear-cut delegation of authority, costs are sure to escalate with a corresponding reduction in productivity. The best remedy is continuing organization study by each manager of his own organizational component with the accompanying thinning and pruning of unnecessary manpower and activities that make for a streamlined and efficient operation.

Effective controls provide a continuing check on the state of health of each part of the company and will flash an early warning when deficiencies in operation begin to develop. Unfortunately, control cannot be exercised through the reading of reports by a few managers at top levels. It requires the development of performance standards for each unit that will spell out unmistakably what is good work and what is unacceptable; it will provide a reporting system that will alert the accountable manager soon enough for him to correct his own variances a large proportion of the time; and it will establish the checks and balances necessary for an automatic check on each significant deficiency.

THE CARBORUNDUM COMPANY. This company states its objectives in this area as follows:

Management. To realize these objectives through the periodic preparation of specific short and long-term programs, carried out through a simple and effective organization, employing proven management techniques and procedures and based on the principle of decentralized operations with centralized control of performance.

THE STOUFFER CORPORATION. In the case of The Stouffer Corporation, the following general objective for the continuing improvement of management has been established:

Management. To manage the business to achieve continuity, growth, profit and public service through:
• Managers skilled in the techniques of professional management and human understanding.
• A sound organizational structure, objectives and policies.
• A communication system that works efficiently and effectively to the public, our shareholders and internally—up, down and across.
• Incentives proportionate to responsibilities, risks and results.

6. *Contribution to Public Welfare.* The corporation that exists only for its own ends has little justification for its continuance. A last-

ing contribution by any company lies in its participation in the responsibilities and obligations of the local community. By providing secure, well-paid jobs, by making use of local resources, and by assisting in the development of community projects wherever possible, the company establishes its place as a good citizen.

The initiative for this must come from top management and is best formalized in the statement of general objectives.

THE STOUFFER CORPORATION. Representative is this statement of intention from The Stouffer Corporation.

Citizenship. To be a good corporate citizen, and encourage individual good citizenship by:
• Participating actively in civic and community affairs, both as a corporation and through members of management.
• Creating a climate that will encourage Stouffer people to affiliate with a political party of their choice and to participate in the party's activities.

7. *Profitability.* The final measure of the company's success is its long-term profitability. Profit, however, is a result, not a means. Profit, in a literal sense, is the difference between the value of the material wealth the company produces and the cost of producing it. Frequently a company asserts that its objective is "to make a profit," and that everything else is secondary. This, of course, is not the whole of the story, for profit will result only if the company consistently improves its product, marketing, and operations; if it manages itself effectively and earns its place as a corporate citizen. In this sense, profit is a measure of the company's ability to accomplish the whole of its mission.

The profit objective is best stated in terms of what the company intends to accomplish with the funds which its accountants label as "profit."

THE CARBORUNDUM COMPANY. This company provides a good statement.

• To utilize funds excess to the needs of the Company to reduce and finally eliminate the Company's long-term debt. Consistent with economy and other objectives, to retire debt prior to maturity.
• To pay regularly the common stockholders of the Company fair and reasonable dividends on a stable basis and to increase their equity in the Company, thus strengthening the confidence of the stockholders and the public in the common stock of the Company as an investment of high calibre and broadening the common stock ownership.
• To invest the earnings of the Company over and above requirements for working capital, debt retirement and dividends in improved productive facilities and new profitable undertakings.

SPECIFIC OBJECTIVES

General objectives identify the long-term end results we expect to accomplish. We need also guideposts along the way that will keep us headed continually in the proper direction. These are provided by short-term specific objectives. For example, if we want to increase our productivity by 12 per cent over the course of two years, we will find it impossible to undertake at once all the activities necessary to achieve this result. Instead, we break down the large job into smaller parts and identify each of these by establishing the interim, specific objectives. This provides us with footstones as well as milestones. For example, we may aim for an improvement of 8 per cent in productivity for the first year, with this divided into weekly and monthly quotas.

Breaking a larger goal that is incapable of current accomplishment into smaller parts that can be undertaken successfully with the resources at hand is a key technique in the use of objectives. The near-term objectives are relatively stable, concrete, and detailed. They are changed rarely and then only for significant reasons. As our objectives are moved ahead, they are stated in more general terms, are less detailed, and are more subject to change.

How Far Ahead?

Specific objectives should be developed as far ahead as it is necessary to make a firm commitment of resources. If we hire people, purchase materials, or acquire capital facilities, specific objectives should be prepared at least to the limit of time it will take us to recover our investment. It is not prudent to spend money unless we have thought through first what we expect to accomplish with it and are justified in our assumption that the expenditure for people, materials, and tools and facilities will yield a greater return than the cost of acquiring and using them.

SUMMARY

An objective is an end result; it is the goal toward which a manager directs his efforts. In establishing objectives, we are determining beforehand where we want to go before we start to travel. This makes for greatest economy of effort and money. Objectives are classified as general objectives, which are the long-range continuing objectives that direct our overall efforts, and specific objectives, which are the shorter-term, measurable, achievable objectives toward which we direct our immediate efforts. General objectives help to shape the character and nature of the company. They should be developed in terms of each of the salient characteristics of the company. Specific objectives identify the concrete goals toward which we direct our short-term efforts.

CHAPTER 12   *Management Programs and Schedules*

Thou shalt show the people the way wherein they must go.   EXODUS

DEFINITIONS

Program: a sequence of action steps arranged in the priority necessary to accomplish an objective. Synonym: series or sequence of activities.

Program Step: an individual action step that is part of a larger program. Synonyms: activity, task.

Schedule: a time sequence arranged to carry out a program. Synonyms: time estimate, activity time.

Management Programming: the work a manager performs to establish the sequence and priority of action steps to be followed in reaching objectives.

Management Scheduling: the work a manager performs to establish the time sequence for program steps.

THE LOGIC OF PROGRAMS AND SCHEDULES

Important as it is to know where we are going, it is also desirable that we determine the best way to get there before we begin to commit people, materials, and facilities. This is particularly important if we want to integrate our action with that of other people and units. It is unlikely that the total work of the team will be coordinated if each individual is intent on doing what he wants to do, according to his own preferences. Before we undertake action, we should establish the sequence and priority of the steps we must accomplish to achieve the end result.

134

Time also is an invaluable asset. How can we make best use of it? We can either do each thing as it comes up, carrying out each step as promptly and efficiently as we are able, and hoping that we will be successful, or we can think the matter through beforehand and establish a time sequence for each activity that will enable us to complete the action within the allotted time.

Programming provides us with a means of exploring the alternative routes to our proposed goal and of deciding the specific steps that will get us there in the most effective and economical fashion.

A program is a series of action steps that must be carried out to reach an objective. Each program step requires the expenditure of mental and physical effort or work. Usually we must utilize the time of people, materials, and tools and facilities to carry out the program, which means that we can determine cost in terms of money.

Scheduling provides us with a tool for making the best use of the time available. When we schedule, we determine the time required to carry out each program step. If what we have programmed cannot be completed within the time available, we can reconstruct our program and schedule mentally and on paper, rather than carrying out the action and using up the time and only then discovering that what we have done is inadequate.

The program and schedule set priorities by listing the action steps to be taken in order of their importance. They enable us to bring the greater part of our resources to bear against the few important things that must be accomplished. At the same time, they throw into proper perspective the less important details which may be contributory but which can also consume energy and expense out of all proportion to their real worth.

If we do not program, we tend to do whatever seems most important at the time. It is easiest to do the small, routine things first. In consequence, we push the major problems back and never seem to get to them. We become overloaded with detail and emergency matters. Unfortunately, the more fire fighting we do, the less time we have for management planning.

ADVANTAGES OF PROGRAMS AND SCHEDULES

Properly prepared, the program and schedule become administrative tools of great value to every manager. Used together, the program and schedule force him to weigh and assess his alternatives for action and to put greatest effort behind his most important problems. Because they bring into focus potential problems before they become emergencies, they enable him to develop, ahead of time, the alternatives and possible answers to these problems and to marshal his resources and facilities so that he can make the most effective action.

Programming greatly facilitates coordination of the operations of different organizational units. If all managers engaged in a common activity have thought through beforehand what they are going to do and have committed their program to writing, it becomes a relatively simple matter for each to compare his projected activities with the others and to reconcile differences where they occur.

The program and schedule are also the basis for effective control. Once a manager has decided the specific steps he expects to complete and the time required, he can use this expectation as a yardstick against which to ensure his progress. By reporting the progress made in comparison with his program and schedule, he has an effective means of planning and control.

Programs and schedules greatly facilitate delegation. Once he has approved the over-all program for his unit, the manager has established limits within which each individual subordinate manager can be delegated a large measure of authority to develop his own methods of getting the job done. Since the program and schedule envisage the total requirements of the unit, they anticipate and prevent overlap and duplication of work by different managers and give each a clear-cut charter within which he can proceed with assurance and initiative.

HOW TO PROGRAM AND SCHEDULE

Programming can be accomplished most effectively if it is carried out systematically. The following sequence is used effectively by many companies.

1. *Review Objectives.* Each programmed step should carry us toward the end results we want to accomplish. Therefore, as a first step, we should review our objectives, making sure that we have clearly in mind the over-all result we want to accomplish. To repeat, if we do not know where we want to go, we can hardly decide how best to get there.

2. *Determine Major Steps.* We should next block out the most important steps we must take to reach our objectives. The major areas of accomplishment should be considered, and we should not become bogged down in detail. The natural tendency to work out each step as it comes to mind should be avoided. Our purpose now is to lay out the course as a whole. Later we can come back to work out the detail, or we can delegate this to others.

3. *Establish Priorities.* Now we have determined the major action steps that must be taken. Since these are probably not all equally im-

portant, we will now want to establish priorities.   Certain things have to be done before others, to work toward a cumulative end result.   For example, we must select and train people for a new project before we get the project itself under way.   When in doubt, a useful criterion is: What contribution does this particular step make toward accomplishment of the objectives I have set?   The more important the contribution to end results, the higher the priority.   To some extent our priorities will depend upon the time we have available.   Therefore, this step and the next will follow closely upon one another.

4. *Schedule.*   We now look to timing.   The first step here is to determine the time limits within which we must work.   One approach is to begin at the end point and work back.   If we know when we must be finished, we have the best means of determining the total time available and how best to allocate it against each of the major steps we must take.   In some cases we will be attempting to meet deadlines set by our superior, or by other agencies in the organization.

5. *Determine Detail.*   Once we have the major area of accomplishment blocked out, together with the timing, we can establish the detail steps.   In those cases where major steps pertain to one subordinate unit, we may want to delegate the detail in full to the accountable manager of that unit, asking him to work out with his people the detail steps together with the attendant schedule.   When we do this, he should be given as wide a latitude as possible.   Our prime concern should be to establish *what* has to be accomplished, delegating the *how* as largely as possible.

6. *Review and Reconcile.*   As a final step, all programs should be reviewed and reconciled to ensure that they are integrated and unified for best accomplishment of the over-all result.   This review and reconciliation can be accomplished at a committee meeting.   When this approach is used, we should be sure to give each committee participant copies of the over-all program and schedule to study beforehand, so that he can come prepared.   It is poor practice to ask committee members to review data or assemble information during the meeting.

PROGRAMMING AND SCHEDULING AT ARMCO STEEL CORPORATION

In Armco Steel Corporation programming and scheduling are used consistently as planning tools by managers at all levels.   One interesting example in Armco is the utilization of programming to help introduce automated equipment in one department.

As a preliminary, it is well to state that in keeping pace with the needs of the business and in making technological improvements in both plants and offices, Armco has maintained foremost the needs of people. Recognizing that the mutual interests of company and employees would rarely be satisfied unless careful planning preceded each move, Armco has managed so that employees are not jeopardized in position or pay by new technology.

To illustrate the point, as early as 1953 Armco identified the potential value of office mechanization and introduced several programs that paid off handsomely in cost savings.

In one case, as a result of the growth of its business, Armco found, at this time, that some of its major customers were dissatisfied with shipment notices of materials ordered. Primary reason was that the plants of the company used a cumbersome invoicing system that required mailing of shipment notices from the plants to Armco's general offices in Middletown, Ohio. By the time the paper work was completed and the customer received notice of shipment, he was often already on the telephone trying to find out what had happened to his order.

Illustrative of sound management is the way the company handled the problem. A careful study showed that mechanization of the payroll and consolidation of responsibilities would help eliminate the difficulty, at the same time increasing efficiency and effecting cost savings. But how to do this without dislocating people and causing unrest and dissatisfaction? With the situation growing increasingly acute, there was growing pressure for rapid action. But a precipitate move, while it might result in fast installation of new equipment, would probably also give rise to resistance on the part of the people involved.

Armco planned carefully. Objectives were established and the program and schedules necessary to implement them were developed. The program was established as follows:

1. One plant of the company was selected for a trial installation of the new system. Selection was based on such factors as capabilities of plant management, employee attitude toward change, and economy potentials.

2. The installation objective and program were discussed with the plant manager and his full understanding and acceptance were secured.

3. The plant manager assigned a staff man to make the local feasibility study.

4. The feasibility study was completed and reconciliation and agreement were reached on potential personnel savings.

5. The finalized installation program was outlined and confirmed for the plant manager with a full explanation of the detailed costs and potential savings.

6. The plant manager held a meeting with all principals actively concerned with the installation and reviewed and discussed it in detail. Since the individuals who participated in the meeting had already contributed to the feasibility study, they were already informed and had actually prepared much of the data presented. As a result, agreement was immediate and complete.

7. All clerical replacements at the plant for the nine-month period prior to the installation were hired on a temporary basis, to ensure that employees already on the payroll would have first chance at the new jobs and to provide job protection above normal attrition.

8. Some twenty people were given intensive training on the job to prepare them for new key-punch machine operator and control clerk positions.

9. Test runs on the new installation were completed several times before the conversion date to minimize possibility of unforeseen accidents.

The installation was completed successfully without disruption of personnel. While jobs were eliminated, careful planning made new opportunities for personnel who otherwise would have lost their jobs. Total savings currently for this one plant are approximately $40,000 annually.

PROGRAMMING AND SCHEDULING AND PERT

In the establishment of objectives and programming and scheduling as we have described them, we find a logical approach to determining what to accomplish and how best to develop the action and time sequences necessary. Any approach relying upon logic would, presumably, resolve itself into similar constituents.

We find an interesting illustration of the universality of this concept in the development of the Program Evaluation Review Technique, also known by the acronym PERT and as networking.

WHAT IS PERT?

While there are varying claims as to the inception of PERT, the first general application was made by the United States Navy Special Projects Office in the development of the Polaris submarine weapons missile system. The United States Navy developed a Polaris Management Sequence which is identified in three steps as (1) the definition of program objectives, (2) program planning and implementation, and (3) program evaluation. Stated in simple terms, this means that in building a vastly complex missiles system, the Navy found it necessary to determine beforehand what was to be done, to do it, and then to check up to make sure it was done properly. Using the semantics of professional management, we can state this as planning, implementation of the plan, and control.

PERT begins with the assumption, common to all sound planning, that before we spend money, consume time, use people and materials, we had better determine precisely what we expect to end up with. Before we set out to build an expensive house, we need to know, for example, precisely what that house will be like when it is completed. If we establish complete specifications as we go along, the costs will mount and our effectiveness will decrease. Simple as this seems, plan-as-you-go is typical of most business, governmental, community, and personal activities. PERT precludes this by requiring that the planning be completed so that it can be *seen* before implementation begins.

The charting technique developed for PERT is a useful contribution to effective planning. It places rigorous requirements upon the planner and literally forces him to think through in detail the essentials of a logical plan.

To identify the sequence of logic inherent in networking, we must keep in mind the rather confusing use of the terms used for objectives, programs, schedules, and budgets. In PERT, these are events, activities, schedules, and PERT/COST. Let us look at how these terms are used in networking.

Events

In the use of PERT, an *event* is a specific accomplishment that has been brought about through directed effort. An event, in other words, is an objective. The PERT concept adds a useful idea in that it specifies that an event happens at an identifiable moment in time but takes no time in itself and consumes no resources. To illustrate, "New Product Introduced" occurs at a point in time, but it consumes no people, materials, or facilities *in itself*. The things that are done to get the new product on the market are what consume resources.

Events form the key points of a PERT network. The things which must be done to accomplish the events are the *activities* which provide the logical basis for determining time, cost, and other matters.

Activities

In basic PERT, an event is separated from other events by activities. In networking, arrows are used to represent activities. An *activity* is defined as the applied effort necessary to connect two events. An activity cannot be started until its preceding event has been accomplished. The event succeeding this activity cannot be considered accomplished until all activities leading to the event are accomplished. This is obvious when we restate it to the effect that an end result cannot be accomplished until the work necessary has been carried out.

Activity Time

Time now must be considered. We have already established that a *schedule* is a time sequence; PERT calls precisely the same thing *activity time*. Activity time is defined as the elapsed time necessary to accomplish a task in a given manner.

PERT now introduces a significant innovation. Three time estimates are made by people competent to evaluate the activity: (1) An *optimistic* time, which is the shortest time in which the activity might be completed if ideal conditions prevail. This time will probably be

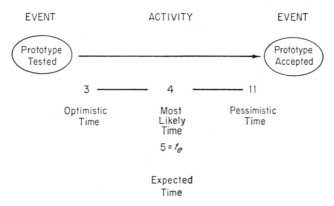

FIG. 12-1. PERT network.

realized only once in a hundred times. (2) The *most likely* time, which is the time that the activity would normally require. This is the time that we could expect to occur most often if the activity were repeated under precisely the same conditions. (3) A *pessimistic* time, which is the time that would be required to complete the activity if everything possible went wrong, excluding such major disasters as floods, wars, and strikes. The pessimistic time would probably be exceeded only once in a hundred occasions.

The three time estimates are at the heart of networking, for the results that follow can be no more accurate than these time estimates. A portion of such a network is shown in Figure 12-1.

The Basic Approach

Derived from the pioneering development of the United States Navy Special Projects Office, we can now show the basic approach to PERT networking in Figure 12-2.

Here *A-G* represent the events (objectives) to be accomplished. The arrows stand for the activities (program steps). The three time estimates for each activity provide the data from which the expected time, t_e, is calculated and shown in each case. The dotted line shows

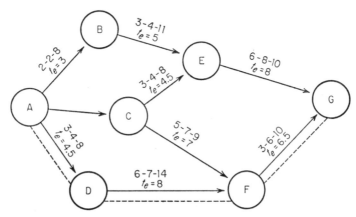

FIG. 12-2. PERT network.

the critical path, or the longest path through the network. All other paths are called *slack paths*.[1]

The Advantages of PERT

How does this relate to the planning and control concepts of professional management? We can see the parallel easily if we remember that PERT is the setting of objectives and the use of programming and scheduling to get a job done. It will quickly become apparent that if the endeavor is already planning logically, PERT will fit perfectly into the planning system; if planning is haphazard and spontaneous, attempts to use PERT will fail until logical methods of planning are introduced. PERT, in fact, will *force* the introduction of rational planning.

PERT requires that the entire plan be thought through beforehand, laid out graphically, and the priority, timing, and interrelationships calculated and reconciled.

The visual display of the plan is helpful. It enables the manager to think through on paper the alternative courses of action open to him and to select the one that will give him greatest probability of suc-

[1] The mechanics in detail will be found in *Program Evaluation and Review Technique*, ASO Exhibit ASOO 61-1, Aeronautical Systems Division, Air Force Systems Command, 1962, and *PERT Cost, Systems, Design*, National Aeronautics and Space Administration, 1962.

cess. Once the plan is graphically laid out, the critical areas can be identified and greatest attention brought to bear on these.

The PERT network identifies the areas in which critical problems are found. It enables us to compare directly our actual performance against the plan and to determine mathematically our probability of successful accomplishment in terms of objectives, program, schedule, and budget.

Because any step in the network can be isolated and broken down into its subsidiary networks without disturbing the integrity of the total pattern, PERT can be tailored to fit the needs of different management levels. It can provide a total picture of progress accomplished for top management, and related reports of subsidiary accomplishment to lower levels, at the same time identifying for each the actual and probable variances of major importance.

Networking has many adaptations. It is particularly valuable in planning and control of large, complex projects in which many new or one-of-a-kind developments are embodied. Using a computer, we can determine what it will take in terms of time and, using PERT/COST, money to accomplish objectives. We can evaluate different options and identify those which have greatest probability of success.

With our plan laid out graphically, we can determine whether it has reasonable expectation of accomplishing what we want. If not, we can focus quickly on those elements which are critical if improvement is to be effected. We can thus anticipate problem areas and prepare for them beforehand. We can determine where more effort must be applied to shorten the total time required for completion, where tasks may be eliminated without jeopardizing the whole, and the cost factors for each alternative.

PERT has the advantage of requiring us to think through first *what* we will do before we determine how much *time* or *money* it will require. Simple enough, but in this statement lies much of the reason for failure in management planning. Illogical as it is, schedules and budgets often as not are developed without the initial formulation of a basic program; in fact, in all too many of the companies we have studied, both scheduling and budgeting are carried on systematically, but programming is unknown.

PERT enables us to identify and evaluate alternatives in a systematic manner. Thus, in making the decisions necessary to sound plans, we can assess and even weight the available options and consciously withhold final decision and commitment until that point in time has been reached where the decision must be made. Using our computer outputs, we can maintain our assessment of the alternatives on a continuing basis.

USING PERT SUCCESSFULLY

As with most management innovations, PERT has assumed many of the characteristics of a fad. Used improperly, it can harm more than help. Three key points need to be stressed in its introduction and application.

It Must Use a Management Vocabulary

PERT workers are rapidly developing a PERT vocabulary which utilizes new terms to describe things which are already familiar and in use. This is giving rise to gobbledygook which makes it virtually impossible to understand what a particular manager means unless we ask for a detailed definition of all the terms used. If the practitioners of PERT, networking, PEP, CPM, line of balance, and other "new" techniques could reconcile the meaning they wish to convey with the management terms commonly used and adopt a standardized vocabulary, both understanding and progress would be greatly enhanced.

It Must Make Managers Accountable

As with automation, budgeting, and other new techniques, PERT is too often being made the special province of staff groups who do the planning of accountable managers and make their decisions for them. The place of PERT staff is to provide specialized staff advice and service, helping managers to understand and use PERT effectively. Staff may develop the networks *for* accountable managers, identify and quantify alternatives, provide coordination and consult on problems. The accountable manager, however, still must make the final decisions.

Education Must Be Provided

If PERT is used, all managers involved or affected should be educated so that they understand the technique and both its advantages and drawbacks. The danger here is that PERT will be introduced as something completely new and will be grafted upon the existing planning system. The real need is to establish the basic logic of professional management planning and to show how PERT becomes an added tool, making the total process of planning and control more effective but not disrupting or replacing it.

This educational process should start at the top and proceed through all levels of management. Only with this understanding can the technique be adapted to differing needs and used to further the management purpose of each component of the organization.

SUMMARY

The management program is a sequence of action steps arranged in the priority necessary to accomplish an objective. A schedule is the time sequence necessary to carry out this program. Programming and scheduling are tools which help the manager to make most effective use of his efforts and time. In programming we think through beforehand the best way to accomplish the objective and establish the sequence and priority of the work to be carried out. Within this framework we can channel all related effort. PERT is an effective means of developing objectives, programs, and schedules by use of graphic networks developed logically.

> *Almost any man knows how to earn money, but not one in a million knows how to spend it.* HENRY DAVID THOREAU

DEFINITIONS

Budget: an allocation of resources.

Management Budgeting: the work a manager performs to allocate the resources necessary to accomplish objectives.

THE LOGIC OF BUDGETING

We know what we want to accomplish, what steps we will follow to get there, and how long it will take. Logically, we can now determine how much it will cost.

Budgeting is an important element of planning. Through budgeting we ensure that we have the resources necessary to reach our objectives and to carry out our programs. Budgeting is defined as *the work a manager performs to allocate the resources necessary to accomplish objectives.*

Every manager has stewardship of a business unit, be it large or small. To secure his results, he utilizes people, materials, tools, and facilities. Since it is difficult to add and subtract such dissimilar elements as manpower, facilities, and materials and since we need a common denominator, we convert all these values to money. As a businessman, it is up to the manager to see to it that the money value of the results he secures covers all of his costs of doing business.

If we keep in mind that the manager is a businessman running his own business unit, the place of budgeting in the over-all process of

146

planning becomes clear. When a manager establishes his over-all objectives, he is deciding what results he expects to accomplish. These results have a definite value. In many cases, they can be translated directly into money or we can arrive at a monetary equivalent. To accomplish this objective, the manager undertakes a sequence of activities or a program. To carry out his program, he utilizes certain units of manpower, materials, and facilities.

If the manager simply spent money for these items as the need occurred, without setting limits to what he could afford, he could quickly find himself spending too much. However, if he decides beforehand how much it should cost for the materials, facilities, salaries, and other expenses necessary to attain his results, he can decide whether the results are worth the expense.

And here is the important point: If the manager discovers he cannot reach his objectives within reasonable cost limits, he can cut back his programmed activities to reduce his expenses, or he can change his objectives to fit the realities of the situation. If he can do this beforehand, on paper, he can avoid committing himself to something he cannot afford.

USES OF BUDGETS

Budgets have many uses. As planning tools, they are of value in developing objectives. Budgets enable us to make the most economical and effective use of the resources available to us because they give us a means of determining the cost of alternative paths of action. Budgets provide one of the best standards for managerial performance because they establish beforehand what it should cost to carry out a given activity. Thus the budget provides a yardstick with which to measure both progress and end accomplishment.

BUDGETING AND PROGRAMS

The first and most important consideration in the construction of a sound budget is to base the budget upon approved programs. What we are saying here, in effect, is that it is neither wise nor prudent to spend money until we have determined precisely what we expect to spend it *for*.

In many cases, managers establish budgets without having first programmed the activities they expect to carry out. When this occurs the budget can have little solid basis. Generally, it is made up on the basis of historical costs or in terms of a series of haphazard guesses as to what probable expenses will be. The budget is most useful as a management tool when it is used to cost out programs and to assess their relative value.

When budgets are not geared to programs, the probable approach to spending will be to increase expenditures as sales increase, cut expenses when volume falls off. While this may have a surface logic, the facts often call for the reverse. Frequently the time to spend more is when sales are at an ebb.

Typical of this approach is one consumer goods company that increases its advertising budget when business is good, slashes it to the bone when sales are down. Complacent when their fortunes are bright, sales managers in the company rarely press for large advertising expenditures when business is good. With a downturn, however, they plan new advertising campaigns with great enthusiasm, only to meet with refusal when an increased budget proposal is presented. Long an also-ran in its field, the company is now struggling to maintain its business at a nominal level.

BUDGET FROM THE TOP OR THE BOTTOM?

Most of the money in the company is spent at the operating level. This is also where the end results are accomplished. First-line managers at the operating level have the closest and most intimate knowledge of what it should cost to attain operating results. For this reason, budgets should be built from the bottom up as well as from the top down. Each subordinate manager should prepare a budget to cover the proposed costs of his unit. Since he does not have perspective beyond his own unit, however, and cannot determine the actual amount of money that will be available to him, he must reconcile his budget at his own level and then submit it to his manager for further coordination.

This process continues until the budgets are finally reviewed and reconciled at the top level of the company. It is here that the proposed total expenditures can be compared to the proposed income. It is here also that the best perspective can be exercised with regard to the relative needs of various parts of the company. Therefore, it is at top levels that budgets must be adjusted and approved. These authorized limits serve to guide each manager in his day-to-day expenditures.

Each manager should understand that his proposed budget is only tentative and that it will have to be reviewed in terms of the forecasted income of the company as a whole. The final decision will have to be made at a higher level of management. In budgeting, managers tend to overemphasize their own needs and to budget more than their proportionate share of the total money available. In other words, the natural tendency is to spend more than we take in. This is particularly true if we find it difficult to measure the money value of the results we accomplish.

Upper-level managers tend to see the whole picture with more perspective, and as a result are more prone to put a realistic value upon the work to be carried forward. Consequently, we generally find that budgets are subjected to progressive pruning as they climb upward. One result of this is that lower-level managers often deliberately inflate a budget request, hoping thus that the pruning will still leave them with as much leeway as they need. Unfortunately, this in turn prompts more rigorous pruning at higher levels, and in the end is self-defeating. The only sound approach is for the managers at all levels to be sternly realistic in their budgeting and in their consideration of budgets.

MANAGEMENT ACCOUNTABILITY IN BUDGETING

Every manager should be accountable for determining the budget covering his own operations. He should make the final decision concerning the budget that he submits to his own superior. Staff agencies such as the accounting or budget departments should not do the manager's work for him. Their place is to offer him advice and service in the technical details, and to help him follow approved budgeting procedures. If the accounting department is asked to develop the manager's budget for him it is placed at a disadvantage. For one thing, the accountant does not have firsthand knowledge of the manager's operation. Since the accountant has not prepared the manager's program, he cannot know what his costs should be. The accountant can do no better than prepare an accounting budget. He takes the historical record of past expenses and adds to this a fixed percentage. When multiplied out, this becomes the budget. As such it is only an approximation and does not accurately reflect management needs.

HOW TO MAINTAIN INTEGRITY OF BUDGETS

Budgets are often treated so loosely that they quickly fall into disrepute. This is unfortunate, for the budget can be one of the most valuable of the manager's planning tools. Frequently a fetish is made of underrunning budgets. Managers are complimented when they spend less than they budget. However, often this is not as admirable as it seems. If we look upon budgeted sums as money put aside for the purpose specified, we can get a much more accurate picture of what actually happens. When the manager does not spend this money, he is tying it up, when, in fact, it could probably be used elsewhere effectively.

Overrunning the budget is equally serious. This means that the manager is spending more than he should. This is often a result of poor analysis and decision making or haphazard budgeting. It requires investigation and corrective action.

When held to budget accountability, the manager should be accountable only for his controllable expense, that is, those expenses over which he has command, or which he has agreed are chargeable to him. In many cases, overhead expenses are also allocated to the manager; he is asked to pay them even though he has little or no command over those expenditures. When this is the case, the allocated items should be made a part of his budget so that he can estimate his total cost picture. Otherwise, he should not be held to account for that over which he has no authority.

SUMMARY

Budgeting is the work a manager performs to allocate the resources available to him. From a management viewpoint, budgeting is the determination of how much it will cost to carry out our programs and reach our objectives within the limits established by the schedule. The budget converts to monetary terms the time of people, materials, tools, and facilities necessary to get the job done. Every manager should be accountable for his own budget, using the accounting or controllership functions to provide him with the specialized help and advice he needs to do the job effectively. In utilizing budgets, it is important that overruns and underruns both be held in check, otherwise the integrity of the budget will be jeopardized.

You won't skid if you stay in a rut. KIN HUBBARD

DEFINITIONS

Procedure: a standardized method of performing specified work.

Establishing Procedures: the work a manager performs to develop and apply standardized methods of performing specified work.

THE LOGIC OF PROCEDURES

It is highly desirable to let people determine the best way to do the job for themselves. However, there are always circumstances which make it necessary to establish in advance a uniform method of doing specified work. For example, if we let each accountant determine how he will keep his books, it will be difficult or impossible to arrive at a consolidated balance sheet; and if each inspector were to work out his own methods of testing for quality, the quality of the product would vary widely.

In every company it is necessary that certain work be done the same way wherever it is performed. In cases such as accounting and quality control, this is necessary so that uniform results can be ensured. In other instances, the prime requirement may be to standardize the handling of routine so that it can be performed most quickly and efficiently. *A procedure is a standardized method of performing specified work.*

ADVANTAGES OF PROCEDURES

Procedures can be of great value in simplifying training. A procedure is a sound basis for breaking down the job into its constituent steps and training people to perform each step in the most effective fashion. Procedures can eliminate a great deal of routine decision making, by predeciding how repetitive work is to be performed. At the same time, because they are standardized work methods, procedures ensure that the same kind of work performed by different people in different units of the company will fit into the same over-all pattern. For example, the use of uniform accounting procedures enables us to determine the cost of our products and to prepare a consolidated balance sheet to show our over-all financial results. If each accountant could keep his records and accounts according to his own dictates, accounting would be chaotic, to say the least.

THE STRUCTURE OF PROCEDURES

Procedures that apply to the over-all operation of the company should be established at the top company level. It is only here that perspective and objectivity exist with regard to the needs of the company as a whole. Since these procedures specify how work is to be performed throughout the company, it is generally necessary to develop company procedures in detail. This means that there is minimum opportunity for interpretation or modification at the local level. Where uniformity and standardization are necessary in the individual units of the company, division, department, and section procedures are developed. In this case, each is authorized by the accountable manager.

PROCEDURES SHOULD REPRESENT THE BEST WAY

A procedure is most valuable if it is based on careful study and analysis of the work to be performed. The total job should be broken down into its component steps, and each step studied carefully to determine the best way to get the job done. The people who are doing the work should be called into consultation as fully as possible. They will have firsthand knowledge of the problems and difficulties that are encountered and will be able to suggest ideas based on their own practical experience. However, since the operators themselves cannot be expected to study new developments in other companies and from outside agencies, a staff group often can be utilized effectively to develop the best way to do the work and to help incorporate it in the procedures used.

Procedures should be consistent. Since a procedure dictates the best way specific work is to be performed no matter where it is carried on, deviations from the procedure should be kept to a minimum. If we are to secure full return from our investment in procedures, all managers should be familiar with those that apply to their operations and should see to it that they are used consistently.

FEWER RATHER THAN MORE

Procedures tend to be restrictive. They hold people to a specified manner of performing their work. This is necessary in some cases, but even here it tends to have a dampening effect upon initiative and innovation. People who are kept to routine performance have little incentive to use their imagination or to develop new and better ways of doing their day-to-day work. For these reasons, procedures should be kept to the minimum. Wherever possible, sound standards should be set and people should have freedom to reach those standards, rather than being held to a prescribed method.

KEEP PROCEDURES UP TO DATE

Once approved and put into use, a procedure can become so much a matter of rote that its significance is overlooked. Often procedures are still followed slavishly after their need has passed. In many cases a complex and involved procedure is used when new circumstances would make a much abbreviated method practicable. The best way to anticipate and prevent these situations is to provide for a periodic review of all procedures. This should take place at least once a year. Through this rigorous screening, unnecessary procedures should be eliminated and those which can be improved or modified should be adapted to current needs.

SUMMARY

A procedure is a standardized method of performing specified work. In developing procedures, we analyze the job to be done and identify the best way to perform it. A procedure then becomes a standardized method that will be followed by everybody doing that work. Procedures have the advantage of helping to ensure that work is done the best way and in a uniform manner; however, they can have the disadvantage of discouraging creative effort and ingenuity.

CHAPTER 15 *Management Policies*

> *Men must be decided on what they will not do, and then they are able to act with vigour in what they ought to do.* MENCIUS

DEFINITIONS

Developing Policies: the work a manager performs to develop and interpret standing decisions that apply to repetitive questions and problems of significance to the enterprise as a whole.

Policy: a standing decision made to apply to repetitive questions and problems of significance to the enterprise as a whole.

Regulation: a standing decision made to apply to repetitive problems and questions of significance to one component of the endeavor.

THE LOGIC OF POLICIES

As a company grows and expands, it finds it necessary to act in a uniform manner in certain fundamental areas of the business. For example, it should be consistent in the way it sets prices, in the credit it provides for different groups of customers, in the manner it compensates its employees, and in the quality of its products. Questions relating to such fundamental aspects of the business as these come up repeatedly at all levels. They could be handled individually by the accountable manager. However, when these are basic questions affecting the entire company, individual managers find it unwise to commit the whole company at their own level and therefore they are forced to refer the question higher.

Eventually such basic questions reach the chief executive office, where objectivity with regard to the needs of the company as a whole exists. A good deal of time would be wasted if these same questions were relayed repeatedly through many layers of organization, finally to get the same answer. It is more satisfactory to have top management think through the basic issue and to provide continuing decisions that will apply to these questions every time they arise. These are policies.

A policy, then, is a decision made by top management that continues in effect and applies to those repetitive questions and problems which are covered by it. A policy, literally, is a command from top management to the company as a whole. It directs every manager to act in a prescribed manner in handling specified situations.

ADVANTAGES OF POLICIES

When thought through carefully, policies enable top management to establish the nature and character of the company in a knowing and conscious fashion rather than letting the company be shaped by external, and often fortuitous, circumstances. The enterprise that knows what it wants to become has the best chance of accomplishing what it wants.

Shape the Nature of the Company

Consider the effect conscious policy has upon one large oil company. Early in its corporate existence, this company decided that it would follow three basic policies:

1. It would specialize in the production of crude oil and stay out of refining and marketing. This enabled the company to concentrate upon what was, at the time, the most profitable part of the oil business. When a glut of crude oil later became available, the company suffered because of lack of balance in its operations.

2. It would use conservative accounting methods. In the oil business conservative accounting means charging off drilling costs as operating expenses rather than capitalizing them. As a result, the company's book value remained at a low level, while the market value and the price per share of its stock climbed steeply.

3. It decided to explore aggressively for oil only within a limited and prescribed geographic area. Concentrated expenditure of funds within this area instead of over the face of the globe enabled the company to build large reserves that constituted a major asset.

The point here is not whether these were the best policies; rather, it is important to recognize this prime advantage—that firm adherence to these policies enabled the company to become the kind of enterprise its top management had decided it wanted.

We can see clearly how policies have shaped the character of some of the leading companies of the world.   For example, Harvey S. Firestone, Sr., built The Firestone Tire and Rubber Company from a tiny firm with $20,000 assets in 1900 by following two basic polices: (1) That the highest possible quality must be built into a product commensurable with the price that the customer can afford.   (2) That the product must be backed by the kind of service that gives every consideration to the customer's welfare and service.   Firmly instilled in every executive, these policies have been followed consistently ever since.

Facilitate Delegation

Policies make it easier for managers to delegate because individual managers do not have to spend time deciding and redeciding repetitive problems.   They are free to concentrate on the exceptional matters that cannot be handled at lower levels.   This frees managers for forward planning and gives them an opportunity to think beyond the dimensions of their own jobs.

When properly developed and authorized, policies enable the top management of a company to make balanced and considered decisions with respect to the basic questions of continuing importance that confront the company.   The opportunity to weigh and consider beforehand eliminates the need for hasty, spur-of-the-moment decisions and makes it possible to bring to bear on these problems the accumulated knowledge and experience of the company as a whole.

Policies improve the over-all quality of decision making.   Since they apply to matters beyond the scope of single individuals or departments, they do not require managers to make decisions for which they are ill-equipped because of their limited vantage point.   Sound, well-considered policies encourage effective teamwork.   Because the vital and often most controversial problems have already been carefully weighed and their decisions made, there is less opportunity for argument or dispute in the heat of a passing emergency.   This helps all members of the team to work together toward a common goal.

DIFFICULTIES IN USING POLICIES

In spite of their potential value, policies are frequently relegated to the background because of certain difficulties that arise in their use. One prime danger is that policies will be too restrictive and may tend to discourage initiative and freedom of action.   This can come about very easily because the top managers who authorize the policies ordinarily have little current firsthand acquaintance with the operating levels of the organization where policies are largely applied. Unless this gap can be closed through participation and communication, the policies may hamper rather than help the people for whom they are designed.

Difficulty often arises because the proper use of policies is not understood. Managers may "invent" a policy in situations where they are not too sure of their ground or want to enforce an arbitrary decision. Again, policies may be made so inflexible and unyielding that they cannot be interpreted properly to apply to local conditions. This leads to disuse. Policies may be ornamental rather than useful when they are stated in such general terms that they cannot be made to apply to specific operating situations.

DIFFERENCES BETWEEN POLICIES AND OBJECTIVES

Misunderstandings occur because of failure to differentiate between policies and objectives. An objective is a statement of intention. It establishes that the company or the individual manager will put forth every effort in the hope of accomplishing a specified end result. The objective clearly defines this end result. It becomes a guide for the actions of every manager to whom it applies.

A policy is more definitive. It is a command from top management to perform in a specified manner. It establishes definite limits of authority. The policy does not spell out the end itself but specifies a means to accomplish this end. Where the objective is a guide, the policy is a specific command.

SUBORDINATE POLICIES

Over-all company policies established at the top level are intended, in most cases, to apply to operating conditions and problems at lower levels. However, since they are company-wide in scope, the broad company policies are often not specific or detailed enough for local application. To be most useful, policies should be interpreted for each component of the company. Thus we find division, department, and unit interpretations of over-all policy for local use.

The important point here is that these subordinate policies are derived from over-all company policy. They must be consistent with the over-all policy. To ensure consistency and coordination of the total policy structure, each written interpretation should be authorized by management two levels higher in the organization.

REGULATIONS

Situations frequently arise in individual components of the company that require a standing decision, which is in the nature of a policy. However, in these cases it may not be desirable to establish a company-wide standing decision. Where this is so, we make use of regulations. A regulation is *a standing decision made to apply to repetitive problems and questions of significance to one component of the endeavor.* For example, one division of the company might require all its salesmen to lease their automobiles, while another division might prefer outright purchase. If there is no over-all company policy, the two divisions could establish their own regulations which would guide and direct their managers to the appropriate action when acquisition of automobiles was in question.

The distinction between policies and regulations can be helpful. If we make use of a policy, we know that a similar directive will be found in all other parts of the company. On the other hand, if a standing decision is identified as a regulation, we know that this applies only to the component in which we are located and a different ruling may prevail in another part of the company. The primary caution with respect to regulations is that they should not contradict or contravene overriding policies.

USING POLICIES EFFECTIVELY

Company policies are developed with the participation of managers at all levels; however, they are authorized by the chief executive and board of directors. Every manager is accountable for interpretation and application of company policies to his own unit. The manager is also accountable for developing the appropriate regulations to apply to his unit.

A manager should review and explain company policies and their local application, together with regulations, to his subordinates. Meetings are a good medium. They should be held periodically to ensure that all are kept informed and that consistent interpretation is being maintained. The manager should interpret new or modified policies as soon as possible after they have been communicated to him. If he has been told about a new policy that applies to his unit, it is his responsibility to ask for the definite information he requires.

Maintain Flexibility

A policy has been defined as a standing decision made to apply to repetitive problems. Although repetitive, these problems will differ.

The situations to which they apply will vary, so also will the people involved. Policies must be flexible enough to meet these changing requirements and situations. At top organizational levels, policies, in keeping with other plans, are longest range in their projection and thus are relatively fixed and stable. At this higher level they should be revised only to meet changes in long-term conditions and commitments. At lower organizational levels, however, the perspective and requirements are both of shorter term. Therefore, the lower in the organization we go, the greater the provision needed for flexibility through interpretation. A policy should be an aid to effective action; it should not be permitted to become an obstacle to fast, direct action at the operating level where flexibility counts the most.

Keep Up To Date

Managers at each level should be accountable for periodic review and revision of policy interpretations and regulations that apply to their groups. This review can be best conducted with the full participation of the subordinate managers concerned. Where policy review is carried out systematically, it ensures full understanding of current interpretations of the policy and helps managers advance questions and make suggestions for improved use.

Provide for Participation and Communication

Managers will not necessarily participate in the development of all company policies. Their prime concern should be with those policies which concern them at their own levels. Here they should be given every opportunity to participate in the formulation of new policies and in suggesting policy modifications.

Effective policies must be stated in writing. It is difficult, if not impossible, to secure participation and effective communication if the policies are not available in clear, complete, and concise written form.

SUMMARY

Policies are standing decisions made to ensure uniform action in the handling of repetitive problems and questions that are significant to the organization at large. Regulations are standing decisions that apply to only one component of the organization. Both policies and regulations provide effective guides to independent action. To be used effectively, it is most important that both policies and regulations be flexible enough to meet changing situations, that they be kept up to date so that they reflect current needs, and that participation and communication be utilized in their development.

PART THREE

Management Organizing

CHAPTER 16 *Management Organizing*

> *Sound organizations must be built on respect for the individual; if an organization plan does not make it easier for people to work together productively, it should not be adopted.* GWILYM A. PRICE, WESTINGHOUSE ELECTRIC CORPORATION

DEFINITIONS

The Function of Organizing

Management organizing is the work a manager performs to arrange and relate the work to be done so that it may be performed most effectively by people.

The Activities of Organizing

Developing Organization Structure: the work a manager does to identify and group the work to be performed.

Delegating: the work a manager does to entrust responsibility and authority to others and to create accountability for results.

Establishing Relationships: the work a manager performs to create the conditions necessary for mutually cooperative efforts of people.

Responsibility: the work assigned to a position.

Authority: the sum of the powers and rights assigned to a position.

Accountability: the obligation to perform responsibility and exercise authority in terms of established performance standards.

THE LOGIC OF ORGANIZING

When many people are involved in carrying out a large and co-ordinated action, the question continually arises as to what work should

163

be done and who should do it. Left to themselves, the stronger or more opportunistic will build empires. Results may be accomplished, but the effort may involve much waste and will probably take its toll in human frustration. A better way to go about it is to decide in advance what work must be done to reach the objectives, and then to establish each major task so that it can be performed most effectively by the people concerned.

In organizing, the manager determines, with his team, the total work that has to be done in order to reach the over-all objectives that have been established. Drawing upon the advice of his group, he decides what positions have to be created, and what should be done by each person in each of these positions. Working with his own superior and with other groups, he arranges and relates the jobs that have been created to form streamlined, balanced positions, units, divisions, departments, and other organizational components.

MISCONCEPTIONS IN ORGANIZATION

Difficulties often arise in management organization because of misunderstanding with respect to certain key questions. Does the organization limit freedom of action to an undesirable degree? How accurately do organization charts depict the real organization? Is an organization people? Our research has developed several basic points that help to clarify the issues.

Does the Organization Limit Freedom of Action?

"We don't have a formalized organization because it holds people down and doesn't let them use their creative abilities." This theme is repeated frequently in companies at a certain stage of growth. It is most characteristic of the strong, natural leader who often is impatient of organizational restrictions. Accustomed to operating with the grand sweep and flair of his personal genius, he sees organization as a potential barrier rather than as a guide to more effective performance. And, for him, this is often true. During the early years of most enterprises, we have found there is very little formalized organization. When there is more work to be done than can possibly be accomplished, the likelihood of duplication and overlap is small.

But with growth must come discipline. Twelve or fourteen managers can wheel and deal with relative abandon, ranging so far afield from one another that there is little conflict. But when the company grows to such size that several thousand managers must work effectively together, this freedom becomes chaos and jeopardizes the very thing the managers are trying to accomplish.

The limits set by a good organization resemble the speed limits and the center line on a modern freeway. These restrictions prohibit drivers from getting in the way of other cars or endangering themselves and others by excessive speed; however, by channeling traffic and keeping it within bounds, the restrictions greatly facilitate the total flow of traffic.

In any large endeavor, along with growth and diversity comes the need for the limitation of individual freedom in pursuit of the greater good of the whole. The balance is fine, for while too much individual liberty enables one person to jeopardize the freedom of others, increased restrictions tend to snuff out the sparks of personal interest and enthusiasm that are essential to truly outstanding performance. A key characteristic of the professional manager is his ability to make a rational determination of what metes and bounds are necessary so that he can, within these obligatory limits, provide for maximum personal freedom of action.

Does an Organization Chart Really Show the Organization?

A manager will often lay his organization chart on his desk, smooth it out, and say: "Here is my organization." This is far from the fact. The organization chart is an inadequate representation of the organization that actually exists. Properly prepared, the chart can identify the large areas of work that are to be performed, it can indicate basic relationships, and it can specify who gives orders to whom. But this about marks its capacity.

Organization charts cannot show the nature and limits of the work that has to be done to reach objectives. An organization chart will not specify the type of authority that exists. It cannot tell us *how* people are to work together.

The chart has other inadequacies when we try to use it to convey the true meaning of an organization. An organization chart cannot tell us anything about *how* the subordinate can work most effectively with his boss, what the boss should do to maintain good relationships with his subordinates, how people on the same level should work together, or what relationships should prevail between line and staff. Perhaps the most serious deficiency of all is the tendency of people and organizations to change so rapidly that most charts are out of date by the time they are published.

Is an Organization People?

Two unsatisfactory ways of thinking about organization are prevalent. One assumes that the organization is, in fact, the people of the company. A more rational approach to organization clearly establishes that the organization is not the people of the company but, rather, the arrangement and relationship of the work to be done *by* people.

So that this will not seem hairsplitting, let us look at a related situation. We recognize that the most important elements in an automobile are its driver and passengers, and in a house, the people who live within it. While it is true that the needs of the people who work within the organization are the most significant consideration in designing it, just as the automobile and the house are not the people involved, so the organization is *not* the people who work within it.

Confusion on this score has led to a great deal of difficulty. In some cases companies have designed organizations which are theoretically ideal and have been nonplused because people failed to do the work, make the decisions, and exercise the relationships required by that organization. At this point there has often been a tendency to blame the "formal" organization and to advocate an "informal" and less restrictive structure. In some cases, this has led to the rather empty gesture of abandoning organization charts and position guides, as if, in doing away with these historical notes about the organization, the situation somehow would be corrected.

In developing an organization we have a design problem similar to that of the automobile designer, who must determine what his potential driver and passengers require for comfortable, efficient transportation, or to that of the architect, who must determine the needs of people before he designs his house.

Organizing is often confused with motivation, communication, and development of people. We differentiate by establishing that organization refers to the *work* people must do, the *decisions* they must make, the *relationships* they must follow. People must understand what they have to do. Securing this understanding is communication. People must be encouraged to take effective action, which involves motivation. People must acquire the skills and abilities necessary to do the work and make the decisions assigned to them, and this is the development of people.

A second source of confusion is a concept that envisages a basic conflict between the requirements of the organization and the emotional needs of people who work within it. The contention is offered that business managers, in particular, tend to organize without regard to this potential source of difficulty and, as a result, seriously impair the motivation of their people. In our studies we have found that, in fact, practicing managers have been very much aware of this potential problem and in many cases have made substantial contributions toward its solution. Looking at the real problem and not at the theoretical and emotional fog that all too frequently surrounds it, we find that it can be stated simply. At issue is the fact that any time we place restrictions upon the personal freedom of people to act and think as they want, they will tend to oppose those restrictions. How can we best reconcile the needs of the organization and the needs of the people who work within it? The answer is not simply one of organization; it encompasses the whole of effective leadership as we have defined it. People get the greatest satisfaction from the work they do under the guidance and direction of managers who know how to plan, organize, lead, and control them in their work.

Our need at present is not for theoreticians to belittle the contributions of practicing managers, nor yet for the hardheaded operating man to ignore the value of soundly conceived theory. Rather, what is required is cooperative effort to develop principles and techniques that will enable us to discover the human needs of people who will man the organization, and to design a structure that will enable them to work most effectively together.

WHO IS ACCOUNTABLE FOR ORGANIZATION?

One of the most important kinds of work a manager should master is that of organization. But we have been continually surprised at the degree of lip service paid it and the small amount of organizing work that is actually done. In our study of more than 2,000 management positions, we have found that fewer than 10 per cent have been delegated organization work as a clearly identified responsibility.

If a manager does not know that he is expected to do organization work, is he likely to do it? Probably not. If we *pay* a manager to organize so that he can get the most work done with the fewest people, should we hold him accountable for doing the work and getting the results we require? Prudence and wisdom would say "yes." Prime reason for this situation most often is lack of understanding of the crucial role organization plays in survival and success.

Typical is one large international company in which managers religiously prepared organization charts but had little concept of what sound organization actually entails. For many years comfortably ensconced in noncompetitive markets, the company gradually acquired the layers of organizational fat that represent unnecessary people doing unimportant work. During the years after World War II, competition began to tighten and pressure on costs and prices became acute. Finally the company called in outside consultants and participated in a rigorous organization survey. In the process it found that it could eliminate more than 3,500 people, ranging from top executives to clerks.

In this case. several millions of dollars were being spent year after year on unnecessary wages and salaries. This money could not be identified on the company's balance sheet or in its operating reports. It represented a steady drain on income which could be tolerated only because lack of real competition shielded the company's organizational inefficiency.

If there is to be maximum productivity at minimum cost, each manager should be held accountable for the daily and continuing performance of the management work of organizing. Rarely can staff groups or other agencies do the work as well as can the manager on the spot. When the organization proliferates, unpruned and unchecked, because of this management failure, the company's assets are wasted and people are subject to massive periodic organizational upheavals which threaten their jobs and cause unrest and dissatisfaction.

THE COMPUTER AND ORGANIZATION

Automation will have a significant effect upon organization. However, in response to many completely unsupported statements that the computer will make obsolete our current concepts of organization, we should point to one inescapable fact: an organization is a mechanism to enable *people* to work more effectively together. So long as people remain the kind of human beings we know, our organizations will retain the essential characteristics they now have. Only when we develop a different and perhaps superior human being will we be able to utilize some of the far-fetched theories that are all too often advanced.

To see the impact of the computer on organization, we should look at some fundamental considerations first. An organization structure is best visualized as pyramidal in form because it is necessary to create an organizational position in which one person, or a group of persons, can be so placed as to make decisions involving all members of the team as they work together to accomplish the common goal. The position at the top of the pyramid is the keystone in the decision-making structure.

Information bearing upon all functions of the business must be fed to this top position for broad decisions affecting the enterprise as a whole. But the decisions made at the top are made primarily to guide and coordinate work carried on at the operating level. Because only at the top can the proper course of the undertaking be plotted, to this focal point also there must be a return flow of the information necessary to correct those errors that cannot be detected at lower levels.

The decision-making structure in a small unit is relatively simple in concept but already complex in its relationships, as shown in Figure 16-1.

Once the major decisions have been made at the top to set the limits and direct the operating positions through intermediate levels of organization, these positions should be able to coordinate among themselves the work they perform within their own sphere of accountability.

As organizations grow, intervening levels of managers are created, primarily to enable individuals to encompass in their minds the data necessary to make sound planning, controlling, organizing, and leading decisions. These intervening levels do not change the basic decision-making structure. The requirement still is to enable the top position to understand and assess enough of the requirements of the total organization to make the broad decisions encompassing all interests.

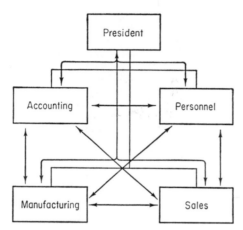

Fig. 16-1. Decision-making structure in a small organization.

Each intervening level now becomes a relay point, a maker of implementing decisions, a correction point, and a regulator of action for errors made at lower levels.

Each added level of management complicates the matter, for it interposes more people who must know and understand in order to act effectively. This is illustrated in Figure 16-2.

Among all positions there is need for a cross flow of information to coordinate matters at each level and across levels. With each new relay point, the information requirements multiply.

Proper filtration and comprehension of this mass of data are beyond the unaided human mind. Until recently, machines have not been of much help in taking over this burden. Because a vertical flow pattern is much easier to channel and limit, the information system has largely followed the command channels of the organization, that is, up and down the lines of accountability. In spite of the admitted inadequacy of the system, it was the best we could devise.

Note here that this deficiency resulted not from inadequacy of the organization but because human capacity is limited and *there were no effective means of compensating for these inadequacies*. To condemn the system—a popular pastime nowadays of theorists who should know better—is the equivalent of a critic damning the propeller-driven aircraft for its inadequacy before the jet engine had been invented.

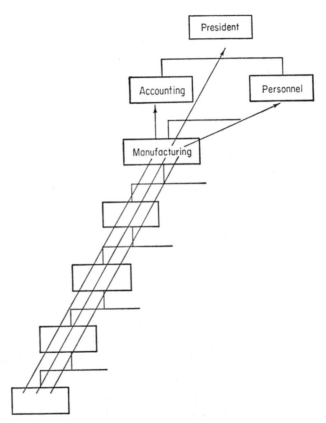

Fig. 16-2. Effect of added levels of management.

With automation and the computer, increased cross flow is now possible.   By this we mean that much greater coordination of decisions can be accomplished at each level of organization.   To illustrate, in the past, if a salesman found a customer who was eager to place a large order for his product but who required a special modification to suit his requirements, the order would climb up and down the functional channels of engineering, manufacturing, and sales and the staff functions concerned before determination could be made of feasibility, cost, and delivery factors.   With the computer, this can be simplified greatly by processing, analyzing, and reporting information as needed through one data-processing center.

In this new approach to decision making, every sales, manufacturing, and engineering activity can be reported, *not to each function separately* but to the one center where the information is classified, summarized, analyzed, and reported to managers who make the decisions.

New Requirements

To use the computer most effectively, we will need to do several things. First we must look to the need for streamlining our management organizations. With the replacement of much routine and detail activity by computerized applications and the increased speed and accuracy of information flow, we will not need as many people in management positions. When too many people handle information it becomes delayed, distorted, and weakened. In the future the span of control will widen and the number of levels will decrease. Bitter as will be the resistance and fierce the rationalization, the process of elimination of management positions is necessary and will proceed inevitably.

Reducing the Number of People. To prepare for effective use of automation in management, we need to identify the key points in our existing organizations where the critical planning decisions must be made. Here we will probably find that we have more people than we need to make decisions; in a great many companies, preliminary attempts to utilize automation to facilitate management show that we have too many managers and too little management.

One large manufacturing company, for example, recently acquired an old-line, well-established firm and discovered that it could get better management in one unit if it used five managers to do the work formerly assigned to eighteen managers, before the introduction of computerized devices for management purposes.

Another large company, a leader in a process industry, was able to save over $3 million in management salaries by streamlining its management team. Still another company discovered that one in every six of its managers was unnecessary to accomplish the required management work. In many companies, we have found that it is quite feasible to prune and minimize management positions, particularly in the middle-management levels and, in the process, to get more work done more efficiently by fewer people. Strangely enough, when managers are given a full load of challenging and demanding work, they generally receive a great deal more satisfaction from it.

Understanding the Business as a Whole. To use the computer effectively in management of any part of the business, each manager will need to develop a systematic understanding of the business as a whole in addition to that part which he manages.   Only when we understand what we are trying to accomplish and how we can best accomplish our goals can we also know what information is needed at each decision point.   The computer pushes back the limits of potential understanding; it can make communication vastly more effective.   But it will take more effort and much greater competence in the work of communication than we have so far envisioned.

ORGANIZING FOR COMPUTER UTILIZATION

An important point is this: Properly utilized, data collection, analysis, and reporting should be done by a *staff* group whose purpose should be to provide advice and service in helping accountable managers *make their own decisions,* not in making their decisions for them. Already there is evidence of an undesirable assumption of authority by some corporate staff planning and control groups.   Where this occurs, inevitably it results in the gradual weakening of the line operation and a corresponding move toward undesirable centralization of authority.

The strategic location for a staff group that will help managers in preparing plans and exercising controls is at the corporate top management level.   Here is a vantage point which makes for a broad view of all operations, is conducive to objectivity, and ensures proximity to the decision-making executives who have greatest need of the consolidated control information.

Assistance from corporate staff planning and control groups has been available in the past in such companies as Koppers Company, United Air Lines, Continental Can, Carborundum Company, and others. Now, however, the use of new information tools greatly augments their potential effectiveness and argues their more general use.

Organization of this staff group will become commonplace within a few years.   Primary reason is that as we learn more about automation, these new planning and control techniques will loom large as competitive weapons and will merit the sharply defined study and attention that can be provided best by a properly constituted staff group at the corporate level.

The Role of the Computer Technician

The novel technological requirements of electronic data processing tend to force the computer technician into a role for which he is not fitted and often does not want.   Problems are even now arising because of it.   Since the computer is technically complex and uses symbolic language and its own code, there is even now a strong tendency for the *programmer* to assume a large share of authority in interpreting and reporting his data. In effect, this puts him in the position of strongly influencing the decision or of actually making the decision for the accountable line manager.

Here we have the same situation as prevailed when the accountant dominated the management of business and saw everything as part of an accounting system, always convertible to dollars and cents and to be judged in terms of visible profitability. We saw the same thing with the vogue of the industrial engineer and the tendency to equate everything with mechanical efficiency and the development of engineered systems. Again our viewpoint was distorted with the prominence of human relations and the common belief that motivation, communication, and training of people were an end in themselves and the most important purpose of the enterprise as a whole. With the advent of the professional manager, we see that the proper integration and balance of the whole are the important thing, and that all these components of the whole must be given their proper weight and balance at varying times.

Prime requirements in effective management are *balance* and *individual* accountability. Therefore, the information specialist should be delegated carefully defined responsibilities that enable him to make a maximum contribution to the team effort, but without usurping the prerogatives of the managers whom he serves. This is one of the most important organizational considerations we need to bear in mind in making effective use of—to do a noble job of scrambling similes—that Alladin in Pandora's box, the computer.

SUMMARY

Organizing is the work a manager does to arrange and relate the work to be performed so that it can be carried out most effectively by people. An organization is not people but the mechanism arranged to enable people to work most effectively together. An organization chart is helpful in showing some aspects of the organization but the chart itself is not the organization. Every manager should be held accountable for his proper work of organizing, for this is how he ensures that the most work is accomplished by the fewest people at the least cost. The computer will encourage simplification and streamlining of organization structure but will probably not lead to radical change in the general forms of structures we use.

Anyone can do any amount of work, provided it isn't the work he is supposed to be doing at that moment.
ROBERT BENCHLEY

DEFINITIONS

Developing Organization Structure: the work a manager does to identify and group the work to be performed.

Organization Structure: the pattern work assumes as it is identified and grouped to be performed by people.

Grouping: putting related work together to form positions, units, and other organization components.

Position: a grouping of work to be performed by a person.

THE LOGIC OF ORGANIZATION STRUCTURE

If work must be done, it will be performed most effectively *if we know what it is.* It is entirely possible to do the work that happens to come to hand and in the process worry through to an end result. Particularly if there is only one, or a very few people, a haphazard approach may even turn out quite well. When many people must work together, however, the rational method is to stop and think through beforehand the major items of work to be performed, who is best placed to perform them, and to make the assignment so that there is a minimum of overlap and duplication.

The organization structure is rarely an acute problem while the company is small and young, for there is generally more work to be done that can be accomplished. With maturity and greater stability, the situation changes. As the number of people increases, there is a

174

growing tendency to perform work that is unimportant in itself or that has little relationship to the basic purposes of the enterprise. At this stage, the need to develop a sound organization structure becomes critical.

In our research, we have found that this difference in approach is sharply exemplified by the strong natural leader and the modern scientific manager. The strong natural leader rarely thinks logically about organization. He does the work he prefers and encourages others to do the same. Because this is his way, it seems proper and natural. Inevitably, however, the organization outgrows this haphazard approach. Positions proliferate, levels multiply, illogical assignment of work leads to waste and inefficiency.

When the natural leader learns to manage scientifically he analyzes jobs logically, makes rational assignment of work, and gets more productivity through people who find much greater personal satisfaction in the results they accomplish.

Note, however, that the strong natural leader must be willing to relinquish some of the satisfaction he derives from exclusive exercise of the important responsibility and authority if a portion of this is to be made available to others at lower levels. The top leader *must give up some of his freedom of choice* if his subordinates are to enjoy the results of making those choices *that he would otherwise have made himself.* It is natural that he tends to resist; firm self-discipline is required if he is to organize in an orderly and logical fashion so that all share in the rewards of challenging work well done.

THE IMPACT OF ORGANIZATION STRUCTURE ON PEOPLE

The organization structure strongly influences the people who work within it. When there is uncertainty as to what is to be done and who is to do it, confusion and overlap are almost certain. In the absence of organizational restrictions, aggressive people will tend to take over work that, logically, they should not perform and to the detriment of the group as a whole. Without a well-defined structure, important work that should be done may receive little or no attention. The inevitable result is a succession of emergencies which crop up with no identifiable cause.

One long-established nonferrous metals company, for example, doubled in size within five years following the development of a new use for one of its basic products. At the end of the five-year period, the company found it necessary to divisionalize its organization structure. It had no suitable candidates for promotion within the company for the new divisional posts and had to go on the outside to find seven key executives. This deficiency resulted from failure of the company's managers to do the work of developing management talent. This failure penalized the company's own people who were not given the opportunity they should have had; it disrupted salary scales as some ranges were widened to accommodate the higher salaries of the new managers; and it added substantially to the salary budget.

Organization strongly influences the motivation of people. In a properly designed organization, jobs will be tightly packed with important work and commensurate authority. They will offer a challenge and give the people who hold them an opportunity to grow and develop to their fullest capacities. A good organization helps to eliminate overlap and duplication, and in the process, removes an important cause of frustration and friction. A properly balanced organization is the basis for sound salary administration; it provides a framework for effective communication; and it facilitates the development of teamwork.

Top-flight people can work effectively in almost any kind of organization. They have the ability to overcome organizational deficiencies through their own energy and resourcefulness. However, a sound, well-balanced organization will make even outstanding people more effective. If the people available are not highly capable, a good organization will help them to attain acceptable results.[1]

THE ALLEN PRINCIPLES OF ORGANIZATION STRUCTURE

Many of the classical principles of organization structure were stated before we had sound knowledge of the relationships between organization and people. We have analyzed these basic concepts, restated those principles which have been in use, and developed new principles to keep abreast of modern requirements.

Principle of the Objective

Organizational efficiency tends to increase as the work performed is directed toward the objectives desired.

The purpose of the organization is to facilitate people working together to accomplish end results. It follows that all the work performed should be directed toward accomplishment of objectives. This is best accomplished by giving primary status and placement to those functions which are directly accountable for accomplishment of end results.

---

[1] Practical application of management thinking to real problems in management organization is described in *Westinghouse Organization Planning*, Westinghouse Electric Corp., Pittsburgh, Pa., 1959.

To illustrate, we have stated that the over-all objectives of Carborundum Company are as follows:

To conduct throughout the world, under all economic and political conditions consistent with the corporate nature of the Company, a profitable, continuous, independent business in the manufacture and sale of

(1) silicon carbide, aluminum oxide, and similar and related basic materials,

(2) a complete line of abrasive products, a complete line of super refractories, metal additives, electrical heating elements and resistors, and other products containing or produced from those basic materials,

(3) similar, related, and auxiliary products, and

(4) other products consistent with the general nature of the Company, which can be undertaken successfully by the existing organization or an appropriate expansion thereof with resulting growth of profits, financial stability, essential productive facilities, quality and quantity of products, reputation, and equitable benefits to the Company's stockholders, customers and employees.

Our principle establishes that the basic line functions of the Carborundum Company are manufacturing and sales. This was true of the earlier functional organization. The company has now divisionalized, but each product division has its own manufacturing and sales functions together with the necessary industrial relations, accounting, and other staff activities.

Principle of Specialization

The more specialized the work assigned to individuals within the limits of human tolerance, the greater the potential for efficient performance.

Specialization is basic to modern organization. It has made possible broad-scale industrialization, assembly-line production, and the vast productive capacity of modern machines and facilities. Specialization has very real advantages which should be exploited as largely as possible in organization design. However, we must also recognize that specialization will be truly effective only so long as it is compatible with the needs of the human beings doing this specialized work. This principle tells us that each person should be assigned work that is logically related. For example, the accountant should not sell, nor should the personnel man handle purchasing.

The human mind is capable of mastering and remaining abreast of only a relatively limited amount of knowledge. People can master only a relatively few skills. If they specialize, people are more productive, they learn faster, and they can do more in a given period.

We must recognize, however, that specialization can be overdone. Its limits of usefulness are reached when people lose interest because the work is made so simple and repetitious that it becomes monotonous and boring. This often is the case on an assembly line. However, even simple jobs can be given variety and made more challenging, and hence more interesting, if a little thought and imagination are applied to the problem of organization structure. For example, a machine operator may lose efficiency past a certain point if he does nothing but operate his machine. His specialization can be broadened if he is also assigned the task of setting up his own machine, keeping it in repair, and making the preliminary quality control inspection of his own work. These related tasks give added variety and interest. They give him a whole job and add to his efficiency.

The question often arises: How can we determine what work is related? Since we are referring to *human* physical and mental effort when we speak of "work," the best means of deciding whether two items of work are related is to determine whether the knowledge and skills necessary to perform them are closely allied and can reasonably be possessed by the same person. For example, we would normally expect a salesman of soap to be able to sell other related lines. However, we would not expect him to know very much about psychological testing.

Management work, in itself, is a specialty. People in management positions should be required to concentrate upon management work. The person who is expected to secure results through other people *cannot be expected, logically, to be an expert in doing their work for them.*

Many companies have found that job enlargement is a valuable contribution to improved efficiency. At Detroit Edison, a large public utility company in Michigan, for example, one group of machine operators printed bills and another group of checkers checked the printed bills. The company found that the billing-machine operators could do both the printing and the checking and not only liked the job better, but put out more work as a result. In the same company, clerks were required to specialize in single jobs such as typing form letters, operating a mimeograph machine, checking results, and filing. Now, each girl is given a job that requires three or four different operations. Again, interest has been enhanced and production improved.

Principle of Management Emphasis

When called upon to supervise two or more differing functions, products, or geographic units, a manager tends to show preferential emphasis in his decisions and choices; the closer to the line of opera-

tions he is located organizationally and the greater the differences in the units he supervises, the greater his tendency toward preference.

There is a human tendency to favor that which we know best. Put an engineer who came up in the company through engineering in charge of sales, manufacturing, and engineering and we will see that his human tendency is to show preference to engineering. This may be positive or negative preference. He may show bias in favor of engineering or he may go to the other extreme and, in his attempt to be objective, neglect engineering and its requirements. The former, of course, more often is the case.

The closer the manager is to the work being done, and the more familiar he is with it, the more likely that he will favor it. If a foreman was once an electrician and is now supervising both electrical and mechanical work, he will tend to favor the electrical side unless he strongly disciplines himself. This principle also points out that since every manager is required to perform both management and operating work, he must make his choice as to which will receive emphasis. If he does not school himself, the operating work almost certainly will get major attention.

To illustrate, a Middle Western aeronautics company was founded in the 1920s by the proprietor of a radio repair shop who invented several devices for use in the budding aircraft industry of the day. Highly creative, the verstile president also had an exceptional ability to sell the products generated by his imagination. While the company was small it was successful because the owner was able to do a large part of the sales work and to make most of the decisions in the organization. When company sales reached the $100 million mark, however, it became clear that the company could not manage itself effectively if the whole focus at the top was on selling and operations. The president brought in several general managers, but he went around his executive in each case to deal directly with his sales, manufacturing, and engineering heads on the operating problems that were nearest his heart. Finally, competitive pressure forced the president out of active control, but not before the company had lost valuable ground.

Principle of Maximum Span

The more people each manager can effectively manage, the smaller the total number required to attain given end results.

A vital question in organizing has always been: How many people should a manager supervise? Answers have ranged all the way from an arbitrary formula to the assumption that if a manager is given more people than he can possibly handle, he will be so busy managing that he will not have time to operate.

In practice, neither extreme is desirable. In our studies we have found that high efficiency results most often when each manager has a little more work to perform than he can accomplish comfortably. This means that every manager should be given the maximum number of people he can *manage* effectively. The key word here is *manage*. The number of people for whom the manager can plan, organize, lead, and control effectively becomes the criterion for his span of control. There is no formula which will enable us to determine what this span should be for any one manager. However, we have found that five factors are most important.

1. *Diversity*. The more dissimilar the work being supervised, the more effort and attention a manager must devote to planning, organizing, leading, and controlling. To illustrate: Assume that a district manager can supervise twelve salesmen. The work of all the salesmen is very similar. The manager does not have to handle twelve different kinds of problems but the same set of problems repeated twelve times. On the other hand, if the same sales manager were called upon to supervise credit, sales promotion, advertising, and sales training as well as direct selling, he would have different kinds of problems to handle and the span of supervision would be correspondingly lessened.

2. *Dispersion*. This is synonymous with geographical separation of the units being supervised. The more widely separated the activities being supervised, the more difficult it is to plan, organize, lead, and control them. Line loss is one factor which limits the supervisory span in this instance. There is also the fact that management emphasis tends to be shown in terms of geography as well as product and function.

3. *Complexity*. The complexity of the work being performed will determine the frequency with which new kinds of problems arise, and the difficulty of handling them. It is more difficult to plan, organize, lead, and control complex work because of the breadth of knowledge and information required to do an effective job.

4. *Volume*. The least significant of the factors affecting the span of supervision is volume. One individual, for example, could supervise a very large number of ditchdiggers or coalshovelers if they were in the same immediate area. However, he would have much more difficulty supervising electricians, steamfitters, and plumbers located in three different towns.

5. *The Ability to Delegate*. This has much to do with the span of supervision. If the manager confines himself largely to managing, that is, planning, organizing, leading, and controlling, he can supervise

far more people than if he insists on doing much of their work for them.

Selecting the proper balance in the number of people supervised requires careful analysis and good judgment. Each manager should endeavor to maintain a reasonable span of supervision. He should avoid the one extreme where he does not have enough work to do and hence takes over the responsibility and authority of subordinates, or the other extreme where he is too busy and becomes a bottleneck for decisions—the indispensable man upon whom every move of the organization depends.

In some cases, companies have gone to great trouble and expense to find out the number of people being supervised in various functional positions by managers in other companies. For example, if the production engineer supervises four subordinates, and this is the average for sixty companies, presumably this is a significant number. In fact, we find this may reflect more than anything else the prevalent inefficiency of managers. It is almost a certainty today that any large sample of companies will show an average span of control that is far below the optimum. Supervisory span can best be determined by requiring each manager to maintain a continuing study of his own organization. If he will do his organizing work properly, he can determine the requirements of his own group.

Principle of Minimum Levels

The fewer the levels within the limits of maximum span, the greater the potential effectiveness of the people involved.

If we have an organizational problem which relates to improving the effectiveness and productivity of people, this principle tells us that we can take two steps that will enhance the probability of greater efficiency: (1) increase the span of supervision; (2) reduce the number of organizational levels to a minimum.

The Principle of Line Loss (page 277) establishes that the more organizational levels we have, the more rapidly communications tend to be diffused, distorted, and weakened. The organization with seven or eight levels will tend to be less efficient than one with three or four levels when people of similar competence are doing the same kind of work.

Since each added level tends to multiply the problems of communication and coordination, it follows that if we want to prolong the usefulness of our current form of organization we can do so by keeping the number of organizational levels to a minimum.

There is a direct relationship between the span of supervision and

the number of levels. The wider the span, the fewer the organizational levels required to accommodate a given number of people. It
follows that one of the best ways to broaden the span is to reduce the
number of levels. In effect, this means giving more operating work to
operating people and requiring managers to do more managing.

Principle of Carry-over

*The early characteristics of organization tend to persist in later
organizational forms.*

As an organizational unit grows, it tends to create positions which
are necessary for current operation. However, as time goes on the
need may pass or the organizational form itself may be changed.
Nevertheless, the unnecessary organizational positions tend to be carried
over intact.

This is very true when a company outgrows its functional form of
organization and then divisionalizes. For example, it is characteristic
of the overly large functional organization that many assistant positions
are created and additional committees are appointed in an effort to
enable top managers to carry the rapidly increasing burden of decision
making. After divisionalization is accomplished, the need for these
organizational agencies is usually minimized or disappears. However,
the assistants and committees tend to persist. Work is found for them
but often this work is unnecessary or a duplication of work being
done elsewhere.

We find that the Principle of Carry-over is important to many other
aspects of organization. For instance, if work improvement studies
are made, new and more efficient methods may be established on paper
but we find that inevitably people tend to go back to their old inefficient ways. Continuing control and discipline are the best remedy.

The general sales manager of a large Middle Western food company provides a good example. Moved from his line position where
he had charge of all the field sales operations of the company, he was
promoted to become vice president in charge of staff marketing at the
corporate level. Although his authority now was entirely advisory
and service in nature, the general sales manager carried over to his
new position a great deal of the authority which theoretically he should
have left behind. When in the field, he continued to give direct orders
to the field sales force. He called frequently upon key customers whom
he had once serviced himself, and was not above countermanding
instructions given by the general sales manager who replaced him.
This, of course, led to chaos. It was corrected only after the new
vice president had been educated in his new relationships and the

company president had maintained firm discipline on his activities for a period of over a year.

General Motors' entry into the diesel engine field provides an interesting illustration of this principle. In the 1920s, C. F. Kettering, chief of GM Research, pursuing the improvement of the internal-combustion engine, turned his attention to the diesel engine. Theoretically the diesel, with its high-compression efficiency, should have been more widely used. But at that time diesels were heavy, with slow speed, and relatively costly. Kettering felt that the diesel engine designers had more or less built them along the lines of steam power plants rather than internal-combustion engines. So he and the GM engineers decided to start from scratch and design an engine that would reduce the size and weight and increase the power and efficiency.

After years of intensive research and development, they came up with a much improved, lighter, high-speed, diesel power plant, two of which supplied the power and light for the General Motors exhibit at the Century of Progress in Chicago in 1933. These caught the attention of Ralph Budd of the Burlington railroad who was looking for such an engine for the Burlington's new train, the pioneer Zephyr streamliner. In 1934 the new train was completed and equipped with one of these new engines. The subsequent performance of the Zephyr in a dawn-to-dusk run from Denver to Chicago at an average speed of 77.6 miles per hour created a stir in railroad circles and heralded the beginning of a new era.

But the large manufacturers of steam locomotives, in spite of the performance of the new diesel, felt that the steam power plant, which had dominated railroading for over a century, was still the best bet.

The principle of carry-over was operative. At that time all of the major companies insisted on building steam locomotives. The companies were large. They had adequate facilities to design and build any type of locomotive that the railroads required, and they had the facilities and finances to carry out any program they wished. All remained wedded to the past.

IDENTIFYING THE WORK TO BE PERFORMED

In designing a sound organization structure, we are concerned with both *identifying* and *grouping* the work to be performed. Looking at the organization as a whole, our first question is: What are the important tasks that must be done? Our answer, of course, stems from the Principle of the Objective (page 176). The scientific manager knows that his best approach is *to determine first what he wants to accomplish, then to do only the work necessary to achieve that which he has already determined is necessary.*

Logically, of course, this cannot be faulted; emotionally, however, we can anticipate that it will meet every resistance because, as we have seen, people are prone *to do the work they like to do,* not that which, intellectually, *they know they should do.* To support this emotional preference, we can expect to find every conceivable rationalization advanced and supported with vehemence.

GROUPING THE WORK

When we *group* work effectively, we see to it that each task is assigned so that it is carried out by the person *who is organizationally placed to do it most effectively.* If we are making our first attempt to accomplish this, we will find, almost inevitably, that logic will come against emotional resistance. Through long and persistent effort, people in the organization will have mastered illogical combinations of work; because they can now carry them out with some facility, they are quite surprised to discover that these procedures are inefficient and difficult, if not impossible, for a newcomer to master in the ordinary course of job indoctrination.

In one large New York food company, for example, the controller had two of the operating divisions reporting to him, together with the accountant, treasurer, internal auditor, the personnel department, and the department responsible for the company airplane. A CPA, a former war pilot and squadron commander, the controller offered a unique combination of talents that could not be duplicated. When he left to become chief executive of a larger company, the president insisted that his successor take over the same combination of duties. Three years of chaos resulted until the controller function was finally divided into logical segments that could be handled by managers with normal background and training.

THE TWO TYPES OF ORGANIZATION STRUCTURE

A key question in identifying and grouping is: What kinds of grouping patterns are there? If we can identify the basic patterns of grouping and classify these as structural types, we will have the best possible basis for determining our own needs in organization structure.

Many varieties of organization structure have been proposed—staff, line, line and staff, centralized, decentralized, committee—to name but a few. In our research, however, we have found that, at the corporate level, there are only two basic patterns in which grouping takes place.

These lead us to conclude that there are only two basic types of company organization structure.[2]

Our later research leads us to conclude that every company, without exception, begins its existence with a functional type of structure and as it expands, diversifies, and spreads geographically, it eventually outgrows it. The company must now divisionalize or suffer the dangers of organizational strangulation. We conclude that every business enterprise that grows and expands successfully should expect to develop in successive stages from a functional to a divisionalized type of organization.[3]

FUNCTIONAL ORGANIZATION STRUCTURE

The functional organization structure is the building block of organization from which all other forms of organization are built. It is formed by grouping all the work to be done into major functional departments. As a result, all related work of one kind ultimately is managed by one top coordinating head. For example, in a functional organization, one manufacturing department, under a manufacturing executive, is responsible for all manufacturing done in all plants and for all product lines. The same is true for marketing, engineering, and other functions.

The small functional organization, or one which is called upon to handle only a limited product line and which has a restricted geographical dispersion, has many advantages. One is that it facilitates specialization. By throwing its resources into one specialized type of work or by emphasizing the engineering, manufacturing, and sales of one specialized product, even the smallest company can compete with the big corporation on quality, delivery, and price.

Paul Dean Arnold, for example, had an idea that he could make bread more tasty and appetizing. In 1940 he started a small bakery in Stamford, Connecticut, and produced a home-baked white bread. Operating within a functional organization, Arnold Bakers, Inc., has been able to specialize and to compete successfully with the conventional loaf even though its bread commands a premium price.

The functional organization is more economical, because it requires only one group of manufacturing facilities, one sales function, and one

[2] For the initial identification of these two types, see the author's *Management and Organization,* McGraw-Hill Book Company, New York, 1958, pp. 77 *et. seq.*

[3] These data have been confirmed in person with executives from 385 companies. All of these experienced managers have agreed that, to their knowledge, there is not a single business enterprise that has developed contrary to this basic rule. We therefore assume that it is valid.

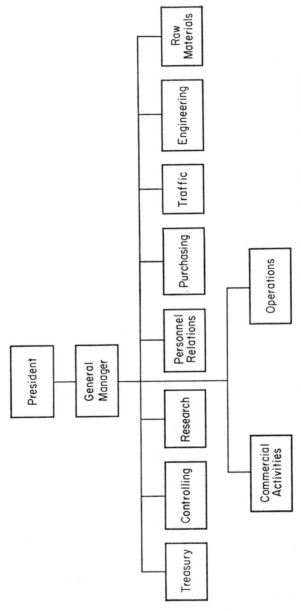

Fig. 17-1. The initial functional organization structure in Armco Steel Corporation in 1923.

set of managers; hence both capital and administrative expenses are held to a minimum.

For example, Armco Steel Corporation grew during its early years with this basic type of functional organization. The pattern in 1923 is shown in Figure 17-1.

Here we can see that all selling is done in the commercial department; manufacturing is grouped in the operations department; and all engineering is the responsibility of the engineering function. When this type of functional organization prevails, any new sales activity inevitably must be placed with the existing sales function, and manufacturing and engineering have only one logical home.

Is Functional Organization Desirable?

There is little point in debating the merits or demerits of the functional organization, any more than it would be profitable to discuss the question of whether childhood is good or bad. The fact is that the new, young endeavor invariably organizes functionally and the functional unit remains the building block from which the other types of structure are constructed.

In our studies, we have found that every large company, logically enough, began as a small, young enterprise with a functional organization. From Ford Motor Company to Toshiba, from Cincinnati Milling Machine to Montecatini to Henschel-Werke G. m. b. H. Kassel, the same pattern prevails. Utilized logically, the functional organization provides the soundest base for future strength and diversity. When it is retained through emotion or ignorance past its point of usefulness, however, the same structure becomes an increasing handicap.

The important requirement is that the company determine how best to utilize this kind of organization and that it be alert to the symptoms that point to the need for change.

WHEN TO CHANGE?

Size is not the only, nor always the best, indication of the need to divisionalize. Continuing analysis should be made of the influence of such factors as diversification, dispersion, production characteristics, and the marketing pattern as well as size in itself.

Diversification

The greater the variety of products and markets, the more complex and demanding the burden of decision making and coordination placed upon functional management, the earlier divisionalization should be undertaken.

General Foods, for example, was founded in 1925 when the Postum Company acquired Jell-O. Until 1929, the company grew by expansion of its basic product lines. However, by 1930 it had acquired two new kinds of business in Birdseye and Atlantic Gelatin, and still a third in Diamond Crystal Salt. To succeed in their own competitive markets, these new products needed sound, expeditious decision making by executives who were thoroughly familiar with their unique problems. Divisionalization provided the answer to this.

Experience demonstrates that the firm which is planning to diversify or which has already diversified must give early consideration to divisionalization and decentralization. Aeroquip Corporation, manufacturer of flexible hose lines, couplings, straps, clamps, and fittings, divisionalized in 1955, when it had a sales volume of $25 million, $14 million in assets, and 1,400 employees.

Geographical Dispersion

The more widely separated the plants and sales offices of the company, the more difficult it is to manage them effectively from one central point through a functional organization. Pushing authority closer to the plants and sales offices in the field where the operation is performed will help. However, this is only a temporizing measure, for there still remains the need to manage the differing functions, and with a functional organization this can only be accomplished at the top level of the organization which invariably must be at the corporate headquarters.

Not only does physical distance become a handicap, there is also the need to understand and cater to distinctly different geographical requirements. With all good intentions in the world, eventually this becomes more than single individuals can accomplish.

Standard Oil Company of California provides an excellent illustration of sound management thinking in divisionalization. Beginning as an integrated oil company, the company operated primarily in the western portion of the North American continent. As it grew, however, Standard of California spread to other parts of Canada and the United States, to the Middle East and other parts of the world. It diversified into petrochemicals and industrial and agricultural chemicals. Divisionalization on a geographic basis provided the framework for continued expansion and growth.

Production Processes

If divisionalization proceeds to completion, both sales and manufacturing will need to be divisionalized together with other primary functions. To facilitate this, it should be possible to separate the production facilities so that each product or group of related products can have its own manufacturing plants for which costs can be clearly identi-fied. In some cases it is practicable to use shared facilities; where this is so, one division will act as the landlord and sell to others at competitive prices, or the costs can be allocated equitably on some other basis.

In the Rheem Manufacturing Company, for instance, when different divisions manufacture their products in the same plant, the division whose product has the largest dollar volume at the particular plant is responsible for the common services and capital of that plant. This is the "landlord" division. It installs a resident plant manager who sells to the other divisions using the required services, facilities, and capital equipment.

Production of heavily engineered, complex products requiring high capital investment and a concentration of top engineering and produc-tion skills will usually indicate product divisionalization. A simple product, such as soft drinks; one requiring commonly available, bulky, or heavy raw materials, such as sand and gravel and cement; or a product depending upon freshness, such as dairy products and baked goods, will spell geographic divisionalization.

Marketing Requirements

If separate divisions are to be organized, an early requirement is the ability to sell the products of the company to different customers in different markets; otherwise, the possibility of holding the divisions to profit accountability will be remote. Preferably, the functional sales group will be divided into divisionalized units, each with its own separate markets. If this cannot be accomplished, the divisionalized sales units should at least be able to compete in similar markets by means of brand name differentiation.

Size

As the functional organization continues to grow, it can increase only by adding layers to the pyramid that goes to make up each function. As new production lines and plants are added, as the sales force takes on more products and spreads into new areas, the span of control of each functional manager tends to become wider and the number of levels increases. As a result, decision making and communications slow down. Action becomes cumbersome and inflexible.

Johnson & Johnson, for example, operated profitably under a func-tional organization for forty-three years and until it had attained a sales volume of some $20 million annually. One day, however, Robert W. Johnson, president, called a meeting to discuss a problem involving one of the company's products. When he found that seven-teen men had to be present to consider all the ramifications of the problem, he recognized that the company had grown too large for its original functional, centralized organization.

Carrier Corporation operated effectively under a functional organization for some forty-two years. However, by the time it had reached an annual volume of $164 million in 1953, with assets of $20 million and 8,000 employes, it found that the volume and variety of problems funneling upon the managers of the functional organization severely taxed their strength and capacity.

Manning, Maxwell & Moore, Inc., manufacturers of gauges, valves, industrial instruments, aircraft engine controls, cranes, and hoists, made the change in 1955, with a sales volume of $34 million, $29 million in assets, and 3,100 employes.

Compare to this the size attained under a functional organization by companies with little diversification. Boeing Airplane Company maintained a functional organization to $853 million in sales, $256 million in assets, and 65,000 employes. In the automobile industry, General Motors divisionalized before 1920, at about the $500 million sales level. Ford Motor Company made the change-over in 1947 when its sales were less than $1 billion.

DIVISIONALIZED ORGANIZATION STRUCTURE

The divisionalized organization structure is the second major kind of organization. This divides the functional organization into relatively small, self-contained administrative units. With proper decentralization, each such division is capable of competing independently with its own line of products in its own markets, both against outside enterprises and even other divisions inside the company. In essence, divisionalization is an organizational means of retaining the advantages of the small, functional type of organization, while minimizing the disadvantages that come with increasing size, diversity, and dispersion.

Divisionalization establishes a series of small, self-sufficient functional units which can tap the combined resources of the corporation through its central headquarters and staff and yet can compete on an equal footing with the flexible, dynamic smaller organization. This form of organization facilitates growth and diversification because products can be added, or new territory added without distorting the basic structure.

Divisionalization at the corporate level is accomplished most frequently either in terms of product or of geography.

Product Divisionalization

Here each major product exists with the functional groupings it needs to operate as an integrated small business. Product divisionalization

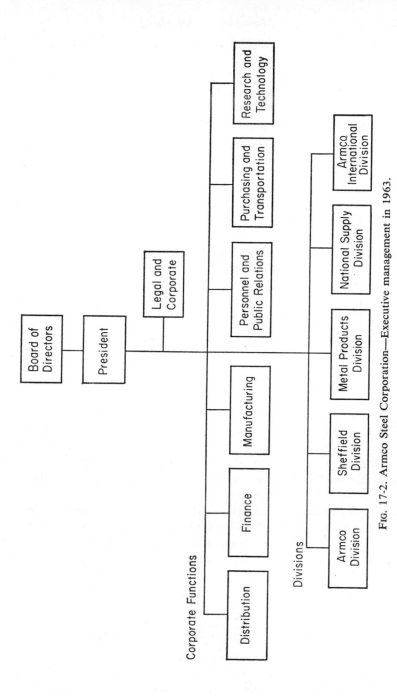

FIG. 17-2. Armco Steel Corporation—Executive management in 1963.

191

focuses on the product itself the total resources of one complete administrative unit. Manufacturing, sales, engineering, finance, and personnel are dedicated to the interests of one or a few related products. This brings great emphasis on product development, market exploitation, engineering improvement, and personnel development in terms of the needs of each individual product.

The divisionalization of Armco Steel Corporation provides an excellent case in point. Expansion of its basic business and diversification into related products stretched the capacity of Armco's basic functional organization, and in a series of well-planned moves it changed to a divisionalized structure with minimum disruption of operations or personnel. Figure 17-2 shows the product divisionalization in effect in 1963.

It should be noted that within an organization that is divisionalized at the corporate level there may be further divisionalized groupings at lower levels of the organization. Eventually, we will find functional units which are grouped in terms of specialized work to be performed.

Geographic Divisionalization

Frequently the special requirements of local markets are a primary factor when the company divisionalizes. Where this is the case, geographic divisionalization makes possible fastest service, undivided attention, and recognition of local needs and traditions.

The purpose of geographic divisionalization is to provide a self-sufficient business entity within the regional area being served, so that most of the decisions necessary to effective management and operation can be made very close to where the action takes place. Geographic divisionalization is most often the structure of choice when the company grows large enough in its international operations to warrant separate organizational entities. The functional sales manager in New York, for example, finds it difficult to keep up with such local requirements as a preference for horizontal rather than vertical packages in Italy, the aversion of English customers for the "hard sell" advertising common in the United States, the dislike of many European customer groups for special deals and large economy-size packages, and the fact that in France and elsewhere the housewife prefers to shop herself and *wants* to spend several hours daily preparing meals.

Geographic divisionalization is also indicated when the company has only one product, or a limited group of closely related products. In the case of Hilton Hotels, for instance, geographic divisionalization is an obvious choice. As another example, the F. W. Woolworth Co. has the problem of organizing some 2,500 stores so that they can compete effectively with myriads of local stores, national chains, and the parallel

lines of drugstores, department stores, and a dozen other types of out-
lets.

F. W. Woolworth has met the organizational challenge by divisional-
izing geographically into eleven districts in the United States and
Canada.   The number of stores in the various districts ranges from
158 to 259.   Each district makes a great many of its own operating
decisions, even to the buying of its merchandise.   By providing this
effective organizational base, the company is enabled to maintain the
advantages of a large, integrated organization yet it can operate with
sufficient speed and flexibility in local markets to compete successfully
with small, local establishments.

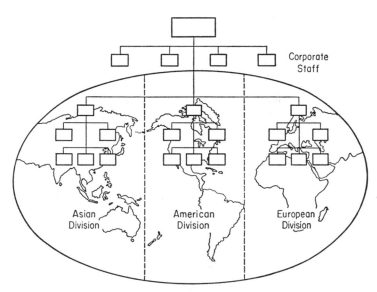

FIG. 17-3. Geographic divisionalization.

The pattern of geographic divisionalization in an international enterprise is shown in Figure 17-3.   Here the process is carried to completion, with line and staff components in each geographical division.
Most often companies divisionalized on a geographic basis have not
proceeded far enough to have arrived at this organizational end point.

THE IMPACT OF DIVISIONALIZATION
IN RADIO CORPORATION OF AMERICA

The Radio Corporation of America clearly illustrates the factors
which lead to divisionalization and decentralization of the organization.
By 1944, in RCA, television was becoming a major market factor.

Other new products were near the distribution phase. The company forecasts emphasized a major growth surge. The question now was: How best ensure that the organization would move ahead of the need? What moves could the company make so that new jobs could be created, people could be transferred and promoted, new product lines developed, new markets penetrated without throwing the existing organization into a shambles? Clearly, the answer was to develop an organization that would move ahead of the forecast need.

This organization should be able to accommodate the uncertainties of growth under forced pressure. Because competition loomed large in every phase of RCA's business, this new organization should clear a field of action for each product group. RCA knew its radios and television sets would be competing against excellent products from many other companies specializing in radio and television. Would a sales department concerned not only with radio and television but also with electronic products, records, tubes, and a host of other products be able to compete successfully against the tightly integrated specialists? The Principle of Management Emphasis, which we have stated on page 178, points clearly to a negative answer. On the basis of logical analysis, RCA arrived at its own conclusion. Organization change was indicated.

RCA's Functional Organization

As RCA surveyed its organization at the time, it could see clearly the pattern the change would take. The functional type of organization which had been the vehicle for RCA's growth up to that time was built around the kinds of work that were of primary importance to the company's success. Looking at the RCA Victor Division (Figure 17-4), for example, we find manufacturing and sales identified by the company as its primary components.

Analysis of this organization, which had served with great effectiveness to this point, indicated several potential areas of weakness, chief among which were coordination difficulties, accountability problems, and personnel problems.

Coordination Difficulties. The Manufacturing Department, in its seven plants, manufactured special electronic products, home instruments, tubes, and records. Most decisions involving any two or more of the interests involved were forced to the top. As a result, the general manager was concerned with problems involving the manufacture of high cost, custom-made electronic products. Here, he competed with General Electric and Sperry. He manufactured mass-produced home instruments in competition with Magnavox, Zenith, Webster, and many others. He had to deal with the artistic problems of

singers and musicians, and how to find a hit song in competition with
Capitol Records.   As if this was not enough, he was also concerned
with the technology of low-cost, high-volume production of tubes in
competition with Sylvania, Westinghouse, and Texas Instruments.

On the marketing side, the general sales manager was selling products to government and industry, and to consumer groups ranging from
the musical aesthete to the housewife trying to decide if the most important characteristic of a new radio was its tone or its suitability as
a piece of furniture.

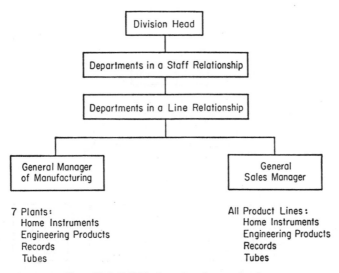

FIG. 17-4. RCA's functional organization.

Coordination of these varying interests *within* the manufacturing and
sales departments was complex and difficult.   Extending this coordination to the problems of adjusting production to demand, of purchasing
materials and components infinite in number and variety, of proper
allocation of capital resources for growth, and the thousand and one
questions that burgeoned on every hand, promised unending difficulty
unless they could be reduced to manageable size.

Accountability Problems.   The functional organization permitted
clear-cut accountability for the total manufacture, sale, and engineering
of a product only at the very top.   It was difficult if not impossible
to separate out the true cost of a jazz record from a radio tube.   If
the newly developing television product line failed to reach its forecast
potential, direct accountability would have to be shared by a dozen or
more managers.

Personal Problems. A tremendous burden was thrust upon individuals by this rapidly increasing business. The organization acted as a funnel, concentrating upon a few people the need for making most decisions of any consequence, of trying to resolve the frustrations and strained relationships which the organization itself generated, and of providing leadership in endlessly varied and complicated problems of finance, personnel, purchasing, and engineering. No matter how capable the individuals, human capacity has its limitations.

Divisionalization

In 1945, RCA took the first major step to organize for the surge of growth that was already becoming evident. The products which were

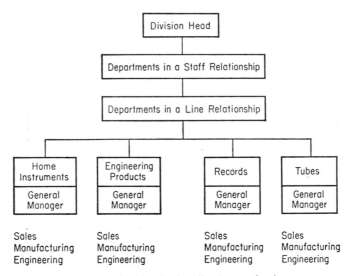

FIG. 17-5. RCA's divisionalized organization.

being manufactured and sold grouped most naturally into four distinct business entities: home instruments, engineering products, records, and tubes. These became the nucleus for four product divisions. Each division was organized so that it could compete successfully in its own markets, with its own products, against other companies which were specialists in these products. This meant that the manager in charge of each business unit had to be provided with the functions he needed to engineer, produce, and market his product profitably as well as the staff functions necessary to successful administration. This was the basic pattern from which the current RCA divisionalized organization has developed with great success, as shown in Figure 17-5.

SUMMARY

In developing an organization structure, a manager determines what work must be done and in what position it can best be performed. In doing this, the work is arranged to accomplish established objectives in the best way and to provide for specialization within the limits of human tolerance. In a sound organization structure, each manager supervises the maximum number of people with a minimum number of organization levels. In grouping the work, the key question is what type of structure should be provided. Every business organization begins as a functional structure; with increased diversification, dispersion, and size, it must eventually change to a divisionalized type of structure. The divisionalization is generally in terms of product or geography.

> *I know of no safe depository of the ultimate powers of society but the people themselves, and if we think them not enlightened enough to exercise their control with a wholesome discretion, the remedy is not to take it from them, but to inform their discretion by education.* THOMAS JEFFERSON

DEFINITIONS

Management Delegation: the work a manager performs to entrust responsibility and authority to others and to create accountability for results.

Responsibility: the work assigned to a position.

Authority: the sum of the powers and rights assigned to a position.

Accountability: the obligation to perform responsibility and exercise authority in terms of established performance standards.

Centralization: the systematic and consistent reservation of authority at top levels of the organization.

Decentralization: the systematic and consistent delegation of authority to the levels where the work is performed.

Divisionalization: the process of breaking large functional organization units into divisions grouped in terms of product, geography, or some other basis.

Dispersion: the physical separation of people, equipment, and facilities.

Consolidation: the bringing together at one physical location of people, equipment, and facilities.

THE LOGIC OF DELEGATION

In our management research we have found that there is almost universal semantic confusion about delegation. In particular, the terms "responsibility," "authority," and "accountability" have had conflicting and sometimes contradictory meanings injected into them.

We have felt it important not to theorize what managers *should* do when they delegate but rather to study and identify what actually happens, and then to define precisely the terms to be used. In this we have found it necessary to do some slight mayhem to ordinary usage, for precedent here has left us with a veritable semantic grab bag of meaning. Let us examine responsibility, authority, and accountability.

Responsibility

By definition, a manager is given or has more *work* to perform than he can do by himself. By this we mean that in his position he is required to put forth more physical and mental effort than lies within his personal capacity. Therefore he must get others to do some of this work for him. Assume that we have a sales manager who is given the work of selling automated presses throughout Europe. The work assigned to him—that of selling the presses—is his responsibility.

Since the sales manager cannot do all this selling work himself, he hires six salesmen to do a share of it for him. He assigns some of *his* responsibility to each of the salesmen; that is, each of the salesmen does some of the selling work that the sales manager otherwise would have had to do himself. The work assigned to each salesman is his responsibility. The sales manager now has a great deal of managing work to do to satisfy the requirements of his position; he still has a certain amount of selling work he is required to do personally. The work of the sales manager is his responsibility.

We need a semantic label or word that will *stand for* or *mean* "the work assigned to a position." Although this is somewhat at variance with nonmanagement usage, we have found in our studies that the term which is most meaningful to managers here is *responsibility*. Therefore we have defined *responsibility as the work assigned to a position.*

Authority

Now let us continue with our analysis and determine what actually takes place in an organization when authority is exercised. To return to our salesmen, if they are to sell automated presses, each must be prepared to do the necessary work of calling on customers, persuading them to buy, arranging for delivery, and so forth.   In doing this work, each salesman will have to make many decisions with respect to such things as which customers to call upon, promises of delivery, prices, and credit.   If the salesmen must contact the sales manager and ask him to make each decision, the sales manager will spend most of his time making routine decisions and the salesmen will use valuable time waiting for decisions when they could more profitably devote it to selling.

The logical answer here is to let the salesmen make as many decisions as possible with respect to the work they do.   Also logically, the sales manager should try to restrict himself to those decisions which, organizationally, he must make because of his unique organizational position and his multiple role.   If he will do this, he will be free to concentrate on the management work he should be doing, and the salesmen not only can do more work but will get more satisfaction from it because they can use their imagination and resourcefulness in making their own decisions.   *The sum of the powers and rights we assign* to the salesmen we call their *authority*.

Accountability

If he is to manage effectively, the sales manager must have some means of control.   He does not want to be traveling all the time in France, Germany, England, Italy, Finland, and Holland, the regions he supervises, constantly inspecting the work done and the results of the decisions made by his six salesmen.

Using the techniques of professional management, he requires each of his salesmen to assume an obligation to do his work and make his decisions in terms of certain specified limits which he, the sales manager, lays down for them after considering their suggestions.

Then the sales manager requires reports which tell him how well each salesman has performed and what results he has secured in doing his work and making his decisions.   *Creation of this obligation to do the work and make decisions in terms of established performance standards* we identify as *accountability*.   Accountability, as we shall develop later, is a necessary basis for scientific methods of management control.

Can Responsibility, Authority, and Accountability Be Delegated?

Responsibility and authority *must* be delegated if we look at the process from a rational viewpoint.   An individual's accountability, that is, *his* obligation, cannot be delegated safely.   Even though a manager delegates parts of his responsibility and authority to others, that manager still remains accountable in full to his own superior; that is, he still has the obligation to see to it that all the work done and all the decisions made, to whomever delegated, are performed effectively.

We can show the process of delegation schematically in Figure 18-1.

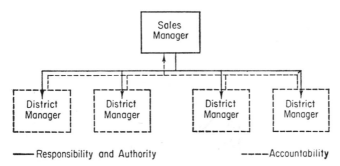

FIG. 18-1. The flow of responsibility and authority and the limits set by accountability.

The flow of responsibility and authority is largely downward; the limits set by accountability always originate from the next higher position.

THE ALLEN PRINCIPLES OF DELEGATION

Skill in delegation requires the observance of several key principles. In our research we have developed and stated one new principle, that of control limits, and have revised and brought up to date to reflect modern business thinking the principles relating to commensurate authority, total accountability, and unity of command.

Principle of Control Limits

Delegation tends to be limited by the availability of effective controls.

Managers frequently attempt to delegate but find it difficult to let people do the work involved and to make the decisions in their own terms. For some reason, it seems imperative that the manager check constantly, and when he does so, his natural tendency is to insist that the work be done and the decisions made the *way he would do it and make them himself.* This, of course, inevitably endangers what he is trying to accomplish. We have discovered that the primary reason for this tends to be lack of controls.

We can entrust responsibility and authority to others only to the extent that we can check up on how well the work is done and on the soundness of the decisions. If we have a sound control system that enables us to control by exception, we can delegate much further and more completely than if we have to observe personally everything that is done to make sure that it is carried out properly. We should look to our controls before delegation takes place. Accountability should be established in terms of acceptable performance standards. An accurate reporting system should be provided and evaluation should be pointed toward identification of variances and prompt corrective action by the accountable manager himself.

Principle of Commensurate Authority

The less the authority, the more difficult the performance of responsibility.

In our earlier research, we established both the practical and theoretical lack of validity in the conventional assumption that "authority should equal responsibility."[1] Further study has clarified the reasons why authority should be commensurate with responsibility; that is, a person should be given the power to make as many decisions as possible with respect to the work he is given to do. We know, of course, he cannot be permitted with safety to make *all* the decisions or we lose control.

This new statement of the principle identifies a basic reason why many organizations require two or three people to do work that, logically, could be done by one. Assume that a foreman, for example, wants to spend $10 for specially threaded bolts and his request for purchase authorization has to go through five levels of organization until it receives final approval from both the corporate staff purchasing manager and the manufacturing manager. Each manager at levels above the foreman *has to know almost as much as the foreman about the need for the special bolts* before he can justify and approve the request. By the time four or five people have handled the authorization, time has been lost, copies have been accumulated in files, and information has been duplicated and repeated endlessly. Add to this instances of company presidents approving clerical salary increases, executive vice presidents endorsing automobile usage, and plant managers authorizing visits from the plant, and the waste frequently becomes rather staggering.

A manager should be delegated not only responsibility, that is, work to be performed, he should also be delegated the powers and rights or authority he needs to make the decisions necessary to carry out that work. For example, we can give a salesman the work of selling to customers, but if we want to get the best performance, we must also give him the right to decide how much time he needs to spend with

[1] Louis A. Allen, "The Art of Delegation," *The Management Record*, March, 1955.

a customer to get the job done, the power to commit the company to delivery promises, and the right to spend company money for such things as travel and selling expenses. To the extent that we refuse to delegate such authority to him, we lessen his ability to perform effectively.

People generally are given sufficient work to do. The prime deficiency is usually a lack of authority to make decisions necessary to carry out the work. If a subordinate has to check with his boss each time he makes a decision, this will unduly impose upon the time of his superior. It will also leach the stimulation and challenge from the job and reduce it to a monotonous task.

Principle of Single Reporting Relationships

The more people to whom a manager reports, the less accountable he tends to become.

One of the most common sources of organizational difficulty is double reporting relationships. The man who reports to two different bosses for the same responsibility and authority is never quite sure of what he is supposed to do, what priority he should give his work, or where he stands. He finds it difficult to delegate because he has no clear-cut charter. Furthermore, as the demands of his different superiors vary, he may find it desirable to play one off against the other. The best solution is to ensure that each person has only one superior to whom he reports and who gives orders to him for any given responsibility.

Principle of Complete Accountability

The more complete the accountability of individuals, the more effective the focus of control.

Our entire process of management control requires that we be able to hold individuals to account for the performance of specific work. This means that each manager must accept accountability for all the work done in his organizational unit. If an error is committed two or three levels below his position, he is still accountable to his own superior. The manager can encourage his team as a whole to decide how they want to do their own work; he can permit them to develop their own methods and set their own pace; he can let them decide how to share the group rewards. However, in the final analysis these are his decisions, even though made for him by his team, and he must stand or fall by the results.

This new statement establishes that if we want to accomplish more effective control, we should first examine how well we have identified and established the accountability of single individuals for the performance of the work that has to be done and the making of the necessary decisions. The more sharply we can identify this accountability, the better we can focus our control effort.

This modernization of the principle of accountability is particularly important with the growing use of automation. In the future we will find that much more work will be performed with fewer people, with greater potential loss from each error. Control now becomes increasingly significant, and we find that this control can be exercised best if we have organizational focal points at which we can hold single individuals accountable for the work that is done and the results accomplished.

Today, when potential reject loss from an improper machine adjustment may be $1,000 per day, we can perhaps tolerate squabbling among the production foreman, the industrial engineer, the manufacturing engineer, and the quality inspector as we try to find who is accountable for the mistake. In the future, when automated production lines will build up that $1,000 loss in minutes, we will not be able to enjoy the luxury of diffused accountability.

BARRIERS TO DELEGATION

Managers often fail to delegate because of psychological and organizational barriers. Psychological hurdles arise primarily because the manager is afraid to delegate. He may be afraid that those to whom he delegates will not do the job properly, and as a result, that he may lose face. This fear is justified if the people on his team are untrained or poorly motivated. When this is the case, the manager should take positive action to overcome these deficiencies.

The manager may be reluctant to delegate because he expects his people to do their work and make decisions precisely as he would if he had the time and energy to do everything himself. When it exists, this attitude is most frequently rationalized. The professional manager knows that, given the proper encouragement and training, people can develop many different ways of doing the same job effectively.

A manager may balk at delegation because he fears that his subordinates may do their work too well, and hence outshine him. However, this attitude overlooks the fact that the most valuable skill a manager can possess is the ability to develop people who, in some respects, are more capable than he is. Good developers of men are among the rarest and most valuable assets in any organization.

Organizational barriers may block delegation. The first of these is the failure to define responsibility and authority. If a manager does not know what work he is to perform, if he does not understand what authority he has to make decisions, it is unlikely that he will be able to delegate parts of this responsibility and authority. Corrective action here involves clear and precise definition of the limits of responsibility and authority. Within these limits a manager can have wide freedom in delegating to others.

WHAT WORK SHOULD A MANAGER PERFORM?

In delegation a key question is: What work should a manager perform himself; what should he entrust to others? Finding the right answer determines whether the manager will use his efforts to provide imaginative leadership and guidance, or be bogged down in detail that his subordinates should be performing for him. There are two points of importance here.

To begin with, a manager should concern himself as much as possible with management work, that is, the work of leading, planning, organizing, and controlling. Next, he should perform this work as it applies to his own position, as it involves the interests of two or more of the subordinate units reporting to him when they cannot coordinate these interests themselves, and when it involves his and other units.

A manager can delegate part of the work of leading, planning, organizing, and controlling necessary to perform his management function if he has the proper people and makes the proper determination of what he must do himself. If we analyze each of the functions of management, we can readily identify the management work a manager cannot safely delegate.

In decison making the manager must identify the real problem. He must make final decisions in matters relating to the unit as a whole. In communicating the manager can delegate much of the media aspects; that is, he can get others to write letters and reports, prepare statements for him, and so forth. However, he must ask, tell, listen, and understand himself, where face-to-face and personal communication is required. In selecting people for his team the manager initiates the request and makes final decision concerning the people he wants.

In developing people the manager must do most of the work of appraisal, counseling, and coaching himself. He can secure help from the personnel department and other agencies in the procedural aspects of development, and in setting up developmental activities such as courses and seminars. The manager must initiate and make final decisions with respect to his organizational structure. He must do most of the work of delegation and establishing relationships himself. These cannot be entrusted to others. In controlling, the manager must initiate and make final decisions himself with respect to setting performance standards, reporting, evaluating, and corrective action.

The manager should delegate as much of the routine and details of his job as he can. He should confine himself as largely as possible to the unique action—that of doing things the first time. After that he should look around for somebody to train to do the work for him.

DELEGATION AND DECENTRALIZATION

Delegation is the process of one manager entrusting responsibility and authority to others and creating accountability for results on a person-to-person basis. Left at this, the process of delegation may stop at any given point or level of organization. To be most effective, there should be a consistent and systematic effort to delegate authority to the operating levels—the point where the work, or responsibility, is actually carried out. Because of its importance, we shall discuss this larger aspect of delegation under the decentralization of authority.

DECENTRALIZATION

One of the greatest failings in organization is to give people work to do but to withhold from them the power to make the decisions necessary to carry out this work efficiently.

One of the characteristics of the matured enterprise is the willingness and ability of the top leadership to give enough authority to people at lower levels so that they can have fullest possible command of their own actions. The more decisions an individual can make for himself, the greater the personal satisfaction he tends to secure from carrying out those decisions.

A question vital to the continued existence of any organized endeavor is: How enable people to make as many decisions as possible for themselves? We have seen the mechanism involved in delegating authority from *one person to another*. In discussing decentralization, we will look at the requirements that must be fulfilled if we are to do this on an organization-wide basis.

We should note first that there can be no question of the need for decentralization. Each person finds the best evidence of his personal freedom in his liberty to make decisions. When people rebel against an established authority, they are rebelling against having somebody else make their decisions for them. There can be no logical question of whether to decentralize or not; the proper questions are: When shall we decentralize? How much? How to control the authority that has been entrusted to others?

THE LOGIC OF DECENTRALIZATION

A great deal of confusion and misunderstanding arises in our concepts of decentralization. We can help clarify this by precise definition of the terms involved. *Centralization* is the opposite of decentralization. It is *the reservation of authority at top levels of the company.* In a centralized corporation most of the decisions are made by top management.

When we build plants, offices, and facilities at widely separate geographical locations, we often refer to this as decentralization. However, to clarify our meaning, we define this as dispersion: *the physical separation of people, equipment, and facilities.* The reverse of dispersion is consolidation. This is the process of *bringing together at one physical location people, equipment, and facilities.* For example, when we collect all our data-recording equipment in one place, this is consolidation, not centralization.

Mistakes and Misapprehensions

Frequently there is a tendency to regard decentralization as a kind of administrative cure-all for companies of any size or stage of growth. Actually, the evidence argues against this conclusion. The small young company, operating under a functional organization, most often does best if it is quite highly centralized.

A little thought will make the reasons clear. A small, new company is almost invariably an extension of the ambitions, dreams, and energies of one or a few outstanding individuals. While it is attempting to establish a niche for itself in the market place, it must battle against established competition. This takes fast, decisive action, maneuverability and economy of operation, all of which can best be achieved in the small, young company by strong, unified direction from the proprietor himself.

Yielding to the urge to decentralize without proper preparation can be extremely costly. Small companies as well as large ones have made sizable investments in this area, only to find that the advertised benefits have not been forthcoming.

The president of a highly integrated manufacturing company persuaded his board of directors to approve a heavy capital budget so that the company could undertake a "geographic decentralization" by building new plants and diversifying into several new product lines. The "decentralization" took three years. Meanwhile, general and administrative expense crept upward. Sales volume increased, but not enough to offset the higher break-even point which resulted from higher fixed expenses. At a recent board meeting, the president found himself forced to recommend sale of two of the plants and a return to "centralized" management. What had happened? The company had assumed that dispersion of facilities would automatically result in decentralization of authority. Instead, the physical separation had merely made communication and coordination more difficult and multiplied the president's burdens.

Examination of company experience indicates that when a business runs into trouble in attempting to decentralize, it has usually been led astray by one or more common fallacies.

It is often wrongly assumed that decentralization can be attained merely by changing the company's organization structure. For example, a large distributing company with Eastern headquarters changed from a functional to a product-division type of organization and waited hopefully for the burden on top management to diminish. One president died of a heart attack and another was incapacitated with a peptic ulcer before the company realized that divisionalization does not necessarily bring about decentralization.

Another fallacy is that if a little decentralization is good, a complete job will be that much better. But, as more than one company has discovered, too much decentralization can be as dangerous as too little.

This is well documented in the case of a manufacturing company with $125 million annual sales which, over the course of some fifteen years, acquired a group of subsidiaries and set them up as operating divisions. In its desire to decentralize to the limit, the company permitted each of the divisions to operate pretty much on an autonomous basis. The slack rein proved a mistake. Expensive and wasteful duplication of both facilities and operations occurred. Eight research laboratories existed, each operating independently. In one case, four laboratories undertook a series of intricate experiments in an attempt to discover a needed catalyst; three continued the work from two to seven months after the fourth had found a suitable material. Since the divisions purchased independently, many relatively small lots of chemicals, bottles, and other materials were acquired at comparatively high prices. Several of the divisions frequently carried abnormally high inventories of similar expensive materials. Marketing problems cropped up. Since warehousing was independent, a customer who bought from two or more divisions might receive his purchases as separate shipments from several warehouses.

The company solved its problem by instituting the necessary centralization. Administrative expense soon dropped, sales improved, and much of the bickering and disagreement that had existed among the divisional managers was gradually eliminated.

Decentralization Is More Than Dispersion

Decentralization is also commonly confused with geographical dispersion. A few years ago, for instance, a transportation company created groups of engineering, maintenance, purchasing, and accounting personnel to service geographically separated locations. It assumed it was decentralizing in the process, but actually authority for direction of these groups remained with the functional departments at headquarters. The problems of coordination soon became so complex that the company found it simpler to transfer most of the staff back to headquarters.

Much of the confusion can be eliminated if we differentiate clearly between decentralization and divisionalization. The two are closely related, but a company can be divisionalized and not decentralized, and vice versa.

Decentralization is *the systematic and consistent delegation of authority to the levels where the work is performed.* Complete decentralization would mean that every person given any work to do would have the power he needed to complete that work and would not be required to check with his superior on any detail. (As a practical matter, of course, the superior must retain certain authority or the operating elements will go their independent ways without common purpose or coordination.)

Divisionalization, on the other hand, is *the process of breaking large functional organization units into divisions grouped in terms of product, geography, or some other basis.*

In speaking of decentralization, most companies refer to the first step of the process—pushing down authority from the top executives of the company to the next level of operating management, usually the divisional or department managers. And decentralization commonly stops there. The division manager runs his shop with a tight grip on the reins. He may recognize that he is functioning better because he has more real authority, but he is unable to realize that his subordinates might be helped in the same way. To the extent that he is strong and capable, he may get away with it. But most companies find that decentralization can and should be a way of life, even at the first-line operating levels of the company.

United Parcel Service, for example, delegates authority down to the manager of each of its stations. Even where several small stations are located in the same building, the organization is so arranged that each manager can maintain his operation as an autonomous unit.

Food Machinery and Chemical (FMC) Corporation decentralizes as much authority as possible to operating levels as a matter of policy. Standard Pressed Steel also decentralizes, in large degree, to the plant level.

WHY DECENTRALIZE?

What prompts a company to decentralize? Study of well over 100 companies that have decentralized since 1907 indicates that there are two basic pressures that trigger the move: company growth and diversification. Essentially, decentralization is a systematic and consistent attempt to ease the burden on top management.

As a company grows, it outreaches the span of a single individual. Sooner or later, decentralization must occur if the company is not to slow down and lose out in the competitive market place. Practically all large companies are proof of this thesis. This was true of Ford Motor Company under Henry Ford, of Du Pont after the death of General Henry du Pont, of Unilever Limited under William Lever, and of many others. If top executives continue to make most of the decisions, sooner or later the proliferating layers of organization impede communication so badly that fast, decisive action at the operating levels is impossible. As a general rule, the broader and more outstanding the talents of the top manager, the longer the company can maintain successful centralization. Sooner or later, however, the break must come.

For example, Paul V. Galvin started Motorola, Inc., in 1928 to manufacture a popular-priced automobile radio. The struggling young company was able to survive only because of strong centralized leadership. Galvin not only supervised his small, talented staff of electronic engineers, but also established the first distributorships, arranged the first advertising campaigns, and kept a weather eye on the bookkeeping.

Leadership was concentrated in one individual. Every decision bore the earmarks of his outstanding talents. During the 1940s, however, the business grew too large for any one man, whatever his capabilities. Accordingly, Paul Galvin began to decentralize. He built up a strong subordinate organization and promptly began to push much of the burden of running the business on to his key managers. Today, Motorola is highly decentralized and rates as one of the world's largest manufacturers devoted exclusively to electronic products.

Staff Needs Multiply

Multiplication of product lines also tends to increase the burden on top executives in geometric proportion. Let a food company market its product in forty states instead of four and its problems are, at worst, multiplied by ten. But let the company branch out into pharmaceuticals, mechanical equipment, and electronics, and the increase is immeasurably greater. As a result, diversification creates a need to redistribute the burden.

Take Carrier Corporation as a case in point. Carrier operated under a centralized management for many years. So long as the company was small and concentrated largely on centrifugal refrigeration equipment, it found this arrangement suitable. Then, before and after World War II, Carrier began to grow at an accelerated pace and to diversify. It spread into unitary equipment completely assembled at the factory, such as room and residential air conditioners, and broadened its lines of commercial and industrial products. This was the cue for the decentralization which has enabled it to grow and diversify with continued vigor.

What to Centralize?

A key question in decentralization is: What shall we centralize? Reference to our basic concept of management will make it clear that the top management group in every company should centralize authority for over-all planning, organizing, leading, and controlling. Unless uniform over-all plans, organization, and controls are established by a central agency and approved by the chief executive, each operating unit will tend to go its own way without regard to the needs or welfare of the whole. This will eventually result in chaos and disintegration of the enterprise. Leadership must also be vested in a central source, if we are to have integrated, consistent movement toward common goals.

HOW TO IMPROVE DECENTRALIZATION

There are as many prescriptions for decentralization as there are companies that have decentralized. Our research indicates, however, that the key factors which warrant first attention are those outlined below:

1. *Balance Decentralization with Appropriate Centralization.* Every move toward decentralization must be matched by an appropriate centralization of authority. A central intelligence must retain authority to guide, coordinate, and control the operating elements so that they will proceed toward a common objective as an integrated whole, not as loosely associated entities pulling every which way to their independent ends.

The centralized authority must establish over-all objectives and policies for the company as a whole, because perspective on the total needs of the enterprise exists only at the top. When properly stated, these corporate plans guide each operating element in planning its own targets.

Effective centralized planning cannot be arbitrary. Subordinate managers cannot be expected to carry out plans with enthusiasm and enterprise unless they have participated in developing those plans. At United Parcel Service, policies covering every major aspect of the business are set forth in a policy book. Every United Parcel Service supervisor and manager was asked to contribute ideas and recommendations when they were formulated. And every supervisor had an opportunity to review each of the policies when they were revised. Because of this participation, the policies are thoroughly understood and receive wholehearted support.

2. *Provide Profit or Cost-center Controls.* The profit-center concept of decentralization involves looking upon each manager as a businessman, managing a segment of the business within the company as a whole. This means that he is made accountable for money which he spends for manpower, materials, tools, and facilities; he is expected to secure definite results and is appraised in terms of his ability to secure those results. Managers can be held accountable for costs as well as for profit or loss. In either case, the accountable manager must be given command over the elements that go to make up his costs or his profit or loss. This means that he must have a high degree of authority to make most of the decisions relating to the operations of his unit.

A classic example—and certainly one of the pioneers—of effective profit-center decentralization is Du Pont. Each of the product divisions operates on a highly autonomous basis. Each manufactures and sells its own products. Divisions buy and sell among themselves, generally on the same terms as outside customers. Their products even compete in the same markets.

At Ford Motor Company, too, each product division is measured in terms of profit and loss. To make this possible, each division is given the staff it needs: manufacturing engineering, production programming and control, plant engineering, quality control, industrial relations, and finance.

Controls directly limit the extent of possible decentralization. As the chief executive of one multiplant processing company put it, somewhat ruefully, after two fruitless attempts to decentralize: "Never try to run a spirited team without a firm hand on the reins."

3. *Identify Key Authorities.* The crux of true decentralization is making sure that the most important authorities are delegated down to the operating level, so that the people who actually do the work neces-

sary to accomplish end results can make most of the decisions related to the work.

While the key authorities necessary to do this will vary with the company and the industry, we have found the following to be worthy of general consideration:

1. Approval of purchase commitments
2. Acquisition of expensed equipment
3. Acquisition of capital equipment
4. Leasing property or equipment
5. Sale of capital equipment
6. Approval of travel expense
7. Approval of donations or gifts
8. Approval of sales prices
9. Approval of price quotations
10. Approval of credit
11. Authority to hire subordinates
12. Approval of wage and salary increases

It bears emphasizing that *complete* authority for carrying out these responsibilities can never be delegated safely. There must always be a balancing centralization.

To make *management decentralization* effective, each manager should have the following:

1. Clearly expressed objectives he is accountable for accomplishing
2. Authority to participate in developing corporate objectives and policies
3. Authority to program major activities and projects
4. Budget limits which are set broadly enough so that he can make final decisions on most activities that are included in approved programs
5. Periodic reports covering both his performance and results, with variances highlighted
6. Performance standards in part based on cost or profit
7. Participation in some form of incentive award which is directly related to his profit or cost performance
8. Opportunity to participate in a company-supported program for improvement of management skills which is initiated and supported by top management and which stresses management on the job

4. *Provide Appropriate Organization Structure.* Decentralization is possible in any type of organization structure, and it can be instituted

by any manager at any level.   But some types of organization facilitate decentralization while others make it more difficult.

Consider first the functional form of organization.   Here a high degree of centralization automatically ensues because only the president is organizationally placed to handle decisions involving all functions. Hence the full weight of every operating problem of any importance inevitably lands squarely on him.   Since the functional heads cannot command all the costs that affect their profits, they cannot be held fully accountable.   Usually the only workable alternative is to hold them responsible only for the *costs* over which they have authority.

A desirable preliminary to decentralization is usually to reorganize the company on a divisionalized basis.   In product divisionalization, each product, or group of related products, is organized as a small business unit in itself.   It is given its own management, sales, engineering, and staffs necessary to operate as an independent entity within the framework of the business as a whole.

Du Pont is divisionalized on a product basis.   Each of the division managers has been delegated authority to run his own manufacturing processes.   He is fully accountable for the company's investment in plants, laboratories, processes, facilities, and personnel assigned to him.

Geographical divisionalization will enable the company to accomplish similar results.   Each region or area is established as a business unit in its own right and given the administrative and operating tools it needs to operate independently.   Then it can be held accountable for its profits.   Prudential Insurance Company of America, for instance, has divided its business into seven geographic divisions.   Each handles its own actuarial, real estate investment, medical, legal, and advertising functions, operating along broad policy lines set by the corporate headquarters in Newark, New Jersey.

Southern Counties Gas Company of California, serving a territory with rapidly expanding population and industry, established its geographic divisions early.   As demand skyrocketed, the company was able to meet it at each step by continually enlarging the responsibility and authority it had decentralized to its operating divisions.   The manager of each geographical division directs and coordinates the operations of his division within the framework of over-all objectives, policies, and procedures set by the general office.   And the division managers, in turn, have delegated an increasing measure of authority to their functional department heads.   Centralized control is maintained as required for the over-all integrity of the organization.

5. *Develop Management Skills.*   The popular idea that decentralization develops managers is true to some extent.   One of the most

effective ways to improve a man's ability to manage is to give him enough authority to carry work through to completion within broad policy limits—and let him stand or fall by the results.

But decentralization can be effective only if the people to whom decision making is delegated are capable of making effective decisions. As one company president put it: "I can't afford to decentralize unless I have some confidence that my management will make the right decisions more than half the time."

The fact that additional managerial talent will be needed means that a company that is planning to decentralize must first undertake a systematic and vigorous program to develop broad-gauge managers who are capable of planning, coordinating, and controlling all the functions necessary to company operations.

Decentralization is a difficult and often costly undertaking. It demands critical self-examination by management. There must be a high measure of psychological conditioning before managers will be willing to delegate, and executives will need self-discipline and a certain measure of humility. But once decentralization is accomplished, it can break the shackles of inertia and give every individual in the company added opportunity to strive, achieve, and win tangible recognition for whatever he accomplishes.

SUMMARY

In delegating, a manager is assigning to others work to be done and decisions to be made and creating an obligation to do this work and make the decisions in terms of established performance standards. The term "responsibility" is used for the work assigned to a position. "Authority" is the sum of the powers or rights necessary to do the work. "Accountability" is the obligation to perform. Responsibility and authority must be delegated but a manager's accountability can never safely be delegated. In delegating, prime consideration should be given to the need for providing for effective controls, for the availability of controls limits the extent of delegation. It is also necessary to provide for single reporting relationships, for the more people to whom a manager reports, the less accountable he tends to become. If we want sharply focused control, we must establish individual accountability through delegation. Important as it is, delegation often fails because of organizational and psychological barriers. A critical barrier is failure of the manager to understand what work he should get other people to do for him. This can best be overcome by recognizing that the proper responsibility of the manager lies within those areas of planning, organizing, leading, and controlling that logically belong to his position. Other work which is primarily operating in nature should be delegated so far as possible.

Decentralization refers to the consistent and systematic delegation of authority to the levels where the work is performed. Decentralization is vital if the company is to grow and diversify successfully. Many misconceptions have arisen with respect to decentralization. The important considerations are to ensure that there is appropriate centralization of planning, organizing, leading, and controlling responsibilities before delegation is undertaken. Most effective control of decentralization can be accomplished through profit or cost centers. Decentralization proceeds most effectively within a divisionalized type of organization structure but it can also be accomplished in a functional organization. The work of managing on an organization-wide basis is more difficult under decentralization, for its requires development of high competence in management skills at all levels, not only the top.

It is better to do thine own duty, however lacking in merit, than to do that of another, even though efficiently, for to do the duty of another is fraught with danger. THE GEETA

DEFINITIONS

Establishing Relationships: the work a manager performs to create the conditions necessary for mutually cooperative efforts of people.

Line Relationship: the relationship of those persons and organization components accountable for objectives and delegated authority to make decisions with respect to those objectives.

Staff Relationship: the relationship of those persons and organization components which provide advice and service in the accomplishment of objectives.

Specialized Staff: those positions and components organized primarily to provide advice and service in one specialized function to other units in the accomplishment of over-all objectives.

Personal Staff: those persons or positions which provide advice and service to one principal.

Line Assistant: a person or position that provides advice and service to one principal in all aspects of his responsibility and assumes part or all of the authority of that principal on specific delegation.

Staff Assistant: a person or position that provides advice and service to one principal in limited portions of his responsibility and does not assume authority.

THE IMPORTANCE OF ORGANIZATION RELATIONSHIPS

Cooperation is a necessary requisite of effective group action. This harmony can be accomplished by working together day by day. Those

217

who cannot make the necessary adjustments and compromises will leave the group, while those who remain learn to be understanding and patient to the extent necessary to function effectively as members of the group.

We find in the modern enterprise, however, that groups form and disband so quickly and there is so much rotation from one group to another, that it is difficult to secure the necessary teamwork by letting nature take its course. Far better is the establishment of definite rules, or relationships, that will serve as guides to everybody in working with other people.

Relationships exist between the subordinate and his superior and the superior and subordinate, between people working on the same level and people in different departments working at different levels, between managers and nonmanagers, and between people inside the company and those outside the company. A basic relationship that is found in most of these situations is the staff and line relationship.

STAFF AND LINE RELATIONSHIPS

Many problems result because of ineffective staff and line relationships. Some companies have advocated the elimination of this concept. However, we invariably find that even after staff and line are abolished from the management vocabulary, new terms are created to describe the relationships that exist. The fact is that there *are* different relationships and they can be discussed and understood most easily if we define our terms in a logical fashion.

The Logic of Line and Staff

A perennial problem in all relationships is "who gives orders to whom." If we look at a group working under a manager, it is clear that the manager gives orders to his subordinates. He does this in full expectation that they will carry out his orders. If they fail to do so, he will have sanctions to apply and can force them to do his bidding. In this case, the manager gives commands and other members of the group carry out those commands. In other words, he is in a *command relationship* to the group. He is *line*.

Line to Staff

Logically, the accountable manager must be empowered to make decisions with respect to the over-all activities of his group, otherwise he cannot fulfill his leadership role effectively. Identifying his relationship as "line" simply indicates to all concerned that he is the one who makes the decisions. Similarly, if two managers work together at any time and one is designated as "line," the other as "staff," this identification establishes that the one who is line will give commands in the expectation that the other will carry them out.

Staff to Line

When a manager is staff to another in a line relationship to him, this is a staff to line relationship. Found most commonly between a superior and his subordinates, it signifies that the one who is staff is primarily concerned with providing advice and service to the one who is line. Literally, staff *works for* the one who is line. This relationship may be permanent, as in an employer-employee relationship. It may be quite transitory, as on a task force, work team, or committee. In all cases where groups are expected to work together harmoniously, however, it is important to designate who is line, that is, who is the boss, and who are staff.

Staff to Staff

Frequently people work together without giving orders to one another and without authority to do so. The sales manager and production manager may be in such a relationship, as may the personnel and the engineering manager. In such a "staff to staff" relationship, matters requiring final decision must be worked out by mutual agreement, compromise, or by carrying the issue to the common line superior.

These varying relationships are shown in Figure 19-1. Here we find the president in a continuing line relationship to everybody else. Since the company is organized to design, manufacture, and sell a specific product line, engineering, manufacturing, and sales are in a primary or continuing line relationship with respect to over-all objectives. This means that they make the decisions related to the basic success or failure of the company, subject to the final authority of the president.

To illustrate, engineering, sales, and manufacturing determine how many and what kinds of people they want and the personnel staff helps them to find these people. The personnel staff group does not tell engineering what kind of designer it should have to do engineering design work; engineering decides what it needs, and the personnel staff group provides advice and help in locating that kind of designer. If engineering does not have the proper people, engineering is accountable. However, if engineering places an order for a design engineer with personnel and personnel does a poor job of finding the person required, personnel is accountable for falling down in its mission of providing expert help and advice.

Is all of this important? Not at all, unless it is understood. Once properly comprehended, it gives us a quick and meaningful insight into the inner workings of some vital phases of the organization. While it is awkward and cumbersome until mastered, just as is shorthand or the writing of prescriptions in cryptic Latin, this at least is the best

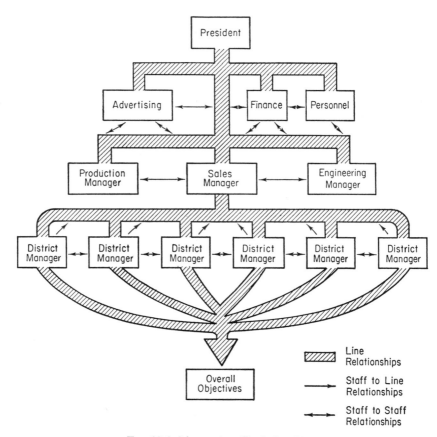

FIG. 19-1. Line and staff relationships.

way we have so far developed to provide a meaningful semantic label for the fast-changing and difficult relationships that actually exist.

When Line Is Not Line

Line and staff are convenient designations, but they do not permanently characterize all relationships among the people of the organization. Relationships change, sometimes with bewildering rapidity. We have said that in all those matters having to do with accomplishment of the group's objectives, the manager gives orders in the full expectation that they will be obeyed. In other matters not having to do with the objectives of the group, however, he may not have this command authority.

For example, several members of a group may want to form a bowling team. Since this is not during working hours and not on company premises, the manager does not have a command relationship here. His subordinates may come to him for advice with respect to the formation of the bowling team, but his authority is limited to advisory authority.

Back on the job, what is the relationship of the members of the group to the manager? As we have seen, they give him suggestions, recommendations, and ideas, and advise and counsel him in any way he requires or that they feel will be helpful. They do things for him which he cannot do for himself because he does not have the time, experience, or special skills required. In this case, the subordinates are in an advisory and service relationship to the manager.

While this is clear-cut in a group with its own manager, it becomes much more complex when different groups are working together. For example, the quality control inspector and the foreman work together in getting out quality production. Who gives orders to whom? Can the foreman let material through even though it does not meet standard? Can the quality control inspector close down the line in spite of the objections of the foreman? Until we determine who has authority and enforce our decision, there probably will be a running argument between the foreman and the quality control inspector.

This is also true in many other situations. For example, the director of staff marketing at the corporate level visits in one of the company's sales territories. While there, does he have authority to tell salesmen in the field what they are to do and how they are to do it? Perhaps the staff marketing manager is a vice president and director of the company. Almost anything he says will be taken as a direct order. Does he have this authority? Should he exercise it? These questions can be answered properly, of course, only if we look at the role we have assigned to the marketing vice president and the field sales force. From the principle of single reporting relationships, we know that if we ask sales personnel in the field to take orders both from their own manager and from the vice president of marketing, we will find it very difficult to hold them accountable for specific results. In every case where we have people from different groups working together, it becomes extremely important to determine beforehand who is to make the final decisions and give orders based upon them.   If we do not do this, there will be endless difficulty and most of the problem will find its way to the boss for his resolution.

THE ALLEN CLASSIFICATION OF RELATIONSHIPS[1]

We have identified *line relationships* as the relationship of those persons and organization components accountable for objectives and delegated authority to make decisions with respect to those objectives.

The *staff relationship* is the relationship of those persons and organization components which provide advice and service in the accomplishment of objectives.

Types of Staff

We have identified two types of staff: specialized and personal. Personal staff, in turn, is further classified into staff and line assistants. Established first in 1956, this classification has been widely accepted and is here brought up to date.

Specialized Staff

This refers to those positions and organization components which are firstly staff; that is, they are organized primarily to provide advice and service to others.   Secondly, they are specialized; that is, they specialize in one type of work such as accounting, personnel, and so forth.   Specialized staff units provide advice and service in their specialized type of work to the organization at large.

Personal Staff

Personal staff positions are organized to provide advice and service; however, they do this for only one person—the principal to whom the position reports.   This is the chief difference between specialized and personal staff; specialized staff is organized to help virtually everybody; personal staff exists largely to help one person.   Personal staff positions are generally identified as assistant positions.   As a comment, the executive vice president most commonly serves in a personal staff relationship and is usually a line assistant, although he may assume a different role as the chief operating officer or chief staff officer.

Line assistants are positions that provide advice and service to

[1] This identification and classification was first made by the author in his three-year study of 150 companies for the National Industrial Conference Board.   See *Improving Staff and Line Relationships,* National Industrial Conference Board, Inc., New York, 1956.   This was continued in the author's *Management and Organization,* McGraw-Hill Book Company, New York, 1957.   New findings are incorporated here.

one principal in all aspects of his responsibility and assume part or all of the authority of that principal on specific delegation. The line assistant has two distinguishing characteristics: (1) He replaces his principal in the latter's absence, assuming the latter's responsibility and authority in the process, but not his accountability; and (2) he has a wide scope and is capable of providing advice and service to his principal in virtually the full range of his job.

We have recently finalized a further classification of line assistants as follows:

Associate (manager, director, etc.): a line assistant who is delegated and exercises specified portions of the principal's authority and responsibility on a continuing basis. (The line assistant normally assumes this only temporarily and in his principal's absence.)

Executive Vice President: a line assistant who reports to the chief executive. (If held accountable for clear-cut responsibility and authority for the operations, staff activities, or other areas, the best professional practice suggests that the position should be called Chief Operating Officer or Chief Staff Officer and not Executive Vice President.)

Staff assistants are positions that provide advice and service to one principal in limited portions of his responsibility and do not assume authority. The characteristics of the position are: (1) The staff assistant does not replace his principal and does not assume his responsibility or authority; and (2) the staff assistant provides advice and service in only a limited area of the principal's responsibility.

We have recently extended the classification of staff assistants as follows:

Executive Assistant: a staff assistant to the chief executive, board chairman, or executive vice president.

Special Assistant: an assistant who provides specialized help in only one kind of work, such as public relations, taxes, or engineering studies. The special assistant is actually a specialized staff position working for only one person.

Management Assistant: an assistant who provides help and advice to a manager primarily in the planning, organizing, and controlling aspects of his responsibilities.

Assistant to: a synonym for *staff assistant*.

Administrative Assistant: an assistant who performs specified routine and detail activities which the manager might otherwise perform himself.

Figure 19-2 shows how these positions are charted on an organization chart. We shall now discuss these staff positions and groups in more detail.

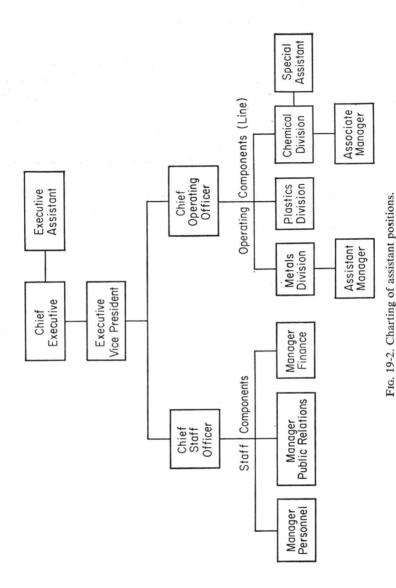

FIG. 19-2. Charting of assistant positions.

THE USE OF SPECIALIZED STAFF

There is no area in management today more fertile of disagreement than the role of specialized staff. We have found that much of this, again, arises from confusion over the meaning of words and from failure to look at what actually happens when line and staff are in question.

To see what is involved in the use of specialized staff, let us first look at a simple organization, as shown in Figure 19-3.

Here we have a small enterprise organized to manufacture and sell metal products. As these managers and operators go about their work of manufacturing and selling under the direction of the president, many problems come up that they find difficult to handle because

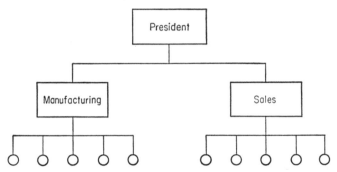

FIG. 19-3. Basic line organization without components in a primary staff relationship.

of lack of specialized knowledge. For example, record must be kept of the money spent and the money taken in. The president may dole out these funds personally and ask his manufacturing and sales managers to keep track for him. He may ask the sales manager to bank the money that comes in from sales and to keep everybody else informed of what will be available for future expenses. This *could* be done, of course, but it would be slow, awkward, and inefficient. The probability is that the manufacturing and sales managers would be so busy doing their own highly specialized work they would have neither the time nor the special skill necessary to do the work of bookkeeping and accounting.

The Line and Staff Problem

How do we solve this problem? If we were to ask the manufacturing head and the sales head, each might request that he be given an accountant to help him personally. But would this be efficient? We would probably find that the accountant for manufacturing, the accountant for sales, and the accountant for the president would all tend to keep their accounts in a different way and that a great deal of time would be needed to integrate and unify the work they do.   A far better solution is to hire one accountant and organize him so that he will do accounting work for everybody.   If we are to accomplish this, we must answer some basic questions.   What work does an accountant do?   What is his relationship to others?   How shall we show him on the chart?

What Does He Do?   The purpose of the accountant is to maintain records and make reports on the money taken in and the money spent by everybody in the company.   The accountant will keep the chart of accounts for the company and will keep the president advised of how much money is received and how much is spent.   He will also let the president know how much the company can expect to take in over the near future.   The president will decide how much money can be spent by manufacturing, by sales, and by the accountant.   Manufacturing and sales will determine what they need in the way of people, materials, equipment, and facilities and will request of the president the proper amounts in the form of a budget.   The president will check this budget with the accountant to make sure that it is in line with their financial expectations.

What Is His Relationship?   The accountant does not tell the president, the manufacturing head, or the sales head how much they can spend or how they should spend it.   He does give his best advice, counsel, and suggestions to all three in helping them make most effective use of the funds of the company.   He will maintain the books of the company, prepare reports, and do other work *for* his three principals.   He *can* decide what reports these three managers should get, but it would be far better if they were to determine their own needs and work out with the accountant a reporting system best adapted to those needs.   Otherwise, the accountant will tend to provide the kind of reports that are best suited to his own particular specialized needs.

The accountant provides advice and service to the organization at large.   He does this not for the purpose of developing a bookkeeping system to fit his own purposes, but rather to establish a system that will help the enterprise in attaining its objective of manufacturing and selling metal products at a profit.

How Shall We Show Him on the Chart?   We could show the accountant on the same organizational line as manufacturing and sales. His work is extremely important and it cannot be done effectively by anybody else.   However, we would like to show him on the chart so we can easily visualize his special role—that of providing advice and service to everybody else.   To facilitate this, we show him on the corporate staff line as in Figure 19-4.

This placement on the chart is a conventional means of telling knowledgeable managers that this particular position is in a continuing staff relationship to the organization at large.   It tells us that the accountant does not give direct orders to manufacturing, sales, or the president as to what they are to do or how they are to do it, but that in every way possible he helps them with their bookkeeping and accounting requirements and problems.

What Authority Does He Have?   The specialized staff, accounting position, has a great deal of authority.   He makes many decisions with

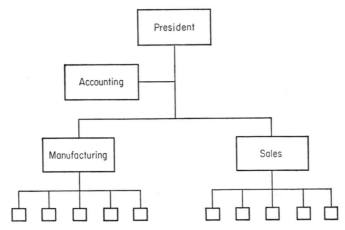

Fig. 19-4. Charting specialized staff.

respect to the accounting work as it is carried on.   However, he does *not* have command authority or line authority over any of his principals.   On the other hand, manufacturing and sales do not give commands to the accountant; they ask him for advice and help.

Neither manufacturing nor sales can tell the accountant what kind of accounting system he is to set up.   This decision must be made by the president.   If he knows how to use staff, the president will ask the accountant to develop the kind of system he thinks will be best suited to the company's needs.   He then will have the accountant carefully discuss this with both the manufacturing and the sales heads until he secures their agreement as to its suitability.   Having done this, the accountant will present his recommendation to the president for final approval, noting any disagreements that may have come up from manufacturing or sales.   At his option, the president will call together manufacturing, sales, and the accountant and reconcile only those few points in disagreement.   Then the president will make his decision and the accounting system will become a matter of company procedure.

When it is established as procedure, in substance, the president is telling everybody, including the accountant, that he wants the accounts of the company maintained in the form upon which he has decided.   He asks the accountant to check up to make sure that this is done.   If there are discrepancies, he requires the accountant to report them first to the accountable manager, whether it be manufacturing or sales.   If the accountant cannot resolve the matter with the accountable manager, then the president expects to decide the question himself.

Here, in outline, we have the major components of staff and line. The president is in a *continuing line relationship* to manufacturing, bookkeeping, and sales.   He gives direct orders to all three of them. These three, in turn, are in a *staff relationship* to the president.   They provide him with advice and service but do not tell him what to do. Manufacturing, bookkeeping, and sales are all in a *staff to staff relationship* to one another; that is, they cannot give direct orders to one another.   These three relationships, line to staff, staff to line, and staff to staff, are readily recognized by anyone who has had management experience.   The logical pattern that has been developed will hold for any set of line-staff relationships no matter how large and complex the organization.   Properly understood and utilized, this is the most effective means we know of maintaining teamwork among the varying and often conflicting interests of people working together.

THE ROLE OF SPECIALIZED STAFF

We define *specialized staff* as *those positions and components organized primarily to provide advice and service in one specialized function to other units in the accomplishment of over-all objectives.*

Specialized staff groups act in several capacities.   Properly organized, they become a decisive factor in maintaining a high level of effective performance in all parts of the organization.

Act as Internal Consultants

Specialized staff groups serve as internal consultants, highly expert in specialized areas of the business.   They bring this knowledge and skill to the help of managers in solving problems and in carrying out their responsibilities.   For example, the finance staff group provides advice and service to other elements of the organization in managing, utilizing, and safeguarding the funds and assets of the enterprise.

Personnel staff advise and help other managers in recruiting, selecting, training, compensating, and motivating people.

Specialized staff departments provide this help and advice to all managers from top to bottom of the organization. For instance, the controller advises and helps the president in financial controls. He does this by recommending objectives, policies, and budgets for the company as a whole, and by preparing consolidated reports. At each lower level, the controller and his group provide advice and service to managers in developing financial plans, applying financial controls, interpreting financial policies and objectives, preparing and using financial reports, and in other ways.

Provide Common Services

Specialized staff may perform one specialized kind of work for the entire organization because it is more effective and economical to carry it out in one place than to set up many units throughout the organization. For example, in one food company, the Market Survey Department provides market research services in the development of all of the company's product lines and in the study and analysis of markets and methods of distribution, new businesses, new product lines, possible acquisitions, and other related problems.

With the advent of electronic data processing, there is generally the question of whether computers should be installed in the separate departments and divisions of the company, or whether one consolidated installation can service the company as a whole. Because of the need for one coordinated clearinghouse for information and the speed and precision with which these data can be gathered, most companies will establish one consolidated unit at the top staff level. This provides electronic data-processing services to all parts of the company.

Provide Functional Leadership

Staff groups advise and help all units of the company. They also provide leadership in helping the company remain at the forefront of new technological and administrative developments. The line operating groups of the company generally are too deeply involved in the day-by-day operating problems to be able to stand aside, study, research, and review new thinking and new developments in the functional fields which are important to them.

The General Electric Approach. In General Electric Company the corporate staff groups are called Services Components. One of their important responsibilities is to provide functional services to all elements of the company in helping them to secure leadership for the company in their specific functional fields. These groups develop a reservoir of knowledge and make available expert personnel who provide advice and service to all other elements of the business.

Illustrative of the General Electric approach is the function of the central staff Manufacturing Laboratory. Recognizing that technological advances are rapidly revolutionizing the manufacturing processes, General Electric decided that it could best maintain leadership if it organized a group that could draw apart from direct operations sufficiently to think creatively and to develop new methods and approaches in manufacturing. The company was keenly aware of the many advances and changes in product design and manufacturing methods. From electrodischarge machining to electron-beam cutting, from low-pressure casting of aluminum and computerized process control, new opportunities for improved efficiency and cost in manufacturing were literally popping up all over the world almost every day.

How to remain abreast, if not ahead, of these fast-moving innovations? Obviously, the line manufacturing departments were incapable of doing their daily job and also studying what the rest of the world was doing. General Electric organized its central Manufacturing Laboratory for this purpose as part of its manufacturing services. The Manufacturing Laboratory develops and builds, under fixed-price contracts, automation and processing equipment for the operating divisions. When new manufacturing techniques such as computerized machining and tape-controlled machine tools are developed, the Laboratory demonstrates these in seminars and workshops which it schedules for interested groups. Since there is always a vital need for competent manufacturing engineers and specialists, the Laboratory trains personnel and makes them available as required. As a consulting service, it reviews appropriation requests, accomplishes plant layout studies, and evaluates metal-conversion facilities. The Laboratory also disseminates information on new developments in manufacturing and provides for the distribution of technical articles throughout the company.

Properly organized, the functional, specialized staff group can provide invaluable service to the operating groups of the company. Because it is not directly involved in the operating situation, it can retain objectivity, accumulate a pool of experience and knowledge, and make this available for the improvement of operations as a whole. In many cases, the staff group can study and analyze specific problems and develop new and more effective approaches that will help to establish and maintain company leadership.

Westinghouse Electric Company. In the Westinghouse Electric Company, for example, inventory has always been a problem of prime concern. Not only do inventories account for a large share of the company's gross assets, but they can also become an expensive liability if they are not turned over fast enough. The production and inventory control department in Westinghouse maintains continuing study of the inventory problems throughout the company. On the basis of this, Westinghouse has developed highly effective means of procuring materials at a rate carefully geared to the processing of parts and assemblies. This affords the company much greater manufacturing efficiency. Calculating inventory turnover by dividing total sales volume by the inventory balance, Westinghouse has been able to improve raw material inventory turnover to twelve times a year, work in process to twenty-six times, and total inventories, including finished goods, from four to six times a year.

Aid in Management

The specialized staff groups help other departments in the planning, organizing, leading, and controlling of their work. For example, the controller should be available to assist managers in developing their budgets, in designing an effective reporting system for control, in forecasting the availability and requirement for cash, in developing accounting procedures, and other related areas of this function. When these plans and controls have been authorized by the chief executive, the controller is then best placed to work with all other groups in the company in explaining, interpreting, and helping them to carry out these plans as they apply to their component.

Provide Audit and Inspection

Specialized staff groups should be constantly on the alert observing, reviewing, and helping managers on all levels to perform most effectively in their functional area.

In the Schlage Lock Company, a leading hardware manufacturer, for example, the manager of industrial relations works with both staff and operating departments to make sure that they are using effective means of selection and placement, that their training efforts are producing worthwhile results, and that new approaches in performance appraisal are understood and used where feasible. He reviews wage and salary data to ensure that company compensation policy and procedure requirements are being met. He looks to planned turnover and mortality vacancies, and audits line activities designed to provide for effective replacements.

In carrying out his audit and inspection function, the specialized staff manager must keep in mind that he is acting for his line principal. It is not his function to correct matters, but to inform the accountable line manager and his own principal of discrepancies so that they can take effective action. A competent staff manager will invariably discuss the findings of his audit and inspection with the accountable manager. This gives the manager an opportunity to correct the situation so that the final report, when it is carried to a higher level, will not only note the deficiency but will also report its correction. This is effective staff work.

PERSONAL STAFF

Personal staff refers to all those positions commonly known as "assistants." An assistant is a part of the staff because he is primarily concerned with providing advice and service, and he is personal because he provides this advice and service to one principal. Questions and difficulties often arise over the proper use of assistants. Sometimes there is dispute over the assistants' authority, while on other occasions their area of responsibility or accountability may be open to question.

Purpose of Assistants

An assistant provides advice and service to one principal. We should note that a specialized staff department provides help in its specialty to all managers; an assistant restricts his assistance to one individual—his superior.

Two Kinds of Assistants

In practice we find that there are many kinds of assistants, which we have classified into two basic types: staff assistants and line assistants. Since each has a specific part to play it is wise to differentiate clearly between them.

Line Assistants. Line assistants commonly bear such titles as "assistant manager," "assistant superintendent," and so forth. The distinguishing characteristics of a line assistant are as follows:

1. He serves only one principal.
2. When his superior is absent, or by special delegation, he steps in and takes over all or part of his boss's job. Depending upon the extent of the delegation, he assumes his principal's authority and responsibility and acts in his stead.
3. The line assistant usually has sufficiently broad scope and experience as to be able to help his principal in the full range of his duties.

Staff Assistants. The staff assistant, depending upon his job, may be known as the "assistant to," "administrative assistant," "executive assistant," or "special assistant." The staff assistant plays a much more limited role than the line assistant. He helps his principal with only specified parts of his job. He does not take his principal's place and has no command authority over other positions in the organization.

How Assistant Positions Develop

A manager usually creates an assistant position when his work load becomes so great that he can no longer perform it satisfactorily himself. This may be due to unusually heavy responsibilities, or to his failure to delegate. Once assistant positions are established, the manager may prefer to delegate to them rather than to his line subordinates. When this is the case, there is a serious tendency for assistants to leach out of the line positions the best parts of the responsibility and authority that should be exercised there.

Do I Need an Assistant?

Assistant positions have their place, but it has been somewhat difficult to determine the role they can best play in the organization. Many an executive has found that a formidable variety and number have multiplied on his management roster, accounting for a disproportionate share of both office space and administrative payroll. The wisest course is to analyze the requirements of the individual manager for help and determine whether he can best delegate to line subordinates, to specialized staff, or whether he should have one or more assistants.

The major factors involved include the need of the executive for assistance with the responsibilities he has reserved to himself, his desire for a sounding board when he is making up his mind, personal and organizational weaknesses, the amount of time the executive spends away from the job, and the methods used in training and developing managers.

The primary advantage of using an assistant to help carry out reserved responsibilities is that the assistant provides the executive with a constantly available, fully committed source of help. He does not have to share his assistant with others; he can train him to his own way of doing things; he can be sure of his attention and loyalty.

These potential advantages are also a source of weakness. The executive may delegate to his assistant much of the meaningful and important responsibilities that would normally go to line subordinates. Or he may delegate to his assistant clerical and minor administrative work that could be handled by his secretary or technical responsibilities that could be performed more effectively by specialized staff.

When the chief must make a decision, he may find it helpful to bounce his ideas off an interested and sympathetic auditor. However, lack of specialized knowledge on the part of the assistant may preclude his offering constructive criticism. At the same time, he may be so dominated by his propinquity to his chief that he tends to "yes" rather than to analyze and criticize.

An assistant may be used to overcome the deficiencies of unsound organization or lack of managerial or leadership ability on the part of an executive. So long as a crutch is available, there will be little systematic investigation of the underlying weakness or attempt to rectify it.

If the executive is absent from the job a large part of the time, there is a seeming need for an assistant to cover home base for him while he is away.

There are two alternatives that have advantages over the use of assistants in covering the principal's absence. First, the manager's job can be organized so that his personal travel is held to a minimum. When absence is unavoidable, the manager is better advised to appoint a subordinate manager to take over temporarily for him, rather than to install an assistant. This will provide an unequaled opportunity for the subordinate manager to shoulder, even if temporarily, the full burden of the top spot.

More Problems

Further problems in the use of assistants should be noted. In many cases, the assistant acts in a one-over-one relationship with his chief. All communications and directions go through the assistant. As a result, the principal may be blocked from his subordinates and quickly lose touch with what is going on. At the same time, the assistant may exercise a great deal of power which should be vested in his principal.

A dangerous situation may also occur when the line assistant becomes a "crown prince" and has first priority on his principal's job. Where this is the case, promotion opportunities are minimized and the interest and initiative of others on the team tend to be dampened.

The proper time to use an assistant is when a manager is so overburdened that he must secure help, or when he personally requires specialized counsel that is not needed by the organization at large. In cases of overload, a manager should carefully examine the work he is doing to make sure that he cannot get the same help from a specialized staff department available to all managers.

Cautions

Assistants should be careful in exercising authority. There is nothing so upsetting or disconcerting to a manager than to receive orders from an assistant who may or may not be speaking for his principal. This danger can be avoided by spelling out very clearly to the organization at large the specific responsibility and authority of each assistant.

Assistants can be useful in carrying out special assignments or projects which are outside the scope of the regular organization. When a manager is scheduled to be promoted, retired, or transferred, he may find it advantageous to appoint a line assistant five or six months before the move is to take place, and from this position gradually work his second-in-command into full responsibility.

SUMMARY

Organization relationships are the rules established to ensure effective teamwork among people working together. The staff and line relationship is most important. The line is the command relationship. It identifies those persons who are accountable for final results and therefore have authority to make decisions with respect to those results. The staff relationship identifies those individuals who provide advice and service in the accomplishment of objectives. There are two kinds of staff: specialized and personal. Specialized staff provides help to managers in specialized areas of work, such as accounting, personnel, purchasing, and so forth. Specialized staff positions act as internal consultants, helping managers with their specialized problems. They provide common services, doing work for managers that they cannot perform effectively for themselves. Staff groups provide functional leadership, aid in management, and provide for audit and inspection of specialized activities. Personal staff refers to all types of assistants. Here we have line assistants who serve only one principal and are broad enough in scope to take over all of his responsibilities when required. Staff assistants are more limited in scope and do not take the principal's job at any time. Need for assistants should be analyzed carefully to ensure effective utilization.

PART FOUR

Management Leading

> *You can buy a man's time. You can buy a man's physical presence in a given place. You can even buy a measured number of skilled muscular motions per hour or day. But you cannot buy enthusiasm. You cannot buy initiative. You cannot buy loyalty. You have to* earn *those things.* CLARENCE FRANCIS, GENERAL FOODS CORP.

DEFINITIONS

The Function of Management Leading

The work a manager performs to cause people to take effective action.

The Activities of Leading

Management Decision Making: the work a manager performs to arrive at conclusions and judgments.

Management Communicating: the work a manager performs to create understanding.

Motivating: the work a manager performs to inspire, encourage, and impel people to take required action.

Selecting People: the work a manager performs to choose people for positions in the organization.

Developing People: the work a manager performs to help people improve their knowledge, attitudes, and skills.

THE LOGIC OF LEADING

Management leading is work. It is the exercise of specific skills which are directed at getting other people to act. Since people are

239

governed most largely by their emotions, this work of leading tends to have the greatest emotional content of all the management functions.

In leading, a manager must do the things necessary to get people to carry out established plans and to act within the limits defined by the organization. Since virtually all action is precipitated by decisions, the *kind* of decisions the manager makes and the *way* he makes them will have a great deal to do with what people do and how willingly they undertake it.

Plans, organization, controls, and action itself depend upon *understanding*. For this reason we introduce a new element into conventional concepts of communication and define it as the process of securing understanding. Since the people he selects will either make of him a heel or a hero, communication is of tremendous significance to the manager. Often left to staff groups, the creation of understanding warrants the personal attention of every manager.

People, by and large, use only a small part of their potential capacity. Therefore, it follows that the manager who can help his people to improve their skills is, at the same time, enhancing his own potential and performance. Often neglected, the vital work of developing people is a critical aspect of scientific leadership.

Even the best mechanism will not operate without a good motor. Motivation is the motor for the management process. The manager who knows how to get people to work hard because they find interest and challenge in the work they do and not because they are driven to it has passed the greatest test—both emotional and logical—of the scientific manager.

In our study of leading, we find that a preliminary question that causes great perplexity and gives rise to much dissension is that of the kind of person a manager should be if he is to be a good leader. Should he have a particular type of personality? Should he be democratic or authoritarian?

IS THERE A LEADERSHIP PERSONALITY?

The literature of leadership is replete with profiles of the "ideal" leader. Presumably, he is dynamic, controlled, tolerant, self-motivated, harmonious, and many other things. The paragon often depicted probably does not exist. Managers, like everybody else, suffer the imperfections of humanity. They must learn to lead with the personalities they have.

Our research shows that different types of personalities can perform effectively the work of management, just as persons with widely varying personalities can be effective doctors, engineers, and lawyers. This assumes, of course, that these personality characteristics are within some reasonable limits of normality.

While we do not minimize the fact that an effective leader must have the necessary vigor and personal strength to make others on the team *want* to follow him, it is clear that the most desirable type of leadership will vary with the characteristics of the group being led. A squad of new recruits in the military will do best under a strong, demanding first sergeant. A group of highly competent scientists would bridle under this kind of leadership and resist it. The manager needs to try to understand how personalities mesh or conflict in a business situation and to match varying personalities so that they can work together as an effective, harmonious team.

THE STYLE OF LEADERSHIP

The *style* of leadership is important. Basic personality types are not to be changed easily. The manager must learn to live with the kind of person he is and find others who can work with him. However, no matter what his personality type, the manager can regulate, to a considerable extent, the *style* of leadership he employs. Here the basic questions are: Should he try to be an authoritarian or a democratic leader? Is the best approach the velvet glove or the iron hand? Should he make decisions and keep people in line by pressure, both overt and subtle? Or should the manager be democratic? Should he give people the greatest possible degree of personal freedom?

These questions have been the subject of much study and two points of view have developed, with many shadings in between. To some, the authoritarian type of leader is undesirable. He decides what his team is to do, develops the plans he wants followed with little or no reference to other members of his team, establishes policy, and directs people in their work, telling them what to do, how to do it, and with whom to work.

As a more desirable leadership type we are often given the democratic leader, who is characterized by the ability to give to the people who report to him the authority to make virtually all decisions governing their own actions. He moderates but does not command, listens but rarely voices his own ideas. The role of the democratic leader becomes that of a catalyst. He helps the members of his team to know and understand themselves He does not initiate but finds out what his people want. He does not decide but helps his people decide for him.

According to this viewpoint, if the supposed strictures of formal organization are removed, presumably the members of any group will have the capacity to solve their own problems and can be depended upon to do so. Given their heads, this viewpoint holds, the decisions arrived at by the group members are usually the best decisions.

Theoretically, this viewpoint can be defended. People *should* be more understanding and tolerant than they are. We *should* be able to secure our satisfactions by giving more, receiving less. We *should* be able to trust the other person always to be fair and honest. But the real world being what it is, there are both logical and human errors in this thinking.

The Logical Error

If we place people together in a group, reason dictates that a leader is needed to do certain work for the group as a whole. Otherwise, the individual members will not be able to work most effectively together on a continuing basis. As we have established, this work involves over-all leading, organizing, planning, and controlling. We have seen that the members of the group cannot do these things for themselves because they do not have the objectivity, perspective, and understanding necessary to see the total picture, as it involves both themselves and other groups within the organization. There has been no validated experiment or actual occurrence which gives us reason to believe that extreme permissiveness and abdication of leadership over the long term by the manager will result in efficient group action in a practical situation. Throughout history, we can find no successful example of pure communism practiced and sustained over the long term.

The Human Error

The permissive philosophy assumes that people do not want to be held accountable, that they are reluctant to face up to a task, to overcome hardship, to discipline themselves to work within the close bounds of an organized endeavor. There is an obvious fallacy to this. Look at any sport, for example. Here, the members participate on the team for the satisfaction they get from the group effort. Each member wants to know the rules; he wants to carry out his part of the over-all play; he expects to be called to account and to be coached until he reaches a high degree of proficiency. The good team player looks to the captain for firm, yet positive, direction.

Debatable also is the proposition that people cannot be held accountable for their mistakes, omissions, or sins because they have been driven to them by their environment, childhood influences, or the boss. The overemphasis upon group dynamics and "democracy" in leadership can easily become an enervating and belittling concept. Man was created to fulfill himself. He is tempered by struggle and trial. He learns to discipline himself so that he may grow and progress. It is an immutable law of life that the strong survive, the weak perish.

One great threat to our modern civilization is our rationalizing of failure and weakness to the point that more time and attention are devoted to excusing failure than are devoted to positive moves to strengthen the weak, to help average people become strong, and strong people become outstanding. The promise of permissiveness is that the weak eventually shall inherit the earth.

The Middle Way

The professional manager has recognized the potential deficiencies of both the authoritarian and the democratic approach. He adopts an approach to motivation based upon the assumption that people are human first. People work because they want to fulfill themselves in their work and in their accomplishment. A man expects to carry his load. He knows he needs guidance and leadership and looks for it. Because he is human, he expects this leadership to be of a type that recognizes his human characteristics, that encourages and supports but does not coddle him. The middle way of the professional manager is to help people make the most of themselves. He uses autocratic and democratic methods both, as the situation requires.

Variations

An effective professional manager varies his style of leadership to suit the needs of his team. The greater the instability of the team he leads and the less his followers are willing to put the needs of the group above their own, the more authority the leader must exert to secure cooperative effort. When his group is sufficiently cohesive to work together as an integrated whole with a common purpose, the manager can turn more decision making over to it. He can then become more permissive and "democratic." We must not forget here that the process of group decision making in itself is a unifying force. The more he delegates, the more the manager finds it possible to delegate.

Principle of Democratic Potential

The degree of effective democracy tends to vary with the maturity and cohesiveness of the group.

We can permit people to govern themselves only when the group as a whole is capable of acting *as a group* with unity and consistency.

This means that the individual members must be indoctrinated in the purposes and culture of the group; they must be educated in its policies and procedures; and they must understand and accept its over-all objectives and programs. To the extent that these conditions do not pre-

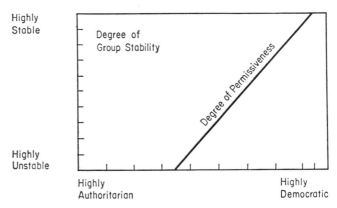

FIG. 20-1. Authoritarian and democratic leadership.

vail, leadership force must be exercised to hold the group together. We show this schematically in Figure 20-1.

Developing Stability

The manager can help to develop a greater degree of stability in the group he leads through education, and by providing for close interaction. Indoctrination is vitally important to get people to understand what they and their group are trying to become.

People need to *learn* the skills of working effectively together. This calls for education. In every organization, knowledge must be acquired, attitudes must be developed, skills must be learned before real teamwork can exist. This *may* occur fortuitously. It is greatly accelerated by conscious education.

Most companies look upon education as a tool for developing such skills as selling, producing, or managing. This comes far short of its true potential. Education should have as a first purpose instruction in the traditions and accomplishments of the organization. People *want* to belong to something bigger than they are, to belong to an aggregate that can accomplish far beyond their individual capacity.

We can help to build stability and integration by requiring people to work closely together. This close interaction tends to act as an abrasive in wearing down points of difference and potential antagonism. It will help to develop personal friendships and to force out quickly those individuals who cannot work effectively with the team.

Is Leading Enough?

We have seen that a leader is a person who guides and directs others. A manager is a leader who specializes in the work best designed to enable people to work effectively together for the end results they *want* to achieve.

Many excellent leaders are poor managers. An outstanding manager is necessarily a good leader. To put it another way, a manager is a good leader who has also become expert in the work of planning, organizing, and controlling.

Important as it is to energize people, to make them want to work hard and productively, it is equally important to make sure that the efforts of the whole team are purposeful, unified, and efficient. When we organize, plan, and control, we are establishing the framework and mechanism which help people to work effectively and productively together. Here we provide the guides to future action, a rational arrangement of the work to be done, and a means of checking up to make sure that the proper results are accomplished.

The initiative, decisiveness, drive, energy, and other personal qualities that make a manager a capable leader are essential also in accomplishing the other parts of the management job. Leadership is not enough. Management is a process, a total pattern made up of many different but interrelated activities. To treat the components of this total process as isolated entities is to lose the whole picture; to confuse one with the other is to confound our understanding of the whole.

THE COMPUTER AND LEADING

Automation will have a significant impact upon people and upon the ability of managers to get results through and with people. In examining the various activities of leading, it is well to note first that the computer will be able to perform a great deal of management work of planning, control, and organization, but to a much smaller degree will it be able to replace human effort in leading.

We shall probably always need a human brain to provide for initiation, for the creative spark that leads to new and improved ways of doing things. But within the framework of established knowledge, the computer will be able to assist markedly in analyzing techniques of management. Even more radical and effective automation devices than the computer will be invented. Even greater changes will occur. But these changes can be used effectively only at the rate the people involved can understand and accept them. The transformation of organized endeavors will be evolutionary and accumulative and keyed to the relatively gradual pace of human acceptance. For this reason, there will be, for the next generations as for the past, a time lag between the availability of these more efficient machines and their most effective utilization.

The lag will result from the same factors that slowed acceptance of the steam engine, the typewriter, and the nuclear submarine—in brief, the humanity of human beings.

SUMMARY

Leading is the work a manager performs to get people to take required action. Leading is the energizing function that makes planning, control, and organizing possible. In studying what it takes to lead, we find that there is no one best management personality. Different people and situations require different approaches. The proper blend of authoritarian and democratic leadership knowingly applied is best. Automation will have a strong effect upon leadership but the key fact to remember is that the computer cannot be more effective than the human beings who guide and control it.

CHAPTER 21

Management Decision Making

> *An executive is a man who decides; sometimes he de-*
> *cides right, but always he decides.* JOHN H. PATTER-
> SON, NATIONAL CASH REGISTER CO.

DEFINITIONS

Management Decision Making: the work a manager performs to arrive at conclusions and judgments.

Conclusion: a terminal point in thinking arrived at from considera-tion of established premises.

Judgment: the verdict arrived at after weighing of evidence.

THE NATURE OF A MANAGEMENT DECISION

A management decision is an intellectual end point—the culmination of a series of mental activities that leads to a conclusion or judgment. This may take place consciously or unconsciously; it may or may not result in action.

Many managers find it difficult to look upon decision making as con-scious work, subject to principles and rules. The professional man-ager knows that a sound decision results from the systematic application of mental effort. He recognizes that decision making is a skill which is made up of separate elements and which can be learned as can any other skill. Just as the firing of a rifle involves more than the touching of the trigger, the making of a decision involves the preparation and make-ready steps as well as the point of decision. In the same man-ner that a rifle may be flung to shoulder, hastily aimed, poorly trig-gered, but yet luckily hit the mark, so may a decision be poorly made and yet result in satisfactory action.

Many an enterprise has discovered that the successful decisions of the past may become a rut in which are buried the undertakings of tomorrow. This often is not for lack of logic; in retrospect, past success usually seems logical. Rather, it results from failure to rethink and redecide continuing problems in terms of new conditions.

The Underwood Corporation, for example, made a typewriter that was unequaled mechanically and dominated its field for some forty years. In the 1930s Underwood was offered an opportunity to manufacture a new and, at that time, unconventional machine—an electric typewriter. Surveying its position of leadership, its profitable growth, and the sterling reputation of its product, Underwood decided that the precedent it had already set was the best possible blueprint for the future. After Underwood turned it down, International Business Machines bought the new typewriter.

Standing resolutely on its record of accomplishment, Underwood tried to relive its years of past glory. But demand changed and the company lost out in its markets. Late in the 1950s, the firm sought to merge with a stronger enterprise and finally was acquired in 1959 by Ing. C. Olivetti & S.A. In the meantime, the International Business Machines Corporation, following a policy of bold but sound innovation, has made the electric typewriter an important asset of its business.

THE ALLEN PRINCIPLES OF DECISION MAKING

Skill in making reasoned decisions can best be developed if we will keep in mind the following principles of decision making. Based on close observation and analysis of the methods of a large number of effective decision makers in business, government, and the military, we have stated these principles as practical tools for making more effective decisions.

Principle of Definition

A logical decision can be made only if the real problem is first defined.
The essence of sound decision making is that the decision reached should provide the best solution to the problem under consideration. Often as not, however, managers make decisions without having clearly in mind the problem they are trying to solve. This is as haphazard and illogical as boosting a space ship into the stratosphere without deciding whether we want it to go to the moon or to Mars.

What happens if we take action without knowing the end result we want to accomplish? For one thing, we have no basis for making best use of people, materials, tools, and money. Instead of purposeful and guided action, we tend to run off in all directions at once. If we don't know where we want to go, we can reach a desirable and profitable goal only by happenstance. And even after we get there, we have no means of proving logically that this *is* the result we want. Once we define our real problem, we may discover that the action we have taken in the past is inadequate.

To illustrate, for decades many retailers assumed that the key problem in selling merchandise was to maintain a suitable profit margin. This was so obvious that nobody troubled to look further. Furniture dealers, as a case in point, most often set their sales price at double the cost of the merchandise they bought. The problem here appeared to be: How to maintain a profit margin of 100 per cent? Appliances, electric razors, and watches were priced in terms of a similar identification of the problem.

The solution involved low sales volume, high costs, and high percentage margin of profit. To maintain the markup, retailers were required to honor the practice; legislation to enforce it was pushed; and many and varied solutions were put into effect with vigor, and at great expense. In the mid-1950s, Stephen Masters of Masters, Inc., a New York department store chain, decided that the real problem was not how to maintain the markup but how to make more profits in dollars. His solution to the real problem as he identified it was high sales volume, low costs, and low profit margins. Put into vigorous action by Masters, the E. J. Korvette chain, and others, this solution gave impetus to the discount store—an innovation that is now reshaping the retail sales industry.

Principle of Adequate Evidence

A logical decision must be valid in terms of the evidence on which it is based.

A management decision should be supported and reinforced by the facts and assumptions upon which it is based. Ask "why" in testing any part of the decision, and there should be facts, or reasonable inferences drawn from those facts, that will support the conclusion itself. Given the facts, many decisions will tend to make themselves. Without a basis of fact, logical decisions are impossible.

In spite of the common sense of this requirement, managers often make decisions which are insupportable if the evidence is examined even casually. Typical is the case of a vice president of a Chicago food company. Seeking a manager for the firm's international operations, he interviewed several likely applicants. One in particular caught his fancy. This prospect spoke several languages. He had a fresh, clean-cut appearance and was poised and forceful in his presentation. He spoke convincingly of several responsible jobs he had filled in the international field in the past.   Impressed with his qualifications, the vice president hired him.

In the course of a routine check of his previous employers, the personnel department found, a few days later, that the new employee had been fired from one company for taking a bribe from a customer, from another because of questionable morals, and he had left the third company because of a large discrepancy which showed up in the auditing of his personal account.   As Supreme Court Justice Louis Brandeis has said, "More erroneous conclusions are due to lack of information than to errors in judgment."

Principle of Identity

Facts may appear to differ, depending upon the point of view and the point in time from which they are observed.

Each of us tends to see the same facts differently.   Our backgrounds, personalities, and prejudices help to change and color our understanding of the people and things with which we deal.   Because what we see and comprehend is vivid and clear to us, we often fail to take into account the differences that result from the other person's point of view. Since management decisions are made to influence the actions of others, these differences in point of view must be anticipated and carefully evaluated.

We can easily demonstrate that, observed from a different perspective or point of view, the same physical object or situation will appear to be different to different people.   Talk about "cancer" to a physician and he sees it from the medical and therapeutic point of view.   "Are there metastases?"   "What is the blood count?" he wants to know.   His interest is logical and objective.   From the point of view of the afflicted patient, the same facts appear quite different.   "Am I going to die?" "Is there anything I can do to cure it?"   His point of view is subjective and emotional.   The closer we are to a situation, the less likely we are to see all sides of it.   If our point of view is limited, we are more likely to act in terms of emotion and opinion.

Because of our particular point of view, we may make decisions which are plausible and even logical in terms of the facts as we see them.   Examined in broader perspective, the same decision may prove to be diametrically opposite to what the situation requires.

In one Dallas, Texas, company, for example, an electrical specialty division manager found that expenses were considerably outrunning the anticipated profit.   An extended session with the division controller convinced him that the only recourse was to slash expenses by 10 per cent across the board.   Before making the decision, however, he talked with the sales manager.   From his point of view, the sale manager thought that the problem was due to the lack of a sufficient number of salesmen to cover a rapidly growing new territory. "Our overhead can support a 25 per cent larger sales force," the sales manager said, "and if we had that much more volume, we'd be well past our break-even point, and our profit picture would be greatly improved." Careful study from all sides pointed to the need for upgrading certain product features and building up the sales force. More investment was indicated, not a slash in expenditure. A careful, setp-by-step utilization of additional budgeted funds proved the logical premise correct.

Failure to make allowances for these differences in understanding can result in some unusual consequences. In one southern United States city, for example, a market test of a new line of ladies' toiletries was made by selling the product in drugstores and supermarkets. Offered at 90 cents per jar, the "secret ingredient face cream" met with a poor reception. Later, sold door-to-door by a sales crew of handsome young men, the identical product sold like hot cakes at $2.75.

Commenting on the matter later, a local minister who had the promotion brought to his attention labeled the whole approach "unethical and dishonest." The sales manager, however, was firm in his belief that this was good business. "We are not just selling face cream," he said, "we are selling a mental attitude toward beauty. If paying a higher price for face cream makes a woman feel she is becoming more beautiful, the psychological 'lift' she gets, the beneficial effects of an improved attitude toward her physical and emotional health, are worth many times what she pays. The extra profit we earn is a reward for thinking of a way to give her this benefit she otherwise would not receive."

One of the most difficult problems confronting a manager is to look at all sides of a problem with sufficient objectivity. He needs to see it in its true perspective and meaning. To do this, he must stay within his management role. If he becomes too deeply involved in the problems of other members of the team, he will tend to assume their point of view and lose his capacity to assess properly the needs of his superior, of others on his own level, and those of staff departments in evaluating the situation as a whole.

The tunnel vision that narrows our viewpoint is often evident in our tendency to judge the boss. From our own point of view, we can quickly see the discrepancies in the decisions he makes. However, if we talk with him long enough to discover the pressures and influences brought to bear upon him by *his* boss and by other agencies inside and outside the company, we often see the same matter in quite a different light. As Mark Twain put it, "When I was a boy of fourteen, my father was so ignorant I could hardly stand to have the old man around.

But when I got to be twenty-one, I was astonished at how much he had learned in seven years."

A PRACTICAL APPROACH TO LOGICAL THINKING

Logic is not always practical; in fact, logical thinking does not necessarily lead us to the truth. However, logical thinking provides us with the most systematic way of arriving at decisions which have the greatest *probability* of being valid and even true.

MANAGEMENT SEQUENCE FOR LOGICAL THINKING

Scientific thinking is logical thinking. For the manager, the same basic approach is mandatory if he is to maximize his successes and minimize his errors. To make the logical thinking process a practical tool that can be utilized effectively by practicing managers, we have developed a modification of the scientific method that lends itself more readily to solving administrative problems.

The Decision-making Sequence

Adapted for management use, the logical thinking process is made up of six steps.

1. *What Is the Apparent Problem?* When we first see a problem situation, or when it is first presented to us, the problem may seem quite apparent. Most often we plunge ahead, eager to come to grips with the difficulty and to get action under way. Many times, however, after we have put forth considerable effort, we discover that we have only been nibbling at the fringes of the problem or even working on the wrong problem.

In solving problems, we tend to observe symptoms arising from underlying causes. Often, we jump to conclusions based on the superficial view. When this is the case, we will probably end up with treating the symptoms only and will never come to grips with the basic problem.

The problem that confronts many businesses in diversifying is typical. Seized with the urge to expand, many a company has set about acquiring other businesses without a clear-cut idea of what it is trying to accomplish. The top management of one New Jersey metals company, for example, undertook a program of diversification with great vigor and enthusiasm. In rapid succession, a footwear company, a clothing manufacturer, a tie company, and a gift distributor were acquired. Within two years, the parent company found it did not have the skills or interests to manage this unrelated assortment. It sold out its acquisitions at a considerable loss.

How can we avoid the mistake of treating the symptoms instead of the disease, of finding a good solution to the wrong problem? Observe a physician, and the answer is clear. If a patient comes in complaining of stomach-ache, the physician does not reach for the paregoric. That spontaneous decision might be fatal. Instead, he questions and probes, searching for facts.

So with the manager. To be sure we have nailed down the *real* problem, we look upon our first identification of the problem as tentative. Before plunging to a solution, we stop and gather the facts necessary to identify or confirm the problem. We test to make sure this is the core or central issue, then proceed in our analysis with assurance.

2. *What Are the Facts?* If we are to identify the problem precisely, we must first examine the circumstances surrounding it. This calls for collection and analysis of available facts, determination of what the facts *mean,* and consideration of assumptions based upon these facts.

Data gathering should be a sharply focused effort. It is rarely possible or advisable to collect *all* of the facts bearing on the problem. Some information may be more difficult or costly to secure than the situation warrants.

Since the time available for fact gathering is limited, it is wise to determine in advance what information we really need, and in what priority we require it. Otherwise, we may find ourselves arriving at conclusions based on large amounts of detail, while we have little information on the most significant aspects of the problem. This becomes particularly important with electronic data processing, for the computer will process all the information fed to it. Just as we can multiply the speed and accuracy with which meaningful information is processed and reported, we can also increase manyfold the flood of unimportant detail which inundates more than it informs.

Facts by themselves are not enough. We must determine what the facts mean, what special significance they have in the problem we are considering. Facts are history. We need to make logical inferences about the future on the basis of the facts if we want to develop creative solutions. In particular, we need to infer from the facts in our possession what will probably happen in the future if current events are carried through to their logical conclusions.

In fact gathering, we can come to focus on the most essential information by investigating systematically each of these decision factors:

THE SITUATION FACTOR. What happened, and precisely how did it happen? Here, we establish a clear-cut picture of the situation as it now exists. So far as possible we rely upon firsthand evidence. The information we gather at this early stage is historical. We should examine the situation from every viewpoint, and we should be satisfied only with an objective and detailed statement of what has actually occurred. This should be acceptable to all who are concerned with solving the problem.

THE CAUSATIVE FACTOR. *Why* did the problem occur? Will the factors that caused the present situation remain constant or will they change in the future? What significance does this have? Facts are useful tools in getting at the causes of problems. Most executives use their facts for an altogether different purpose, that of assessing the results they want to achieve. This can give rise to expensive mistakes.

For example, one large Middle Western metalworking company found its accident rate creeping up, costs for lost time, machine stoppage, first aid, and hospital care increasing. Intent on improving safety, the company instituted a company-wide safety campaign, bought a poster service to make everybody safety conscious, and put all foremen through safety-training refresher courses. Accidents still continued. Renewed investigation of the causes of the accidents showed that 29 per cent of the accidents were occurring in one department using high-speed machine tools, and that over 45 per cent of the machine operators were "moonlighting." They had taken advantage of temporary job offers from a competing metalworking firm a half-mile distant. This firm was offering high pay for short-time night jobs so that it could finish a large contract on schedule. Once the facts were in and properly assessed, the nature of the problem and the best decision became clear.

The causes of the problems will appear to differ, depending upon our sources of information. For this reason, the more different sources we can tap in securing data, the more varied the viewpoints consulted, the more accurate and objective the information is likely to be.

THE PEOPLE FACTOR. Who is involved? In what way do the people affect the situation? Consider the point of view of each person who is important to the problem and determine what special significance this may have. Anticipate what may happen in the future because of the involvement of these people.

People change and their varying interests and preferences may have a great impact on the problem under consideration. Put one or more persons into a problem situation and it acquires unique features. We can solve the problem effectively only if we know and understand the people and can make logical assumptions as to their probable behavior.

We tend to lose sight of the importance of people as automation and mechanization become a way of life. However, so long as one human being is involved, our assumptions must take into account the people factor.

As a case in point, the Atomic Energy Commission, in considering the problem of how to safeguard the operation of atomic reactors for commercial use, built in automatic safety devices until its accident record was nearly perfect. It appeared that an automatic reactor was as safe as any conventional power plant. Then an unanticipated human factor entered the picture. At the Arco, Idaho, atomic reactor testing station, the operator who controlled the operation by pushing the buttons on a console panel pushed the wrong button. The reaction ran out of control, the reactor was wrecked. No life was lost, but a new safety device had to be devised that would protect the machine from the people who operated it.

THE PLACE FACTOR. Where did the problem occur? Does the location have any significance? Are future changes expected which will affect the place factor? In making decisions and solving problems, we sometimes forget that the United States is not Japan, New York is not Los Angeles. This misapprehension can lead to faulty conclusions.

As a case in point, the Los Angeles Times-Mirror Company had in mind the typical metropolitan, New York-style, suburb-oriented reader when it launched its afternoon tabloid, the *Mirror,* in 1948. Visualize this potential reader and you see him in his millions, rushing home from work on the subway or suburban train, eagerly snatching glimpses at the small, breezy paper he has picked up on his dash to the train, and reading as he hangs to a strap or is wedged between two neighbors.

This picture was good for New York. But the anticipated public transportation facilities did not materialize and the commuter who used public transit in New York became an automobile driver charging precariously through congested traffic on the freeways of Los Angeles. Where competition was somewhat stabilized in New York, in Los Angeles some twenty-seven daily newspapers proliferated, almost all of which were and are evening newspapers. Add to this 170 weekly and semiweekly newspapers, plus the then three other metropolitan dailies and seven television stations, and it was clear at the time that what was good for New York was not necessarily good for Los Angeles.

More than this, the prospective *Times* reader was better educated and he earned more. His family interests had broadened from local gossip, crime, and divorce sensationalism to a wider and more mature interest in the state, the nation, and the world. Studying price disadvantages and spiraling costs, the *Times* management closed out the *Mirror* and proceeded to stress the news and editorial content preferred by their prospective audience in the new metropolitan and suburban orientation of Southern California.

THE TIME FACTOR. When did the situation occur? Has the time factor particular significance? How will the time factor affect the decision we reach and the action we will carry out? Just as the nature of a problem may vary because of its physical location, it may also have different implications because of the time period in which it occurs. Time changes all.

For example, Lever Brothers sells Lifebuoy soap in part on the basis of its clean, antiseptic smell. Twenty years ago, a "clean, antiseptic smell" had a pronounced germicidal odor. Today, as epitomized in the new smell of Lifebuoy, it has the light fragrance of an afternoon breeze wafted from spice-laden fields.

Decisions made in terms of the precedent set by the successful action of yesterday, or ten years ago, may be as outmoded and inapplicable as a horse and buggy on a superhighway. Because our orientation to time is so intensely personal, we often overlook this important factor in making assumptions on which to base decisions.

3. *What Is the Real Problem?* After we have thoroughly digested the facts and the inferences we can draw from the facts, we are in position to review the problem as we first identified it. We may find, in view of the facts, that we had only identified symptoms of a deeper, more fundamental problem. Or we may now be satisfied that the problem, as we first saw it, is really the central issue.

As a case in point, the Upjohn Company, a leading ethical pharmaceutical house, faced the question of how to sell the largest volume of its ethical drugs at the best profit. Should it cultivate drug wholesalers by offering them a lower wholesale price? This would solve the immediate problem by encouraging wholesalers to stock more Upjohn pharmaceuticals. But the end result did not lie in the wholesalers. This first part of this pipeline leading from company to customer was large, but it could be filled rapidly.

How about drugstores and hospitals? Drugstores and hospitals stocked what doctors prescribed. The end result depended upon what doctors preferred. The real problem was how to get doctors to prescribe Upjohn products as frequently as possible. If the doctor ordered, the retail druggist, hospital, and wholesaler would all fall into line. Upjohn organized a sales force of some 1,000 detail men, primarily university-trained. These salesmen make a million calls a year on physicians. Armed with the latest valid technical data, they give doctors up-to-date and useful information on products like new steroids, antidiabetics, and antibiotics, and make Upjohn a leader in its field.

If Upjohn had seen its problem as selling to wholesalers, it would have been focusing on only 7 per cent of its market. If it had concentrated on hospitals, it would have reached 13 per cent. By catering to the special needs of 240,000 doctors and the 50,000 retail druggists who serve them, the company reached the heart of its problem.

As much time and effort as necessary should be invested in identifying the basic underlying problem. Our solution of the problem will probably not be better than its identification. If we do not know what is wrong, we can hardly take positive steps to correct it. The real problem is the key problem in the situation which, if solved, will satisfy us both over the short and the long term. In coming to grips with the key problem, we should keep in mind several factors.

THE LIMITS OF THE PROBLEM. We need to identify the limits within which the problem is to be solved if we are to focus our efforts upon the key factors involved. Many times, in a given situation, we try to solve most of the problems of the world. Much wasted effort may occur if we try to solve problems for other people or try to extend our solutions beyond the limits required by the situation. At the same time, we should keep in mind the four-way aspect of every management problem—its relationship to others on the team, to our own superior, and to others on our own level, as well as to ourselves. A manager's accountability extends beyond a blind and selfish consideration of the interests of himself and his own unit. A professional manager considers his problems and solutions in terms of their implications for the company as a whole.

TIMING. The right solution at the wrong time is no better than the wrong solution at the right time. We can give full consideration to the time element if we make sure we identify the problem as it now exists and then project it as far into the future as we can to see what its long-term implications will be. The best possible solution for today's problem may be the worst answer for the continuation of that problem as it will appear a year or two from now. An important skill of the professional manager is the ability to distinguish between the short-term and long-term aspects of the same problem.

RELATED PROBLEMS. In most problem situations, we find a constellation of problems, one of which is central, the others ancillary. Of these, probably one will seem the most urgent and will demand first attention. This often is the fire, blazing merrily. We can see it plainly. It requires immediate and forceful action. Action should be taken, but we must make sure that the action reaches deep enough and is intensive enough to get at the cause of the fire—the real problem—as well as put out the blaze. Otherwise, new fires will spring up continually.

Fire fighting generally involves operating action. Ferreting out the longer-range implications of the problem requires management action; that is, a renewed cycle of organizing, leading, planning, and controlling.

ONE PROBLEM, MANY CAUSES. In getting at real problems, we frequently discover that there are many reasons why the problem occurred. Often, there is no simple cause and effect relationship. The danger here is that we will come to focus on each causative factor and try to solve it as a separate problem in its own right. This may encourage us to take prompt and vigorous action. But the noise and bustle, while reassuring, may prevent us from coming to grips with the basic issue.

MANY PROBLEMS, MANY ANSWERS. Our identification of the problem and our statement of it will tend to vary, depending upon the point of view, background, personality, and experience that we bring to bear. Several people looking at the same problem will probably come up with different statements of the problem and different solutions. Surprisingly enough, all may be correct.

Our great need in decision making is to recognize that *our* decisions are not necessarily the only right and perfect ones, that it is entirely possible for others to arrive at different decisions that will work for them just as well as or better than ours. The criterion should be: Is it logical? not: Is it the decision *I* would make?

4. *What Are the Possible Solutions?* Now we have clearly identified the real problem. At the same time, we have developed a clear picture of the end results we want to accomplish. At this point, we can profitably direct our efforts toward ways and means of attaining this goal. If we have done a good job, the answer may appear obvious. But even the obvious answer may be improved. Our need, now, is to consider and analyze as many possibilities as we can develop, including the obvious ones, and to select the best of these as our decision. In developing the possible solutions, the following points should be kept in mind:

NO ACTION AS AN ALTERNATIVE. We sometimes think that if we do nothing about a problem the decision will thereby be delayed. In reality, events move and the decision is made for us. To do nothing *is* a decision. The only question is whether it is a conscious or an unconscious decision. It is far better to take this alternative into account and weigh its possibilities than to let events decide for us.

If sufficient data are not available or if an alternative cannot be developed quickly enough, it may be wise to temporize. Use this time, however, for positive action. Make sure that all concerned know that the decision will be postponed for a definite period of time. Set a new deadline to ensure that the decision will be made within the time available.

SECURING PARTICIPATION. Other people on the team, staff specialists, and others on our own level may be a fertile source of ideas and suggestions in developing alternative solutions. If we will take the time and make the effort, we can generally develop ideas that will encompass many differing viewpoints in the problem being considered. The larger the number of people who know about the problem and the more they recognize its complexities and implications, the better able they will be to put forward suggestions and the more effective they will be in carrying out the solution when it is finally made.

Group participation can bring many minds to bear on a problem, thus stimulating and modifying individual thought. Where one man may produce a brilliant skeletal idea, another may excel at refining and implementing it. One New York manufacturing company, for example, saved $196,000 by turning one problem over to a group to discuss. A plant superintendent and two foremen were asked to analyze plans for a conveyor system, for which $200,000 had already been appropriated. One member of the group was asked to assume that the plan proposed was all wrong and to suggest an alternate which the others, in turn, were to criticize. In the end, they emerged with a conveyor system that cost approximately $4,000 to install.

USING BRAINSTORMING. The techniques of brainstorming can be used effectively at this stage of problem solving. Brainstorming is carried out in a group meeting. First, all members are fully informed as to the facts and the real problem. Then, each is encouraged to offer his suggestions and ideas rapidly and without restraint. The aim at this stage is to get as many ideas as possible written down without critical review. Then, we can go over the lists, either by ourselves or with the help of the group. We can eliminate those which are obviously unsuitable and come to focus on those with real merit. These should be analyzed and given proper weight in making the over-all decision.

MAKING USE OF THE SUBCONSCIOUS. The subconscious mind can be an effective tool in developing alternative solutions. We have stored in our subconscious a great wealth of experience and ideas. Properly brought to focus, the subconscious mind may present some brilliant, intuitive insights if permitted to do its work. The trick is to fill the conscious mind as completely as possible with the problem and its implications, carry our conscious thinking through to the point of diminishing returns, then forget the problem, go for a walk, or turn to some other activity for a few hours or even days. When we come back to the problem we will probably find that new alternatives readily appear and can be incorporated into our thinking.

5. *What Is the Best Solution?* The professional manager decides, not by pulling an idea out of the air, not on the basis of hunch, but by rational selection of the best of the various alternative solutions he has analyzed and considered. This is the point of management decision.

Here, judgment is the critical faculty. Selecting the best solution requires objectivity. This is the loneliest and most demanding part of a manager's job. Looking at the total needs of his group, balancing the requirements of top management, his subordinates, and those of his own level, he must select the alternative that will give greatest promise of maximum returns to all.

The best solution can be tested before it is put into effect by carrying it through to its logical conclusion and determining whether it gives good promise of enabling us to solve the real problem we have identified. If we can make this reasonable assumption, we have the best justification for going ahead. However, in proving this out mentally, if we discover that the action we take will not logically bring us out to the result we want, probably we have not found the proper solution. When this is the case, reconsideration or further search is indicated.

6. *What Course of Action Shall We Follow?* The decision by itself is worthless unless it is put into effect. Often, we spend great time and effort arriving at a sound, logical decision; then, because we fail to provide for a means of putting the decision into action, our investment is largely dissipated. To make a decision fully effective, we should establish a thoroughly detailed course of action. Here, the following should be considered.

OBJECTIVES. What are we trying to accomplish? We should spell out our goals in measurable terms. The more participation we can get from those who are to carry out the action, the better understood and the more effective the action will be.

POLICIES. What policies apply? Virtually all decisions must be carried out within the framework of other guiding and limiting decisions made at higher levels. It is important to establish clearly the limits of action before other people are given their assignments. In some cases, over-all policy decisions have not been made. It then may be necessary to go to upper-level managers to secure the necessary primary decision.

PROGRAMS. A sound course of action contains a statement of the action necessary to attain the end results. Here, we develop the sequence and priority of the steps to be taken. If the situation is unstable or if new and unanticipated conditions are likely to arise, it may be necessary to develop alternative programs that can be put into effect in case of later developments.

SCHEDULES. Time is always an important consideration in developing a sound course of action. Whenever possible, we should specify the date for the beginning and ending of each programmed step. We should make sure our people understand that they will be held responsible for accomplishment within these time limits. Participation is most important in programming and scheduling. So far as it fits within our over-all course of action, we should encourage each individual to determine for himself what he will do and how he will do it, in order to reach the goals we have agreed upon.

PROCEDURES. Some of the work to be accomplished may have to be performed in a standardized and uniform manner. Where this is the case, we should develop and specify the procedures to be followed or make provision for using procedures already in effect.

BUDGETS. Almost always there are expense limitations within which the action must be accomplished. If people are left to themselves, they will tend to spend more money than the results warrant. We can best hold the cost down to the desired level by determining in advance what we can afford to spend in terms of people, materials, tools, and facilities. Converted into money terms, this becomes our budget. We should keep in mind that the budget is only as effective as the understanding and acceptance of the people who must live within it. It follows that a high degree of participation is a most necessary step if we wish the budget to be a useful guide.

WHAT DECISIONS SHOULD A MANAGER MAKE?

Who should make a particular decision? The theoretical and practical answers may vary widely. The availability of information, capacity of the manager, time, and other factors have their influence. However, even with these considerations, it is well to know the theoretical framework within which the manager should be able to make his own decisions.

If work is to be performed effectively, enough authority must be delegated to make the decisions necessary to carry out the job. Theoretically, authority may be delegated for all aspects of planning and control except for initiation of the work to be done and the final or implementing decisions as to the specific forecasts, objectives, programs, schedules, procedures, and policies.

Decision making may be delegated for organization structure except for initiation and final or implementing decisions dealing with the short- and long-range organization structure, and the steps to be followed in putting it into effect. The manager cannot delegate effectively his own authority for delegation or for establishing relationships.

In control, the manager can safely delegate authority for decisions in establishment of performance standards, measurement, evaluation, and performance correction, except for initiation of the activity and the final or implementing decisions in each case.

Decisions that apply only to the internal activities of his own group should be made by the manager himself, within the limitations of the planning and control framework that has been established.

Management decisions should be coordinated at the lowest possible level. When we ask our subordinates to participate in decision making, we should insist that they time, unify, and integrate their recommendations at their level before passing them on to us. We owe the same service to our own superior.

What if the decision involves our own and other groups? Here the superior will reserve the authority for the final decisions. But we can be of great service to him in reaching a sound decision. We can apprize him of the nature of the problem, secure his permission to go ahead, then prepare a sound and balanced recommendation for his review and final approval. To do this, we will want to consult with other groups, develop alternatives with them, and consider their suggestions in the recommendations we prepare for our superior. If there is disagreement on important points, the boss should know of this and should be informed of the pros and cons in each case.

To conclude our discussion of deciding, we can say that, in many ways, a decision is a management summation. Examine the decisions a manager makes and you see accurately reflected there his ability to reason, his powers of observation, his attitude toward people. His decisions spell him for what he is—positive, logical, and forward-looking, or uncertain, confused, and defensive. Great undertakings find life in sound and venturesome decisions; failure decides its own illogical and inconsistent grave.

SUMMARY

Management decisions pervade all of the functions and activities of management. Important to the making of sound management decisions is the identification of the real problem before a conclusion is sought and the accumulation of evidence upon which to base a valid decision. It is vital to remember that the facts which are gathered may appear to differ, depending upon the point of view and the point in time from which they are observed. Management decisions can best be made by following a process of logical thinking. This requires first a differentiation between the apparent and the real problem. This is accomplished by careful development of the available facts and their assessment in terms of the problem situation. Once the key problem is identified, alternatives are developed to project the possible solutions. The best of these solutions becomes the management decision, which is really a conscious choice among alternatives. The decision can be made operative only if it is carried out through a well-formulated course of action.

CHAPTER 22 *Management Motivating*

> *Lack of something to feel important about is almost the greatest tragedy a man may have.* DR. ARTHUR E. MORGAN

DEFINITIONS

Management Motivating: the work a manager performs to inspire, encourage, and impel people to take required action.

Inspire: to infuse a spirit of willingness into people to perform most effectively. People are inspired through the leader's personality, his example, and the work he does, consciously or unconsciously.

Encourage: to stimulate people to do what has to be done through praise, approval, and help.

Impel: to force or incite action by any necessary means, including compulsion, coercion, and fear, if required.

THE LOGIC OF MOTIVATING

Motivation is the work a manager performs to get people to do what has to be done. Most often the manager encourages his people; frequently he can inspire them; but when action is necessary, he sees that it is undertaken by whatever means of motivation the situation requires.

The most effective motivation is self-motivation. If we can get people to work because they *want* to, not because they are driven to it, we will secure most effective and enduring performance. Considering motivation from the rational viewpoint of professional management, we must keep in mind two key points:

1. As human beings, we are prone to weakness and errors which, intellectually, we recognize and may deplore but which, emotionally, we

263

can do little about. The human material with which a manager works is at once the weakest and the strongest of the resources available to him; the best way he can keep these assets and deficits in mind is to remember that other people tend to have as great virtues as he does himself and their weaknesses, while many, should be regarded as tolerantly as his own. The human tendency is to require of others much more than we require of ourselves.

2. Real attainment is unnatural in that it requires, to some extent, conquering ourselves. To lead effectively demands that we consider others as much as ourselves; to manage requires that we do what our minds tell us, not our emotions. Management leading can be accomplished best through the application of *logical* thought and *conscious* action.

METHODS OF MOTIVATION

What motivates people has been more a matter for conjecture than actual knowledge for most of the history of the human race. For centuries, fear and coercion were taken as the prime motivators. Man was a driven animal. He was goaded and pushed into action by physical, economic, moral, and psychological pressures. If he did not act as his leaders dictated, he could be whipped, ostracized from the community, drawn and quartered, or damned to an eternity of fiery brimstone. Since these methods forced people into the desired action with little argument and great expedition, the common belief was that fear was an excellent way to get people to do things. It was effective—up to a point. But history footnotes the disadvantages of this approach. The more people are pushed and threatened, the more they tend to resent and resist the pressure. In human affairs, every action tends to have an equal and similar reaction; force breeds more force, hate generates more hate.

Mechanistic Motivation

If people could be driven only to a point, what other means could be found to get them to work productively? The next move was to look upon man as a machine that could be made to work better. The goal, now, was to study the *way* people worked and to improve the efficiency of their movements. The assumption was that people would work more if the work was made simpler and easier. Since the end product was the amount of work completed and not the happiness or satisfaction of the people involved, this conclusion seemed logical at the time. Also, it proved effective—up to a point.

Frederick W. Taylor, a pioneer in scientific management, made some of the early discoveries in this approach while working in a steel mill.

Taylor noticed that workers were very haphazard in the methods they used. Some were inefficient in the way they handled their machines. They duplicated and retraced many of their movements, and lost a great deal of time in waste motion. On the other hand, some were direct and economical in their movements and seemed to be much more productive as a result.

Taylor undertook a systematic study of different tasks to see if he could find the one best way to perform each. In working with coal shovelers, for example, he assumed that the strongest men, who could use the largest shovels, would shovel the most coal. However, he found this did not hold true. Experimenting, he had men use shovels holding a maximum load of 34 pounds. Production started high, then tapered off. Next, he had the shovelers use shorter, smaller shovels. Finally, he found that men would consistently shovel the most coal in a day when using a shovel holding a 21-pound load. Above and below that the total fell.

By continuing such studies, Taylor was able to separate many jobs into their component parts and to train people to specialize. They became highly proficient in their individual tasks. The scientific study of methods efficiency began. It resulted in a widespread revolution. However, the emphasis was largely on the work itself. Little attention was paid to the worker. Taylor had warned of this danger, but his cautions were at first disregarded.

Eventually the limits of improvement through work study alone were reached. People could achieve high working efficiency but this, in itself, was not the whole answer. Slowdowns, strikes, apathy, and disinterest were commonplace. The moral seemed to be that machinery and processes would run no better than people *wanted* them to operate. What was the answer?

A CLUE TO A NEW APPROACH

One of the first insights came at the Hawthorne Works of the Western Electric Company. In an effort to increase the output of girls doing assembly work, Western Electric experimented by putting a number of girls to work in a room where the lighting was varied from one extreme to another. The production rates of this group were then compared to those of girls who had been left undisturbed.

Strangely enough, production went up no matter what kind of lighting was used. It should have dropped under poor lighting, but it continued to rise. Greatly puzzled at this seeming contradiction to "scientific management" principles, the company called in the great Australian sociologist, Elton Mayo. He discovered that the girls put in the test situation were so stimulated and interested by being singled out for special attention that this alone was enough to ensure increased productivity. Here was a new insight into human behavior; from it we have learned much.

THE KEY FACTOR IN MANAGEMENT MOTIVATION

For the manager, the important considerations in motivation are emotional and psychological. On the job, we can identify a vital psychological need that, more than any other, causes people to do what they do. This is the desire of each human for ego recognition and satisfaction. Each of us wants to become what he is capable of becoming; we want to feel worthwhile and to be recognized as important in our own right; we want to fulfill our interests and capabilities. As Ralph Waldo Emerson said, "Our chief want in life is somebody who shall make us do what we can."

We get this feeling of importance and fulfillment in different ways. Some of us look for attention, praise, and material rewards. The more of these we receive, the greater our satisfaction and motivation. Others, perhaps more mature, get this feeling of importance and recognition from the ability to give to others. We look for opportunities to contribute of what we have and of ourselves.

The task of a manager is to understand what gives his people this feeling of recognition and importance. Knowing this, he has the key to the mainspring that prompts high achievement.

MOTIVATION AND MONEY

Most of our actions on the job are influenced by this basic need. Often we mistake the end result for the need itself. For example, people do not work primarily for money. They work for the feeling of importance and recognition they can buy with money. The amount of money a person receives determines the kind of house he lives in, the type of automobile he drives, and the other things he can buy to spell out his importance.

If he does not get it on the job, the individual may seek this recognition by devoting much time to membership in clubs and to civic and community affairs. But if he can get this feeling of recognition from the *work* he does, money may not be the most important element.

SATISFACTION FROM TEAM MEMBERSHIP

People can secure the feeling of recognition and importance they need by working with other people. To a degree, we are as important as other people make us feel. The groups to which we belong, and the satisfaction we get from our membership in these groups, become a dominant factor in our motivation. This applies particularly on the job.

If people are not organized into groups, they will form their own groups. If they do not receive the satisfactions they want from their group associations, they will become dissatisfied and will look elsewhere. A primary qualification of an effective manager is his ability to build a close-knit, effective team. If he can do this, often he can get results with his group in spite of poor pay, inadequate facilities, and other handicaps. Lacking the ability to create a team, however, the manager will be plagued continually with low morale and poor productivity.

We can conclude that the effectiveness of a manager depends in large measure upon his ability to help the members of the group of which he is a leader to satisfy their needs. To the extent that people he supervises feel that he will help them do this, they will follow him willingly and enthusiastically.

THE ALLEN PRINCIPLES OF MOTIVATION

The principles which tell us how to inspire and encourage others to highest endeavor are written large and in similar terms in most major codes of philosophy and religion. We are beginning to discover that these truths are not simply injunctions to be good. They are concrete and effective ways of helping ourselves and others to gain greater satisfaction and rewards from the work we do. The extent to which a manager understands and applies these principles can, in a large measure, be a determining factor in his success. We define them as follows:

Principle of Participation

Motivation to accomplish results tends to increase as people are given opportunity to participate in the decisions affecting those results.

Participation involves making systematic provision for consultation with subordinates in those matters directly related to their jobs. In developing participation, a manager asks his subordinates for their suggestions, recommendations, and advice in matters that affect their work. Psychologically, he develops a "mutuality of interest."

Participation has a powerful motivational impact. It received concerted theoretical attention only after World War II, but much earlier such pioneers as Armco Steel Corporation, Standard Oil Company (N.J.), and McCormick & Company were putting into practice the activities which later became the subject for theory. As early as 1919, for example, the board of directors of Armco Steel Corporation recognized the critical importance of mutuality of interest and participation in a basic statement of company policy that they would "encourage such organization activities as will clarify and enlarge the mutual interests of all who are working with the management of the company." Armco's board of directors continued with a statement which might well be found in the most recent text on industrial psychology: "Mutual interest is the cement that binds a group of men and women together in every sort of productive effort. Without a true mutual interest there can be no serious application, no real loyalty, no cordial cooperation, and little chance for concerted and effective effort."[1]

Charles P. McCormick, chairman of the board of McCormick & Company, Inc., a leading company in spices, condiments, and other flavoring ingredients, pioneered many practical applications of participation. As early as 1932 he emphasized the basic need of every person to be a liked and contributing member of a group. Long before "group dynamics" had become a psychological cliché, Charlie McCormick had identified the essential requirements and put them into practice in running the world-wide business which he headed, through use of group or council meetings, management boards, including his highly effective Junior Board of Directors, and sharing of profit with employees. As he said in reference to the program of "multiple management" which he originated, "No man can take full credit for everything he has done. Others are a part of our success, and private enterprise can be at its best only if all feel that way about it and are proportionately rewarded according to their contribution. We owe our ancestors much and our followers even more."[2]

As the concept of emotional ownership establishes, to the extent that people have a part in making decisions, these decisions become their own. We are much more interested in goals *we* have set, in decisions *we* have made, than in those made for us by others.

However, participation is not to be undertaken casually; it must not become abdication, or more harm than good may result.

Principle of Communication

Motivation to accomplish results tends to increase as people are informed about matters affecting those results.

The more a person knows about a matter, the more interest and concern he will develop. When a manager makes an obvious effort to keep his people informed, he is telling them, "I think you are important.

---

[1] *Armco Policies,* Armco Steel Corporation, Middletown, Ohio, Dec. 12, 1919.
[2] Charles P. McCormick, *The Power of People,* Harper & Brothers, New York, 1949.

I want to be sure you know what is going on." If he withholds information, he makes it quite clear that he feels it is of little importance whether or not his people know what is occurring.

Communication helps make work purposeful. It gives meaning to the job. It is much more satisfying to sit up front in the driver's seat where you know about things that are happening than to be perched in a rear seat where you get only sporadic and fragmentary glimpses of what is going on. If we know what the goals are and what progress is being made toward them, it is not difficult to feel a real and vital part of the team.

HOW TO IMPROVE MOTIVATION

The principles of motivation we have already discussed provide the foundation stones for sound motivation. The following points will also prove helpful.

Know Your People

A manager can best help his subordinates get the satisfaction they want from their jobs if he knows their special needs. Perhaps one person secures his feeling of recognition and importance from money, another from status, still a third from new challenges and experiences. If we want to know our people, it is necessary to develop a personal relationship that encourages confidence on both sides. This should be informal, but not so personal that we lose objectivity. It is a good rule for the manager to avoid becoming emotionally involved in the personal problems of his subordinates. This is certain to lessen his effectiveness.

The manager can learn about his people through observation and study. He can ask questions. During the course of appraisal interviews and in counseling and working with his people, he will find out what they want from their jobs, what their goals are, and something about their home life and families. This will give him an insight into the mainspring of their motivations and help him become a more effective leader.

All this requires careful handling. Most of the information we secure is highly personal, and necessarily subjective. We must keep in mind that people tend to present their own side of the story—and it is usually in their favor. Often, too, they will tell us what they think we want to hear, not the literal facts. If we are not sure of the accuracy of our information, we may want to verify it from other sources. This requires tact and caution. Divulging a confidence will automatically block off the source of supply.

Help Develop a Feeling of Proprietorship

Being human, we tend to show greatest interest and concern in things that belong to us. If something is ours, we have full control of it. We can shape and build it as we think best. This is one reason why the independent businessman gets such satisfaction from running his own enterprise.

We can help people capture much of this feeling of proprietorship on the job by proper motivation. Give a person a chance to participate. Keep him informed about matters that concern him. Let him make most of his own decisions. Give him an opportunity to develop the knowledge and skills he needs. All of these are building blocks in helping him become an entrepreneur in managing his own business unit in his own interests and those of the company.

Encourage Teamwork

People want to feel that they are part of the team. They want to be accepted and liked by their fellows. The greater this team feeling, the more strongly they will feel impelled to work hard and productively to achieve the goals of the group. Some managers are accepted as members of their groups and get their results by working with the team. Others are on the outside, giving directions and commands. Over the long term, we know the team effort gets the best results.

How can the manager encourage this kind of teamwork? One approach is to create as many opportunities as possible for members of the team to work together and with him. Often only certain people are in daily contact through their work assignments. The creation of task forces for special projects, delegation of specific tasks to small work groups, and committee participation are effective methods of providing closer working relationships.

The manager himself should work closely with individual members of his team as often as he can. Use of a line assistant may be a handicap because it tends to screen the boss from personal contact. Frequent discussions on the job, counseling and coaching to improve skills, and other job-related activities also help develop this team feeling.

Develop Friendly Competition

Competition is a strong motivating influence. It helps to generate keen interest in results and stimulates initiative and ingenuity in getting the work done. When a competitive situation is established, keep in mind that results must be comparable if the competition is to be fair and equitable. The best way to make sure of this is to ask the competing individuals to establish the ground rules themselves. If you stage a sales competition, for example, your own salesmen will be quick to establish conditions that guarantee a fair chance for all involved.

In competitive situations, somebody must lose. To minimize the disappointment, offer as many awards as you reasonably can. And try to hold out further competition of the same kind as an immediate incentive to those who did not win at first.

Motivate Down, Up, and Across

We have no difficulty recognizing our accountability for motivating those who report to us. But most often we overlook our obligation to inspire and encourage our boss and the people at our own level to undertake necessary action.

Often the boss must be motivated. He may fail to take certain steps or to perform work that he should undertake on our behalf. When this is the case, the professional manager does not retire into his shell. By utilizing the tools of participation and communication, he can awaken the boss's interest and energize him to take the necessary action.

Recognition can be practiced upward as well as downward. When the boss does a good piece of work as it relates to our responsibilities, a sincere and honest compliment will help to motivate him to accomplish other good work on our behalf. Often enough, the boss is the one who works in the kitchen. He ladles out recognition, but rarely receives it.

People at our own level also must be motivated. This is largely a matter of utilizing the recognized principles of motivation. When staff people are asked to participate in solving a problem, for example, if we give generous appreciation for their contribution, this will help motivate them to sustained efforts on our behalf.

SUMMARY

Motivating is the work a manager does to inspire, encourage, and impel people to take required action. Motivation is the energizer for all management activities. On the job, people are most largely motivated because of the things they do to establish and maintain a feeling of personal recognition and importance. This can be facilitated by the manager in many different ways, as exemplified in the basic principles of motivation. Here we find the importance of participation so that people become a part of the decisions they are expected to carry out and the need for communication to help people understand and appreciate the significance of the work they do. We can improve motivation by knowing our people, developing a feeling of proprietorship, encouraging teamwork, and developing friendly competition.

CHAPTER 23 *Management Communicating*

> *There is a great difference between knowing a thing and understanding it. You can know a lot about something and not really understand it.* CHARLES F. KETTERING, GENERAL MOTORS CO.

DEFINITIONS

Management Communicating: the work a manager performs to create understanding.
Understanding: comprehension of meaning.

THE LOGIC OF COMMUNICATING

A great deal of information is conveyed about communication without much real understanding taking place as to what is meant. Many a book has been written on the subject with never an attempt to define the term.

As we have studied organizations and managers, we have discovered that some companies have policy and procedure books, organization charts, company newspapers. These enterprises are busily engaged in transmitting great masses of information in the prescribed up and down channels. Yet little real communication takes place.

In a large Eastern service organization, for instance, managers spend up to 25 per cent of their time in committee sessions; a management bulletin marked "confidential" goes to every manager each Monday morning; virtually every letter is typed in quadruplicate so that those concerned may have their copies. Yet the constant complaint is "poor communication."

272

In an even larger Middle Western manufacturing company there are only a few committees and little attention is paid to the conventional media of communication.   However, everybody understands that orders are off this quarter, that technical difficulties have cropped up in the installation of the newly automated assembly line, and that the controller and treasurer functions will be integrated to form a new finance office the first of the month when the controller retires.   In other words, communication is excellent.

Our chief difficulty in arriving at a logical understanding of communication has been our tendency to become so involved in the techniques of communicating that we lose sight of what communication is required to accomplish.

Communication has been defined as the use of language and signs, the transmission of information, and as a means of influencing behavior. These are all part of the meaning.   However, when we communicate, logically we want to do more than use signs and symbols or to transmit information, more even than to influence behavior.

If we give somebody instructions, we are not satisfied just to say the words to ensure they are heard, or even to cause the other person to act. We want the other person to do *what* we intended the *way* we intended it to be done.   In other words, we want the other person to *understand* what we want done, *the way we understand it.   The end result of communication is understanding.*   Following this analysis, we are led to define communication in a new but simpler way.

We define communicating as *the work a manager performs to create understanding.*   Mental and physical effort must be exerted to communicate effectively.   From the standpoint of the professional manager, it must result in comprehension, the *sharing of the same meaning* or it is not true communication.   Communicating is what a manager does to understand other people and their motives, to get others to understand him.   The important considerations are these: for true communication to take place, the manager must understand other people as they understand themselves; he must get them to understand him the way he sees himself.

Difficult though this work may be, a moment's reflection will show that the effectiveness of a manager rests in large measure upon his skill in communication.   Plans can be acted upon, organization can be made effective, motivation can take place, controls can be exercised only if we can convey our meaning about these things to others and understand what they are trying to convey to us.

Every time we want to work with, or through, others, we must establish a bridge of meaning, that is, communications.   This holds true in every phase of human contact.   What we know of our subordinates and our boss, how we appear to them, depends in large measure upon the facts, impressions, and feelings that are communicated.

THE PROCESS OF COMMUNICATION

At one time most managers looked upon communication as the process of *telling*. They told others what they wanted them to know, what they wanted them to think, and what they wanted them to do. In so doing, they thought they were communicating. But in spite of their telling, they found that people still did not understand. Later, communication was regarded as a two-way process—one person talked to another and got feedback to find out if he was understood. But our research shows that two-way communication is inadequate, as is our conventional approach to the subject. We have established that communication is a four-way process. It involves asking, telling, listening, and understanding.

Asking

As managers, we often overlook the key activity necessary to get the communication process under way: that of asking other people for the information we don't have but feel that we need. This applies at all levels. The professional manager does not wait to be told. He asks. He asks his subordinates for their advice and suggestions on common problems. He asks to find out about their points of view and to make sure they understand his. The manager asks his superior for the information and advice he requires. He asks those on his own level for information and suggestions on matters of common interest.

Telling

Before we can be understood we must transmit our message. This calls for telling which, in itself, is four-directional. We must know ourselves. We must keep our subordinates constantly informed about matters that concern them. Our superior needs to be told about problems, developments, and activities that affect his responsibilities. And if information is available which relates directly to the responsibilities of those on our own level, we should tell them as promptly as possible.

Listening

If we wish to communicate fully, that is, to understand what others are trying to convey to us, we need to listen. This is a most difficult skill to learn and one that we do not always associate with the communication process. It requires self-discipline and rigorous control of our own urge to talk. When mastered, however, the skill of listening is the best guarantee that we will receive and understand the messages that are being transmitted in our direction.

Understanding

The most important aspect of communication—and the one most often overlooked—is understanding. Most communications have both an emotional and a logical meaning. Often they must be heard by both the head and the heart. To understand in this sense, the manager must have a keen insight into human motivation and must be able to hear or read not only the words, but the meaning behind the words.

WHY FAILURES IN COMMUNICATION OCCUR

These four activities of communication are difficult to accomplish because they require us to make effective contact with other human beings. Consider the problem involved in reaching only one individual. This person is barricaded behind his own doubts, fears, and frustrations. His actions are single-mindedly devoted to the things *he* wants to do, and it takes much effort to bring him to consider our needs and ideas. Habitually he talks and thinks of *himself* and is impatient when forced to consider *us*.

Communication rarely breaks down for lack of our own *wanting*. Most of us want to be understood, often desperately so. But we may find it difficult to cut through the opaque cloud of misunderstanding that seems to block us from making effective contact with another person. One reason we misunderstand is because we mistake the thing we use for communication with communicating itself.

Mistaking the Form for the Function

Why do we so commonly mistake the *form* of the communication for the communication itself? Think of the word "communication." What do you associate with it? Most likely a telephone, somebody talking, or a letter. Acceptable enough, but generally, this is as far as we go in our understanding. On this basis, if we see the need to improve communications, most often we look to the installation of more and better telephones, more talking, and more letters. This is about the same as saying that if we want to improve our ability to play golf, a good way to do it is to buy two sets of golf clubs. We may take it for granted that the letter we send, the bulletin we put up, or the notice we circulate is communication itself. This is the same as assuming that you can offer a guest his dinner by letting him observe a steak on a platter. He has to eat and digest it before it really becomes his.

Again, we mistake the form for the function by assuming that *telling* people what we have in mind, by itself, is communication. But this may be no better than assuming that a Frenchman speaking French, and an Italian speaking Italian, can talk on the telephone between Paris and Rome and communicate because each is saying something.

Selfish Understanding

Communication often fails because we are single-mindedly concerned with getting other people to understand us—what we want and how we feel. Understanding is rarely alone and entire in itself. To understand ourselves properly, we also must make some effort to understand others. This viewpoint is particularly difficult for managers to accept. Accustomed to command, we tend to think others have an *obligation* to understand us and will work hard to do so. The contrary is more often the case. Effective communication begins with understanding what the other person wants and needs.

Emotional Blocks

Emotions may block communication. Our attitudes and feelings may be so strong that they drown our understanding of what the other person is trying to convey. If we are saddled with prejudices or think of people different from ourselves in unfavorable stereotypes, this will twist and distort our understanding of what they are trying to communicate.

What we *feel* about things is often as important as what we *know* about them. Most engineers, for example, know factually that newly developed direct-current motors have great advantages for many in-plant uses. Yet one of the large electrical equipment manufacturers found that an important reason many of its customers failed to use DC motors was because their engineers still associated, emotionally, the direct-current motor with its old fashioned and outmoded predecessor. The engineers could not properly understand the advantages of the new type direct-current motor because as soon as they heard the words "direct-current motor" their emotional response was "inadequate" or "no good."

The person who distrusts his boss probably will not understand him. The boss who fears the ideas or changes proposed by his subordinates will not accept them. As a case in point, the organization department of a Middle Western food manufacturer proposed an organization change involving divisionalization into five product divisions. The sales vice president fought the idea doggedly. He cited every reason why it could not work. The real facts were that he feared he would be moved to head the staff marketing department in the change-over and that his large and important sales function would be fragmented.

The company president confided in the sales executive that if the change-over were accomplished he would need an executive vice president to help him carry the added burdens of top management. He wanted to know if the sales head would be interested in the promotion. At the executive committee meeting the next morning, the sales vice president came out strongly in favor of the new plan. He now understood it perfectly.

Selective Listening

We *hear* a great deal but we *understand* only what we want. Even though people are in the proper listening posture, their eyes alert and their faces interested, often they understand only part of what we say to them. Psychologically, it is entirely possible for a person to hear two sentences, one spoken right after the other, of equal weight and intensity, and to understand one and apparently not even hear the other.

The president of a small company in Georgia, for example, hired a secretary, a competent, well-experienced girl. In his interview he mentioned that the pay range for the job was $400 to $525 per month. "Newcomers and people with minimum experience start at $400," he stated explicitly. After she had received her first paycheck, the young lady approached the president indignantly. "You told me experienced people get $525 for this job. I'm experienced and you are only paying me $400," she said. The president's explanation did not placate her and she quit in a huff.

Where these failures in communication occur, the most significant result is lack of understanding. We fail to understand the thoughts and feelings of others; they do not understand our meaning or intentions. When people do not understand, friction and frustration are likely to be the twin handmaidens of error. Personal relationships then often deteriorate and the prevalent tone becomes one of apathy and disinterest.

THE ALLEN PRINCIPLES OF COMMUNICATION

In our research, we have developed several basic principles which will serve as useful guides in establishing sound communications.

Principle of Line Loss

The effectiveness of a communication tends to vary inversely with its extension.

The more people through whom a communication passes, the more the meaning tends to be delayed, diffused, distorted, and lost. The most effective communication is person-to-person and face-to-face.

When a message is communicated from one person to another, each human brain and tongue that relays the message tends to alter or weaken it. Unintended meaning may be added or the original sense may be changed. If plans, orders, recommendations, or control information are transmitted through several levels of organization, there is the tendency for each person in the chain to hedge the message with safeguards as he passes it on and to add reservations designed to protect him if there are repercussions. This tends both to diffuse the sense and delay the transmission.

Line loss multiplies as the company grows in size. This is one important reason why the expanding functional organization tends to become slow-moving and inflexible. Corrective measures center around the improvement of communication and include reduction of the number or organization layers and decentralization of authority.

What if multiple organization levels must be maintained because of the nature of the enterprise? In this case, line loss can be minimized if each manager becomes a booster station. In acting as booster stations, as managers our purpose is to augment and reinforce the information we receive with our own special knowledge of the needs and requirements of our own group. To do this effectively, we must first understand and appreciate the requirements and the point of view of our own boss. If we lack this, we should *ask* for the information we need. Frequently, upper-level managers will attempt to bridge this communication gap by talking directly with people at the line of operations. This can be effective when the top manager is speaking for the company as a whole. However, top managers cannot perform communicating work effectively for accountable lower-level managers with respect to matters that apply to their own jobs, because the top manager does not fully understand the local operating situation and does not have the time or the resources to explain general conditions in local terms.

Principle of Emotional Appeal

Appeals to emotion tend to be communicated more readily than appeals to reason.

We tend to think with our emotions. If you want a person to comprehend your meaning, look for an emotional peg upon which to hang that understanding. Even if your message is factual and impersonal, people will listen and understand better if you introduce the idea by relating it to their personal interests, their desire for advancement, their jobs, and their families. The way we *feel* about things strongly influences the way we *think* about them. Most people buy both ideas and goods with their emotions, not their minds.

Managers often feel that emotional appeals are somehow unfair or unscrupulous and tend to avoid them. However, if it is honest and sincere, an emotional appeal can produce understanding and subsequent action most quickly and effectively. Keep in mind that the great ethical and spiritual messages that have most profoundly influenced human action throughout the centuries have been emotional in tone.

THE MANAGER'S RESPONSIBILITY IN COMMUNICATING

Every manager is accountable for communicating downward, upward, and at his own level. Most often we wait for some "communication system" to take over. Or, if our people complain that they don't know what is going on, we urge the development of a "communication program."

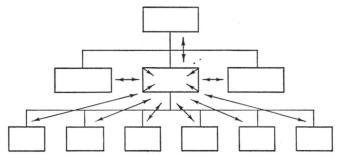

Fig. 23-1. Four-directional communication.

Unfortunately, these cannot do the job for us. If poor communications exist in his area of accountability, the manager must first look to himself. The probability is that he is failing in his personal responsibility of asking, telling, listening, and understanding.

The first step in assuming this responsibility is to understand it. Here, we should keep in mind that effective communication is four-directional. First, the manager must make sure of his own understanding; second, he communicates to other members of his team; third, he communicates on his own level; and fourth, he communicates with his boss. This is shown in Figure 23-1.

Self-understanding

As managers, we are the center of the communication network for our own unit. In surveying our communication needs, we must first make sure that we thoroughly understand ourselves and the plans, organization, and controls that apply to our unit. This is the formal network that provides the skeleton for the dissemination of other pertinent information. If a manager finds that information is blocked in the line ahead, he goes after the understanding he needs. This is his work. One way to make sure he has this understanding is to plan person-to-person contacts with the key people with whom he works.

Communicating Upward

The manager is the main channel for carrying requests, ideas, and suggestions upward. Often, he needs to augment and reinforce the information he receives with his own special knowledge of the needs and requirements of his own group. He is the decoder. Managers at upper levels must depend upon him for both the quantity and quality of the information they receive. If the message is diluted or distorted or if it does not get through, the manager most often is the bottleneck.

In communicating upward, we should satisfy ourselves that we thoroughly understand the point of view of our own boss. If we lack this, we should take positive and continued action until we find out. In many cases, managers above us do not know precisely what information *we* require. Unless they take this work over for us, the only way they can find out is through the information and requests that we feed upward.

Communicating Downward

A competent manager keeps his people informed of the plans and organization that guide their activities. He makes sure they receive the control information they need so that they can evaluate and regulate their own operations. Effective feedback from communication downward will give him the information he needs to keep posted on variances and exceptions that require his attention.

An important part of communicating downward is the establishment of an atmosphere that will encourage others of the team to come to us for information they need. People will not complain of lack of information if they feel free to go to the boss and ask him for it.

Each person is primarily concerned with his own job, his own stake in the company, and his own problems. He is interested in hearing about matters that affect and concern him. An important requirement of communication downward is to translate and interpret top-level plans, accomplishments, and new developments so that they will be understood by each person who works with us in relation to his own job and responsibilities.

FORMAL AND INFORMAL COMMUNICATION

Formal channels of communication are provided in every organization. Orders and directions flow along prescribed lines. Reports are routed to specific individuals. Information has official sanction only if it is properly endorsed. A hard core of such formal communication is needed to make sure that information gets to where it is needed, when it is needed to establish a sound structure of planning and control, and to maintain the integrity of the organization no matter how rapid the transfer, rotation, or turnover of people. Formal channels of communication ensure that only the proper people give orders and that there are no overlaps in authority.

In every organization, a great deal of informal communication also takes place. This is communication which has no official recognition but which occurs when people exchange information, suggestions, and ideas on a personal basis. We are all familiar with the fact, also, that in many groups a "thought leader" emerges who tends to dominate a good deal of the group thinking and who may actually give "orders" through his suggestions and comments.

The "grapevine" is part of this informal communication in that it consists of the passing of specific information from individual to individual and from group to group. This communication is rapid and it pays no attention to organizational lines. The grapevine carries news, rumor, and gossip; its communication in some cases may be contrary to company interest. What it does carry is usually of intense interest to employees and captures their attention as the formal communication may not.

Too much is generally made of this distinction between formal and informal communication. The assumption is made that formal and informal communications exist as two different systems, often antagonistic. Much effort is devoted to identifying what is formal, what informal. Much of this intellectual labor moves molehills, not mountains. While useful, the distinction between "formal" and "informal" communication is about as significant as the difference between dining at a formal dinner and eating a picnic supper as a means of feeding. Both end in precisely the same result—the ingestion of food and drink. All good communication, formal or informal, points to the same end— better understanding. Formal and informal communication can both be tools to that end.

WORDS—THE TOOLS OF COMMUNICATION

Most of our communication takes place through the medium of words. Unfortunately, words are often very inadequate for the tasks they are called upon to perform. Understanding of the peculiarities of words will help us to anticipate and overcome some of the hazards in communication.

When we communicate, each of us has a series of pictures in his mind. These we try to have understood by one person, a group of people, or a thousand. Our task is to enable other people to see these mental pictures of ours in exactly the same way as we see them. If we could use a motion picture apparatus to project these thoughts, the problem might be simplified. But the primary tool we have is a set of words—a verbal code we have developed to stand, in a symbolic way, for the things that actually exist. The words we use have special meanings that we inject into them. They are rarely understood in exactly the same way by any two people. By use of these fragmental, changing verbal symbols, we try to describe the mental pictures we generate in our minds so that others will comprehend them precisely as we do. This is much like trying to get a visitor from Mars, who has learned our language but who has never seen the painting, to *understand* the "Mona Lisa." Touching only the fringe of meaning, stereotyped and devitalized by use, hackneyed through familiarity, words yet remain our prime tool to convey meaning.

The difficulties are clear. Add to this the fact that, frequently, we are not quite sure ourselves what we mean or why we are doing things. Our meaning often becomes clear to us only after we get the work done, but we want other people to understand *before* we begin. The clincher is the fact that other people often don't want to understand us. They are so deeply involved in getting themselves understood that they may not hear our words or will misunderstand them if they do. Moreover, even if the words do penetrate, they are almost certain to be decoded in a way that gives them a final meaning different from what we intended. We can avoid some of the pitfalls of semantics if we keep in mind that words are not things, and that words can mean what we want them to mean.

Words Are Not Things

We often use words as if they were the things we are talking about. If we say "budget," for example, we take it for granted that the person to whom we are talking has the same mental picture, that he visualizes the same budget as we do. But this may be far from the case. What he has in mind may be closer to what we would call a "forecast." If this is so, it is clear that we are talking about different things and we are not likely to understand one another.

As we have indicated, words are symbols. They are semantic labels that we apply to specific things. When we talk about those things, we use the symbols. And here problems begin. The first problem is to make sure that the other person sees the same thing we do when we use the same words. For this we need precise definition. When discussing any subject in which there is the possibility of confusing these verbal labels, it is a good idea to define precisely what we are talking about. What do we mean by "budget" or "forecast"? If we can't describe exactly what we have in mind, there is a fairly good possibility that we don't quite know what we're talking about.

Change is a second problem in the use of words to represent actual things. We know things are continually in the process of change. Today's objective may be stated in identically the same numbers as yesterday's objective. But even though we use the same words, it is no longer the same objective. From day to day our markets, products, customers, and other related factors change to some degree and so does the essential meaning of the word "objective."

We must have this factor of change large in our minds if we are to use words effectively in communication. The Principle of Identity, which we discussed under Decision Making (page 250), helps to confirm the need for establishing clearly what our words mean both in terms of point of view and point in time.

Words Have the Meaning Given to Them

In using words, it is well to note that we can inject into them almost any meaning we want. If we go from one company to another, for example, we may find that the same kinds of departments are called "auxiliary departments," "service departments," and "staff departments." The word "staff," in turn, may also mean our subordinates, an authority relationship, or our assistants. Clearly, if we wish to practice as professionals in management, we should adopt a common language with terms precisely defined so that we can understand one another.

HOW TO IMPROVE COMMUNICATION

The vital things that happen in communication generally lie in what the manager does or fails to do in getting his people to understand and in understanding himself. While a great many words are spoken and printed with regard to improving communication, relatively little *work* is done to accomplish it. In most cases when a manager complains of poor communication, he will find that a good part of the cause lies in himself. The vital factors here are the need to achieve real understanding, and to make sure that what is understood is remembered.

Getting Real Understanding

People will comprehend what we are trying to communicate the way we understand it if we can make them *want* to understand it our way.

The first hurdle is emotional.   The best way to overcome it is start with agreement.   From an emotional viewpoint, we know that once a person begins to nod his head in affirmation, he is on our side of the fence. He has geared himself to understand.   Sooner or later, we may come to a point of disagreement, but if we have built up to it by first seeking out the things upon which we can agree, we have a much better chance that the other person will see our point of view.

It is easiest to agree upon things that actually exist or actually happened, but it is much harder to agree upon opinions.   In most cases it is easiest to get that important first agreement if we begin with a statement of fact and not with our conclusions with regard to the facts. Facts are most easily understood; the value judgments we place upon them often are not.

The second hurdle to achieving real understanding is more mechanical.   It arises from our normal tendency to say much more than people can assimilate and understand.   The reason is that if we have an idea we want to communicate, we are usually full of it.   We know every detail.   In communicating to others, we may assume they know as much as we do.   As a result, we may pour out our idea in one large mass of information.   Often this proves highly indigestible and is not understood.

The larger the helping of information, the more likelihood that some part of it will run into emotional blocks or contrary opinions.   At the same time, since our minds tend to be highly selective in what they understand, the more possibility that parts of the communication will be overlooked or misunderstood.

When information is communicated in small bites, mental digestion is much faster and more complete.   If the listener can familiarize himself with our ideas little by little, he is much more likely really to understand and accept them.

Finding Out What People Understand

Communication does not take place effectively in a vacuum.   We can be most certain of what people have heard, what they understand, and what they will remember if we provide for feedback.   This is the process of making sure that the listener understands what you want him to understand.   It requires skill in listening and in questioning.

Learn to Listen.   The ability to listen is one of the basic personal skills every manager should master.   When we are talking, we are probably repeating some thing we already know.   When we listen, we may learn something new.

Listening encourages other people to talk.   It enables us to find out how they are reacting to our message and what they understand.   The first requirement in successful listening is to learn to press both lips firmly together. If pauses ensue, relax. The build-up in tension will encourage the other person to talk if we don't rush in with our words.

When either listening or talking, we should keep in mind that the other person can think much faster than we can talk. The danger here is that the listener's mind will wander to the constant magnet of his own thoughts. The conclusion: *work* at listening. We need to try to understand not only the words, but the meaning behind the words.

Ask Questions. Questions prompt the kind of responses that will enable us to determine whether our communication is being properly received. When asking questions we should remember to begin with "what, where, when, who, why, or how." This will head off the tendency to a "yes" or "no" answer. Ask a person, "Were you at the accident?" His "yes" tells you little. But ask, "What happened at the scene of the accident?" and you are prompting a full response.

Helping People To Remember What They Understand

People forget much of what they hear in a surprisingly short time. Tests indicate that people tend to forget about 25 per cent of what they hear in the first twenty-four hours, and up to 85 per cent or more within a week. Since time and effort are needed to help people to understand, it follows that the investment will pay off best if enough additional effort is made to ensure that as much as possible is remembered. Repetition and association will help improve retention.

The more times we hear something, the more likely we are to remember it. The Rule of Four is useful here. This states that we should have four tellings if we want people to remember. (1) Before trying to get an idea across, tell your listeners what you are going to say. (2) Say what you have to say. (3) Tell them what you said. (4) Get them to tell you what they understand.

Repetition cannot be monotonous, however, or it will create boredom. The best way to overcome this is to repeat the same thought in different ways. Phrase it as a question: "John, have you given thought to that new gauge installation yet?" Cite a case, "When we put in the last installation, you remember we had these problems." Get feedback, "Now, how do you plan to handle the gauge installation, John?"

We may feel that this approach will bore the other person. But if the work is important to him, he will appreciate the opportunity to think it through and to be sure he understands.

Association is an excellent way of securing retention. If we link a new idea with something we already know, it will be much easier to remember the new idea. Many systems for improving memory are based on this principle. It goes without saying that when we do make use of association, we should try to make the familiar idea one that is well regarded and that is looked upon favorably by our listeners.

SUMMARY

Communicating is the work a manager does to create understanding. Communication can be accomplished best by accountable managers in a face-to-face relationship with the people who report to them. Effective communication is made up of asking, telling, listening, and understanding. Communication often fails because of semantic and other barriers; however, utilization of basic principles will help to remedy this situation. A four-way process of communication requires first the development of real understanding and then the ability to ensure that people remember what they understand.

CHAPTER 24

Selecting People

> *Let there be men and the government will flourish;*
> *but without the men, government decays and ceases.*
> *With the right men, the growth of government is rapid;*
> *therefore the administration of government lies in find-*
> *ing the proper men.* CONFUCIUS

DEFINITION

Selecting People: the work a manager performs to choose people for positions in the organization.

IMPORTANCE OF SELECTION

We look to the acquisition of capital assets as a decision of grave importance. The spending of $10,000 for a machine merits much investigation, analysis, and discussion. However, when we hire a man, we are dealing with an investment of perhaps $250,000 during his career with the organization. Yet often the work of selection is given little more thought and attention than the filing of a letter.

Not only is the selection of a person a financial investment, it is also a human one. When we hire a man, we are investing in his own happiness and that of his family. We are committing ourselves to a course of action that is difficult to reverse. The process justifies as much time and effort as we can give to it.

As G. J. Dusseldorp, chairman of Lend Lease Corporation, a large and enterprising Australian property and construction firm, points out, in a very real sense, a company is what its people make it. Each time a manager hires a new employee or promotes a man, he is at that time making a critical decision that will strongly influence the future characteristics, the success and profitability of one segment of the company or, quite possibly, the company as a whole.

ACCOUNTABILITY FOR SELECTION

A manager should have responsibility and authority for selecting the people he wants for his team. Often, we minimize this duty and do not give it the priority it deserves. However, it is clear that the people who come into the company and who are selected for promotion from internal ranks will largely determine the future success and capability of the enterprise.

When managers do not face up to their selection responsibilities, people may find a berth on the company roster in spite of inadequate ability. This is an injustice to both the individual and the company. Such a person will inevitably get beyond his depth. He will struggle to maintain his position and status, and, in the process, suffer both frustration and continued anxiety. If he is kept on as a manager, not only are the responsibilities of his position inadequately discharged, but his subordinates are penalized through the weakness of his leadership and the poverty of his example.

Selection requires the broad view of a manager. As opportunities ripen and the capacity of his people enlarges, he can expect them to move ahead. Thus, he must have in mind not only people to fill immediate openings, but also candidates for progressive advancement to positions of constantly widening horizons. He selects people with the capacity to grow within the company.

In carrying out his responsibility for selection, the professional manager gives careful attention to these three aspects:

1. His obligation to find the best people available to fill every position on his own team.

2. Careful screening, against the highest standards, of every person he accepts from another part of the organization.

3. Willingness to recommend for promotion from his own group the best people he has available.

THE ALLEN PRINCIPLES OF SELECTING PEOPLE

The manager who wants to do a professional job of selection should keep in mind three basic principles.

The Principle of Potential

The success of an endeavor over the long term tends to be proportional to the abilities of its members.

Think of it this way. Each time the manager selects a person for employment or promotion within the company, he is staking part of his future and his own reputation upon his choice. If the manager's selection is good, through his talents and energy, the new man will help the whole team to drive ahead. He will create opportunities for himself and for others on the team. On the other hand, if the person who is selected is not interested in working hard, if he will not make the effort to develop top-grade skills and abilities, he will handicap not only himself but also everybody who works *for* him or *with* him.

The Principle of Job Satisfaction

An individual's contribution to group objectives tends to be proportional to his ability to find personal satisfaction in the work he does.

During his career with the company, a person will tend to be productive to the extent that his work gives him personal return and satisfaction. When selecting a new man, we owe it as much to him as to ourselves to determine whether he will be able to work productively with others in the group. Is the work such that he will get satisfaction from it? Will he have an opportunity to grow and progress? These are questions that only the manager can answer. He should explore them fully before selecting a new person for the team.

The Principle of Future Characteristics

An individual's past performance tends to foreshadow his future characteristics. The best way to determine how a person will probably act on a new job is to find out as much as we can about his performance in other positions that he has held. If he has been a consistently good worker, if he gets along well with all kinds of people, we can anticipate that the same pattern will continue. However, if he has been in trouble continually, if he shirks his job, the possibilities are that he will do the same in a new position. Of course, there are often extenuating circumstances to consider, particularly if we judge only on the basis of one job a person has had in the past. However, it follows logically that the more we can find out about a person's job characteristics in previous positions, the better we can make informed judgments as to how he will probably work out in the position for which we are considering him.

THE MANAGER AND THE PERSONNEL DEPARTMENT

In performing the work of selecting people, managers can get a great deal of help from the personnel department. However, in order to make best use of this staff advice and service, the manager should first understand clearly what part of the work of selection he must do himself and what the personnel staff can do for him.

The answers are clear. A manager must initiate the selection; that is, he must decide what people he needs and what qualifications they should meet. A manager must also make the decision on the people he wants for his team and the people he will recommend for promotions or transfer, subject always to company policy and procedure.

The manager can get others to help him in most other aspects of selection. He may want to secure the participation of others on his team or delegate to them. Personnel staff members are trained and expert in selection work and they can provide invaluable guidance and aid in finding people, interviewing, testing, checking references, and other aspects of the selection process.

The personnel department can help best if the accountable manager describes clearly the job he wants to fill and the kind of person he will require to fill it. Also, the personnel department will want to coordinate in each part of the selection process. To maintain a good relationship, the manager should ask for personnel help as far in advance as he can anticipate his needs. This will give personnel staff an opportunity to survey potential candidates within the company and to make sure that the requirements are coordinated with those of other departments.

North American Aviation, Inc., fast-expanding in the aerospace industry, has continuing need for new management personnel. In North American, line managers *select* their own people; however, the personnel staff provides valuable help in a number of ways. It compiles information on candidates, administers psychological tests, obtains ratings of candidates, and evaluates and prepares summaries of candidate qualifications. Personnel develops and maintains the procedures for the selections system and remains abreast of new techniques and developments, which it presents and makes available to accountable managers for their use.

THE PROCESS OF SELECTION

To do a professional job of selecting people, a manager should have clearly in mind the over-all sequence of steps to follow. These are outlined below. While the specific order will vary for different companies, our research shows that the steps given are almost universally recognized in well-managed companies.

1. *Organize the Job*

Before selecting a person for a job opening, we should make sure the job itself is necessary. When a position becomes open, our first temptation is to call the personnel department and say, "Find me a man." However, this hasty approach is rarely satisfactory. It makes better sense to review the work that is being done and make sure that this same job is necessary. If study shows that the position should be reorganized or the work changed, far better to do it *before* we begin to look for a new person.

Even if we are sure that the job is necessary, we need to analyze it carefully to see if we can streamline it. If the organization has grown haphazardly, each position may have accumulated a grab bag of responsibility and authority. Through chance or personal ambition, some members of the team may have acquired responsibility and authority that could better be discharged elsewhere. This is the time to define responsibilities, specify the limits of authority, and clarify the relationships. We also want to make sure that the person who holds the job will report to only one person.

This organizational information can best be put in writing in the form of a Position Guide. The guide will become a charter for the position and will help us to find the best person to fill the spot. It will be useful also in orienting applicants to the job and as a guide to staff agencies who will assist in the selection.

2. *Plan Personnel Needs*

We need to plan well ahead in anticipating needs for people. In this planning, we should keep several points in mind. Careful forecasting of personnel requirements is important, both on a long-term and on a short-term basis. To forecast our long-term needs, we should estimate for five years in advance the retirements that will occur, the transfers, promotions, and other movements of people. Since this long-range forecast may not be very accurate, it should be kept flexible. But it does force us to think ahead and it is much better than not forecasting at all.

The long-range forecast should be backed with a more specific, concrete, and dependable short-range forecast, covering the twelve months to come. This should provide an accurate picture of the number and kind of people we need to start looking for *now*. As time advances and we use up this annual estimate, we should continue to project our five-year forecast for an equal period.

In planning for people, we will want to program and schedule so that we will be sure to give proper priority to this work and complete the necessary steps in good time. Waiting until the last minute usually results in wasted effort, throws an unnecessary burden on personnel staff, and often means that the process is so rushed we don't get the best person.

If we determine personnel needs well in advance, we can budget the money we will need much more realistically. Also, this gives us an opportunity to check procedures. The personnel department, in particular, will have standardized methods for doing many parts of the selection job. If we use these procedures, they will save time and help make our job easier.

3. Prepare Qualification Specifications

Now we know what work is to be performed. The next step is to determine what kind of person we need to do this specific work. The best way to do this is to prepare a qualification specification. This is a written check list of the qualifications of the person we need. It will serve not only to clarify our own requirements but will also provide a guide for the personnel department. In drawing it up, we will want to include such items as the following:

Personal Specifications. We must formulate qualifications as to age, sex, family situation, and related matters.

Education. The educational background required of the selectee should receive careful consideration. The educational requirements of the position being filled should be stated. If we are looking ahead to other positions to which the successful candidate can aspire in due time, we should make sure these also are noted in our requirements. After a man has worked for us for five years is no time to tell him that he lacks the education to move ahead. If in doubt as to the probable route of progression, we can confer with our superior or the personnel department. We must remember that every job we fill puts a man on the lower rungs of a ladder that may reach into the highest and most vital positions in the organization.

Previous Experience. What experience is necessary for the job? If we make this clear, we will remove the probability of considering people who lack the needed experience. This will save our own time and that of those helping us in the selection quest. However, we should not overbuild the experience factor. Training and development can compensate for experience deficiencies, provided the necessary intelligence and willingness are present.

Radio Corporation of America uses a man specification form which gives pertinent data on the position opening, including position title, reporting relationship, geographical location, salary grade, and a brief description of position responsibilities. The man specification also outlines "search specifications" including education requirements, age, language requirements (if pertinent), and necessary and desirable work experience.

These "search specifications" are used to extract, from a mechanized manpower inventory, those persons who appear to be best qualified based on the information provided. Performance appraisal summaries on these persons are then reviewed to develop a list of candidates who are qualified based on current job performance as well as the information previously outlined.

4. *Locate Candidates*

Now comes the task of finding candidates who will satisfy the qualifications we have outlined. Here, the personnel department can be of great assistance. For outside candidates, the personnel department will turn to employment sources such as application files, employment agencies, college recruitment, and other appropriate points of contact.

For locating candidates within the company, personnel staff can draw upon personnel audits, management appraisals, inventory charts, and contacts with other divisions or functions. The personnel department can help locate candidates most effectively if they know precisely what is wanted, and what talents and skills are available within the company. Specifying precisely what he wants is, of course, up to the manager himself. Information about outstanding candidates within the company will be available only if each manager does a good job of preparing personnel audits and management appraisals.

In the Crown Zellerbach Corporation, for example, candidates for management positions are found through use of the company management development program as well as through the more customary personnel assistance. Upon request, the management development staff group prepares lists of people from within the company who have the requisite background and experience to be considered for the position vacancy. These internal candidates are always considered before recourse is made to hiring on the outside.

5. *Review Applications*

Now the work load piles up. A list of candidates will probably become available within a reasonable period. These applications should be reviewed and sifted.

Here, the manager can use the services of the personnel staff, particularly if he wants to avoid the deluge of application forms, letters requesting employment, telephone calls, and personal inquiries which are part of the process. All applications must be screened in a systematic and careful manner, giving full consideration to each. If the manager has been explicit in stating his requirements, the personnel department can do a good job for him, winnowing out the chaff and bringing to light the best potential candidates. Whoever does the work, the best rule to follow is to put the greatest effort into choosing among the most highly qualified candidates.   There is not much point in administering psychological tests or conducting extensive personal interviews with people who are obviously unsuitable.   The manager who knows how to work with personnel effectively will find this staff help invaluable in helping him get greatest returns for the least expenditure of his personal time and effort.

When people are rejected, we should be sure that they are handled properly.   They should be thanked sincerely for applying.

6. *Administer Psychological Tests*

Psychological tests can be helpful in the selection process.   However, they must be used properly by competent specialists.

Psychological tests require standardized administration and careful interpretation.   The task demands skilled and competent psychologists or others trained for the work and should not be undertaken by the manager himself unless he has these skills.

Tests are not the whole of the selection process.   However, companies that use them successfully find them an extremely valuable tool.   Sears, Roebuck and Co., for example, which has an outstanding program, finds that psychological tests enable them to identify characteristics in a manager *before he is hired* that could otherwise be learned only through years of observation.   Sears looks for the following characteristics in its managers:

Mental Ability: Of prime importance here is the speed with which a person can learn; a good manager learns quickly.

Administrative Skill: A manager should be able to make objective decisions without becoming emotionally involved.   He should be co-operative, tolerant and open-minded about other people.   He should be able to show firmness in dealing with others.

Sociability: A manager should *want* to work with other people and to help them.   He should meet people easily and take the initiative in group activities.

Stability and Predictability: Key characteristics of a manager are a cheerful and optimistic outlook.   He should feel confident in himself.

Ambition: To be an effective manager, a person should want to better himself.

The Fisher Body Division of General Motors uses psychological tests widely.   A typical battery may include such tests as the California Test of Mental Maturity, Minnesota Paper Form Board Test, Purdue Industrial Mathematics Test, Bennet Test of Mechanical Comprehension, Kuder Preference Record, and the Adams Personal Audit.

7. *Conduct Preliminary Interviews*

Now we have screened out the obvious inadmissibles. We are coming to focus on a narrow field, which will probably yield our successful candidate. In conducting preliminary interviews, the manager may want to leave the matter to the personnel department. Or he may find it desirable to participate in the interviews himself.

If the manager does interview himself, he should avoid the tendency to make his judgment on the basis of a casual chat. Often first appearances are deceiving. It is far better to follow a prepared interview outline that will help to develop a meaningful estimate of the person in the shortest possible time. If the interviewing manager will ask a few difficult and penetrating questions, he can see how the individual reacts under stress. Or he can outline a job problem and ask the candidate what he would do. Interviewing techniques such as these take time, but they bring into sharper relief the critical characteristics that will help the manager make a discriminating final choice.

In this initial interview, our studies show that the following questions will probably help get the most significant responses.

Why are you interested in this job? Has the person a real interest in the position? Does he know enough about it to match his own capabilities against what the job requires? Or is he just looking for a job? If he doesn't have a good answer to this question, help him to make up his mind before continuing with him.

Which, of all the jobs you have held, did you like best? Why? Here the interviewer can get a good indication of the person's real interests. It is important to make sure the candidate really *wants* the job, that he will be really interested in it.

Where do you expect to be at the end of your first year with us? Your fifth year? Here the interviewer can get an idea of what the applicant thinks of himself and his own abilities. Does he have a 1-horsepower or a 150-horsepower motor? His answers to these questions will be revealing.

What are your strongest characteristics? Your weakest? The applicant's own estimate may be surprisingly informative. The manager interviewing can follow up any leads with further questions.

Would you go back to the last job you had if offered the opportunity? Why or why not? Answers to this question should be appraised carefully. They will probably bring out information that will tell a great deal about the person being interviewed.

8. *Investigate Previous History*

Before finalizing his selection, the manager should look into the previous history of the applicant. It doesn't help to find that a person is a rascal if he is already on the payroll. How did his previous employers regard him? Why did he leave? If the manager or the personnel staff can reach two or three previous employers or supervisors, it should be possible to piece together a typical pattern of the candidate's behavior. Was he aggressive, ambitious, and hardworking on previous jobs? He will probably be so also with his new employer. Did he have trouble getting along with his previous boss? If so, possibly this may be as much the boss' fault as his own. Did he have personality difficulties with four or five previous supervisors? Then, the odds are that he will be a difficult customer to handle.

In talking with other people about the applicant, the critical question to ask is: Would you hire him again? The response to this question, and the way it is given, can be very helpful if properly interpreted.

Pay little attention to personal references that are offered voluntarily. Almost anybody can find one or two people who can be coerced or entreated to put down a few favorable statements in a general letter of reference.

9. *Conduct Final Interview*

The final selection usually requires a detailed personal interview on the part of the accountable manager concerned. Valuable as is the help he has received from the personnel department, this is a step he must accomplish himself. The final interview will satisfy the manager that the candidate is right for him and will also give the man an opportunity to size up his potential employer. Where practicable, multiple interviews may be helpful, as a composite judgment may be more indicative of the candidate's over-all suitability for a variety of potential assignments.

The General Electric Company follows this procedure fairly closely. The personnel staff in General Electric aids in screening candidates, but the final choice is made by the accountable manager. The manager facilitates the personnel job, however, by providing enough information about the job to be filled so that a list of job specifications can be developed. While the personnel staff may interview the candidates and prepare summaries and check lists, it is up to the manager concerned to make the final choice. If he wishes, he makes telephone checks and interviews himself also.

10. *Provide Physical Examination*

Before the candidate is hired, he should receive a physical examination. His own statement of health may be sincere, but it is always possible that he has a condition of which he is not aware. Frequently, the examination is given after employment, but this may amount to locking the door after the horse has escaped.

11. *Maintain Follow-up on the Job*

Once a new manager is on the payroll, he is often treated immediately as an old hand. However, the first few days and months are an important transition period and should be carefully handled. These steps are most important.

Alert the Team. Other members of the team should know about the new man, before he appears. It is a good idea to give them his background, tell them what his job and work will be, and how he will fit into the team. This will help to make sure that he is expected and will be welcome.

Introduce the New Man. When the newcomer first appears on the job, he needs to be introduced to every member of the team and to others with whom he will work. The superior can best do this himself. To help the new man get started properly, one member of the team can be asked to act as his sponsor for the first day or two. The sponsor will be a source of information. He can help the new man adjust to a strange situation and can advise him on minor problems before they grow into larger ones.

Train the Man. Almost certainly the new member of the team will need training and development if he is to perform at peak effectiveness. This means that we must begin careful appraisal of his performance and maintain continuing counseling with him on the job. Very early, he will want to know: How am I doing? We should be prepared to offer suggestions and to help him get properly established. The first few weeks are critical. If we can help the new man adjust successfully to his new job and teammates, we will have then accomplished a major responsibility as a professional manager.

SUMMARY

People are our most **important** asset. The selection of people for current positions and promotion is one of the most vital responsibilities of every manager. The principles basic to sound selection can best be implemented by following a clearly defined process of selection. This begins with establishing a sound organization for the job that is to be filled and then planning personnel needs over the long term. A qualification specification should be prepared for each position to highlight the characteristics of the person desired. This specification can then serve as a guide for the personnel department and other agencies which will help to locate candidates, review applications, administer psychological tests, conduct preliminary interviews, investigate previous history, and bring the matter to a point of final interview by the accountable manager so that he can select the person for the job. Physical examination should be a part of the process and effective follow-up should be provided on the job, so that the person selected will fit properly and will be assured of a satisfying place on his new team.

CHAPTER 25 *Developing People*

> *A strong leader knows that if he develops his associates he will be even stronger.* JAMES F. LINCOLN, LINCOLN ELECTRIC CO.

DEFINITIONS

Developing People: the work a manager performs to help people improve their knowledge, attitudes, and skills.

Management Development: the work a manager performs to help managers and candidates for management positions to improve their knowledge, attitudes, and skills.

Performance Appraisal: the work a manager performs to evaluate the performance and capabilities of himself and his people.

Performance Counseling: the discussion of his performance with a person whose work has been appraised.

Coaching: the personal activity of a manager in instructing and helping employees to develop on the job.

Knowledge: cognizance of facts, truths, and other information.

Attitude: reaction to things, people, situations, and information.

Skill: the ability to put knowledge into practice.

Since our studies deal with management, in this chapter we will discuss only one aspect of developing people—that of developing managers and candidates for management positions.

FALLACIES AND FAILURES IN MANAGEMENT DEVELOPMENT

Hundreds of millions of dollars are spent in business and industry every year to develop management talent. The manifestations of this effort are many and often plainly visible. Typical is the periodic dispersal of executives to conferences and seminars to upgrade their management skills, and the periodic rotation of people from one position to another to "broaden their viewpoints." Rare, in fact, is the up-and-coming manager who does not bear service stripes on his family escutcheon to mark two or more forcible uprootings and transfers from one plant or office location to another. Cumulatively, the time and effort spent by managers on company courses devoted to leadership, human relations, and related subjects would undoubtedly be sufficient to run an enterprise of great size.

Despite this wholehearted devotion to a vitally important objective, many companies are finding that all of this management development effort does little to improve the knowledge, attitudes, and skills of managers.

CAUSES AND CORRECTIONS

Most causes of these failures are easily identified. And, in most instances, proper attention to the real problem has generally brought effective correction.

One reason many management development programs have failed is a blind faith in a set of procedures which purports to turn out well-machined, perfectly integrated management talent. The assumption here is that if people are appraised, counseled, coached, required to attend their quota of conferences, and shown in two colors on a managment replacement chart, they will inevitably develop as managers. The reason this assumption is so frequently unfounded is that it fails, at the very outset, to answer the key question: *For what purpose are these managers being developed?*

Why are we developing people? Do we want to help them to increase their personal range of knowledge? Or are we developing people so that they can make a greater contribution to the successful operation of the company and, as a corollary, to their own personal welfare? If we relate development to the purposes of the company, we can be more certain that it will be properly focused, purposeful, and productive.

The failure to develop managers may be due also to other causes arising from a company's own special circumstances. Whatever the reason, however, the fact remains that many company management development programs are not producing the expected results. In divisionalization and decentralization, it is not uncommon for companies to find that their developmental programs have produced functional specialists instead of managers. As a result, a great many key jobs go to outsiders who have developed *managerial* as well as *functional* skills.

Again, there are many instances where capable men have served their companies efficiently and well, working themselves up, position by position, through the ranks of manufacturing, engineering, or sales. Eventually, after fifteen or twenty years, the culminating opportunity opens up—a divisional vice presidency perhaps, or the position of executive vice president.   Time and again, the faithful retainer is found wanting, and the prized opportunity goes to someone else.   Yet, on investigation, the failure is often found to be due not so much to personal inadequacy as to the fact that the man has been hammered into such a narrow mold during his long years of service that he cannot expand himself to master real management responsibilities.

Another reason for failure is the assumption that managers can be trained to manage *away from the job*.   While courses, seminars, and conferences are an indispensable part of the training process, the most they can accomplish is to fill gaps in knowledge and provide a certain amount of practice in management techniques.   In the final analysis, managers can learn to manage only through the direct application of managerial knowledge and skills to the responsibilities of their jobs.

Finally, management development fails because of undue emphasis on *promotion,* not *development.*   The common theme in executive development is the building of people for bigger jobs.   The background music centers on promotion, advancement, progression.   But the facts of life are that everybody cannot advance; for some, promotion will never come.   This is normal.   Managers need to understand that the management development program is not an escalator; it is an *opportunity.*

Great as is the need for people who can demonstrate potential, greater yet is our requirement for people who want to do outstanding work where they now are, who have the craftsman's feel for performing their currently assigned *management* work in a superlative manner.

All people are not emotionally and psychologically suited for promotion.   Everybody can do better where he now is and secure real satisfaction from his accomplishment.   Properly accepted, this is as great a challenge as that offered by any responsibility in the top executive suite.

We sometimes tend to push people past their natural range of abilities and their temperamental capacities by this increasing emphasis upon advancement.   The social and competitive pressures that result lead some to engage in the petty strategies of office politics and drive others to frustration and embittered apathy.

Industry needs as many candidates as it can find for the jobs of presidents and vice presidents, board chairmen and directors.   But it needs, just as badly, outstanding department foremen and superintendents, chief clerks and engineering managers. A first-line supervisor who does his job to the very limits of his ability makes as great a contribution, within his limits, as the chief executive of the company. Each, according to his measure, deserves as much recognition and respect for his accomplishment.

PREREQUISITES TO DEVELOPMENT

Before undertaking the improvement of managerial skills, we must make sure that the necessary background is laid. This calls for satisfaction of certain prerequisites.

Top Management Support

Management development is a tool for improving management skills throughout the company. The way the company is managed, the principles, tools, and techniques utilized in planning, controlling, leading, and organizing the affairs of the enterprise must inevitably be determined by the chief executive and his immediate staff. Yet, in company after company, we find that the top executives do not know what precepts of management are being taught the people who report to them and, often, do not practice this kind of management themselves.

Effective management development trains managers in the skills by which the company is to be managed. Where these programs are successful, we find that the process begins with the chief executive and the board of directors. This group carefully studies and reviews the techniques and principles to be utilized in managing the company at lower levels. Since managers will tend to manage in the same terms as they are managed, the top group first sets its administrative house in order, then continues the process down the line. In companies such as Armco Steel Corporation, Ford Motor Company, Schlage Lock Company, Cincinnati Milling Machine Company, and many others where this approach has been followed, it has been highly successful in aiding top management to improve management excellence at all levels.

In the Standard Pressed Steel Company, leading manufacturer in steel and electronics, the chief executive and top executive group first studied and reviewed the company approach to management and compared this to the most advanced and productive techniques as used in a representative cross section of other leading companies. After careful analysis and reconciliation, the company then established and authorized, at the top level, the principles and techniques of professional management to be followed by managers at all levels.

Each manager, again beginning with the top executives, reviewed and analyzed these concepts with his own team. The net result was that every manager had an opportunity to evaluate his own approach to management in terms of the highest standards of professional competence. Since the boss always did this before other members of his team participated, he first put into effect the precepts he later taught to his own group. This example, of course, served as a potent multiplier in itself. From this level-by-level approach, with its consistent percolation of advanced thinking and techniques throughout the organization, every manager in Standard Pressed Steel studied, appraised, and upgraded his own approaches in such key areas as:

How to forecast
Setting productive objectives
Programming and scheduling his work
Interpreting and applying policies and regulations
Budgeting for improved cost performance
Making most effective use of procedures

He had an opportunity to stand back and look at the way he analyzed problems, his use of logic, the effectiveness of his communication, his ability to motivate his people, and the methods he used in selecting and developing his people.

In the course of this program, every manager studied and streamlined his own organization structure, critically appraised his delegation of responsibility and authority, and clarified his own organization relationships. Finally, each manager reviewed the performance standards he had established and analyzed his methods of performance measurement, performance evaluation, and correction.

Phoenix-Rheinrohr A.G., a leading West German steel, tube, and pipe company headquartered at Duesseldorf, in its approach to developing managers, stresses the futility of instructing the lower-level members of management in the use of the best management principles since they will most often return to the job and find themselves unable to use these new ideas because they are not practiced by senior members of management. To overcome this, Phoenix-Rheinrohr stresses the need for beginning the process of management improvement at the executive levels of the company.

Sound Organization

We should ensure that we have a sound organization before we begin developing people. There is sometimes the feeling that it is best not to hold people down to specified responsibilities so that they will have an opportunity to expand their talents as widely as they wish. This approach may be desirable and even necessary in a poorly organized company. If people are not quite sure of their responsibilities, if the work has not been properly delegated, it may be the better part of wisdom to encourage people to reach out in all directions. This is one way of making sure that the most important things get done.

Unfortunately, in the process much empire building goes on, and odd grab bags of responsibilities are put together. While the architect of these organizational hybrids is still in charge, they may work well and even efficiently. But when he leaves, the artificial structure most often falls apart.

In one company, for example, the controller, a strong and domineering individual, took command of all operating divisions during the early stages of company growth. He ran the divisions efficiently until his retirement. The new controller put in the same position was equally strong as an individual. However, he was overly conscious of expense. He throttled research expenditures and sliced operating expenses and, in the process, debilitated manufacturing and sales until they lost their competitive edge.

A sound, balanced organization, stable through continuing generations of managers, is imperative if people are to be developed effectively. Managers should know what management work they are required to perform. Their responsibilities, authority, and accountability should be carefully defined. They should know to whom they report, and who reports to them. They should be able to perform their work without duplicating or overlapping similar work done elsewhere. They should delegate effectively and have sound working relationships with their subordinates, superiors, and other units.

Management Accountability

As a preliminary to developing managers, we should make sure that they are held accountable for management performance. They should be required to achieve their results primarily in terms of the leading, planning, organizing, and controlling work that they do. If they are held accountable for results in these terms, they will place greater stress upon this kind of accomplishment. This will lead naturally to development of management skills.

Accountability demands standards of management performance. We want people to know for themselves where they are strong and weak. They need yardsticks to measure their own performance. Given this information, they have one of the best incentives for sound self-development.

Companies with strong professional management evaluate managers from day to day in terms of their ability to apply professional management methods and to secure management results. Managing is part of the job, not something reserved for classroom teaching. The effects of establishing *management* accountability are clearly evident. We can see this best by contrasting the results with companies that stress *operating* accountability.

Many organizations place primary emphasis on the operating or functional skills of selling, engineering, and manufacturing all the way to the top. The chief executive then generally regards himself as the leading salesman or engineer or production expert for the company as a whole, not its leading manager. One result is emphasis on operating work all the way to the board of directors. While the company is small enough, this can be highly effective. When the top executives of competing companies are also operators and not managers, the struggle then is held at this lower level of effectiveness. But when one company learns how to *manage* itself more effectively, it tends to break into the lead. And once a hard and firm pattern of management is structured into the company, it will be learned by each succeeding generation of managers and become part of the culture of the company itself.

Ford Motor Company provides an excellent example. Ford well expresses this accountability in a formalized manner by spelling it out as a part of the job of every manager. In evaluating the manager's over-all contribution to the company for both performance and compensation purposes, Ford considers this responsibility as important as such other key aspects of the job as cost, quality, and production.

In Ford, *every manager is held accountable for developing and maintaining an organization of fully qualified personnel. In meeting this responsibility, he is expected to:*

1. Make certain the best man available is assigned to each position.

2. Take steps to plan for and assure that adequate replacements are available to fill vacancies which may develop in key positions.

3. Include within his organization an adequate number of men with management and technical-professional potential.

4. Periodically review the performance and potential of every subordinate.

5. Plan and take action to develop every subordinate to the full extent of his abilities, both as to performance on his present assignment and for greater responsibilities.

6. Periodically review and take action to improve the assignment and definition of job responsibilities.

Each division and staff head has established the necessary controls to assure that these responsibilities are met within his organizational component. The Industrial Relations Staff is responsible for providing such staff assistance as is necessary.

Balanced Compensation

Balanced compensation is a basic requirement. People want to feel that greater financial rewards await them if they upgrade their skills and abilities. Of particular importance is the provision of separate avenues of promotion for people in technical or functional and management positions. Increased technical requirements in a job should be recognized by increased financial rewards. A person should not feel that he has to get onto the management ladder to improve his financial standing. Management positions, on the other hand, should contain constantly increased management responsibilities, so that, as an individual moves higher in the chain, he will be paid for greater breadth and competence in his management work.

THE PROCESS OF DEVELOPMENT

We can best help managers to improve their knowledge, attitude, and skills by focusing on the three activities of the developmental process: performance appraisal, performance counseling, and developmental activities.

Performance Appraisal

Performance appraisal is *the work a manager performs to evaluate the performance and capabilities of himself and his people.* This is a responsibility which a manager must carry out in large part himself. It does not lend itself well to delegation. Performance appraisal is of critical importance because it literally weighs a man and his future career in the balance. Because we have not as yet perfected a means for scientific determination of how well or poorly an individual is doing on the job, management appraisal in the final analysis becomes a matter of personal judgment. It makes great demands upon the objectivity and analytical capabilities of the manager; the way he appraises others is a very good measure of the performance of the manager himself.

Managers often say, "I appraise people all the time." This is probably true. We tend to note examples of good and bad performance and to file them mentally. Most of us have a definite opinion as to the capabilities of each of our people. Unfortunately, these evaluations are not always well based. There is a very human tendency to permit personal emotions to dominate our good judgment. Often, we base our over-all impression of the individual on one outstanding trait. For example, if the individual is a hard and conscientious worker and we like him for it, we may not only rate him high on this trait but also on everything else. On the other hand, if a man has once made a bad mistake, or turned in a poor job, we may let this color our subsequent judgments of him and thereafter he is consigned to the "poor performance" category.

These informal appraisals are useful. However, at intervals we should come to a full halt, carefully review performance, and make a fair and conscientious appraisal of each of our people.

Appraisal not only provides a good picture of the individual's capabilities, it also gives to the person who is systematically appraised the feeling that he is not lost in the crowd. The Kroger Company, a leading food chain, stresses this need for reassurance, particularly for young managers who have not yet had an opportunity to show the full range of their abilities. Kroger sees to it that each person has frequent contact with a variety of senior executives, especially during this critical early period. In the Kroger Company the manager's performance is thoroughly evaluated with him throughout his career with the company. This helps to bring his assets to attention so that both he and the company can capitalize upon them, and, in areas where improvement is needed, it provides the necessary focus upon improvement.

Appraise Both Current Performance and Potential. The question: How well is the man doing on his present job? should be tackled separately from the evaluation of his potential for advancement. The primary reason is that some people who are doing well where they are will have little potential for moving ahead; others who are mediocre in their current jobs may, for reasons that can be discerned, have real promotability.

Appraisals in which two or more people review and discuss the performance of the individual being rated tend to be most objective. One of the best approaches is for the accountable manager to invite one, two, or three other managers on his own or a higher level to form an appraisal group with him. The group then undertakes joint discussion and analysis of the individual being appraised. However, the accountable manager makes the final decision. The appraisal group counsels and advises him. This method is perhaps best designed to enable managers to arrive at a logical and equitable composite appraisal.

Self-appraisal can be used profitably in conjunction with the group appraisal. Here the individual evaluates his own performance, most often using a copy of the standard appraisal form. When he appraises himself in parallel with the appraisal by his superior, the employee is required to think through his performance in terms of the standards by which he is being measured. This encourages self-examination and may lead him to critical conclusions with regard to the kind of job he is doing. In practice, the subordinate will most often appraise himself lower than does his manager. Where he rates himself consistently higher, investigation is in order.

Although it should not be used by itself to evaluate performance because it is entirely too subjective, the self-appraisal is an excellent adjunct to any other method of appraisal adopted.

Performance Counseling

To realize the full value of performance appraisal, we need to discuss the findings with the person involved and to help him develop his own program of self-improvement. Counseling with his people on a formal basis at least twice each year should be a responsibility of every manager. The better he does this, the more he will motivate his people to top performance.

Effective counseling interviews do not occur spontaneously. More is required than to invite a man in to talk about his job. Proper advance preparation should be made. This should include careful planning of the interview: what is to be covered, what points will be made, what kind of action will be decided upon, and the time needed. A quiet, private meeting place should be arranged, divorced from jangling telephones and minor interruptions.

Actual conduct of the interview is most critical, for it will have an important bearing on the relationships that the manager develops with his people. Various approaches can be used to discuss performance. A good way to establish a sound base for the counseling discussion is to ask the subordinate to appraise his own performance beforehand. When asked to review his own performance, the employee will probably identify most of his own important deficiencies and this will provide an excellent basis for productive discussion.

In counseling, the rule of the manager should be to listen more and say less. His role is to ask questions, to encourage his employee to talk out his problems, and to give him the help he needs to analyze his own performance and to develop his own program for improvement.

Many of the problems that arise in counseling can be avoided if the manager will talk consistently about *the work being done* and the man being appraised. As soon as personalities are injected, the discussion will tend to become a verbal wrangle and not a constructive session.

Every counseling session should conclude with a mutual affirmation as to what the employee will do to improve his performance. To do this, it is desirable to isolate in turn each area of performance in which improvement is to be effected. It is most important that the subordinate decide for himself what he will do. Preferably he should put his improvement plan in writing.   When this is done, it will provide the best possible means of follow-up to ensure that the improvement steps decided upon are actually followed through.

At this juncture, comment is appropriate with respect to the common advice to managers that they should not discuss a man's weaknesses with him, but rather, should concentrate upon building up his strengths.   Reviewed from a practical standpoint, this advice has little to commend it.   People in management positions want to know where they are falling short and few, if any, appreciate the camouflaging of their deficiencies with circumlocutions.

DEVELOPMENTAL ACTIVITIES

In counseling subordinates and in helping them to develop, the manager should have in mind a range of developmental activities that he can suggest to them.   Generally, he will find the advice and service of the management development or personnel department of great value to him in providing the necessary facilities.

Importance of Example

The most important developmental influence is the example of a good boss.   The manager who plans, organizes, leads, and controls as a part of his normal, day-to-day job will find that his subordinates tend to emulate him.   If he concentrates on the operative aspects of his job and holds his management subordinates accountable for personal accomplishment of operating work, he will find that this becomes their emphasis.   It is clear that people tend also to pattern themselves after superiors they respect in their approach to people.   If he is a firm, understanding, participative leader, the manager will find that other members of the team tend to adopt the same pattern.

Coaching

Coaching is the personal activity of the manager to instruct and develop employees on the job.   Coaching involves creating opportunities on the job to help an individual improve his strong points and overcome weaknesses.   This requires that the manager observe his subordinate on the job and point out methods and opportunities for improvement.

Coaching requires that the manager create developmental opportunities.   He may assign his subordinate to new and different tasks or he may give him a special problem to work out on his own initiative. The important criterion is that, in coaching, the manager personally observes and follows up the assignment so that he can instruct his subordinates. This requires a great deal of his personal time and attention. However, it is one of the most important responsibilities of the manager and will result in improved performance more quickly perhaps than any other method.

Job Rotation

Job rotation is the purposeful movement of an individual from one position to another on the same organizational level for purposes of development. Job rotation should not be taken up simply for the sake of rotating people. This is hazardous and may unduly penalize organizational efficiency. Rotation should never become a game of musical chairs with people moving about at random. Each rotational move should be planned on an individual basis. The purpose should be to increase the knowledge and experience of the individual in line with the company's needs. Job rotation should improve the over-all efficiency of the organization, not detract from it.

Rotation from one function to another at the first level of supervision is particularly difficult because first-level supervisors are called upon to perform the largest proportion of operating work. If the supervisor or manager who is being rotated has been doing a good deal of the work for his subordinates, his rotation may mean the loss of a key operator. If the replacement does not have an equivalent operating skill, a real loss of operating effectiveness may result. However, if supervisors are in the habit of doing their subordinates' work for them, it is well to note what is taking place and to insist upon more effective delegation as a prerequisite to job rotation.

Build from Bottom Levels. Since a strong supporting organization is necessary for effective rotation of upper-level managers, job rotation should begin at lower supervisory levels. This has several advantages. For one, it ensures that managers will receive functional experience in lower-level positions. A person who has once had this experience retains it no matter how high in the management ladder he rises. He will always be able to bring this operating insight to the management decisions he will make. Rotation at lower levels is also less expensive. Salaries are lower. The potential loss due to temporary inefficiency is more restricted, and the impact of learners' mistakes is localized.

Get Suggestions of Subordinates. The suggestions of subordinates should be given every consideration in job rotation. The best approach here is to involve subordinates directly in planning rotation possibilities, both inside and outside the department. If they are to participate intelligently, employees will have to understand the purpose and method of rotation. As they contribute their suggestions, they will develop a proprietary interest in the undertaking. This will help to forestall and overcome possible feelings of anxiety and frustration and will ensure enthusiastic participation.

Courses and Seminars

Management skills are rarely improved simply by attendance at courses and seminars. Sitting through three days or three weeks of presentation and discussion does not necessarily result in the improvement of on-the-job activities. What is required is a sincere desire and motivation of the manager to carry over and apply to his work the information he has secured.

The more the manager participates in the educational process, the more he will probably take away from it. Work assignments, case discussions, and other group activities are valuable means of involving participants and ensuring full absorption of the concepts and principles being taught. Most helpful in this regard are seminars and courses which are based upon practical operating experience and relate to the requirements of management in real life.

Correspondence courses are a helpful means of self-development if used consistently. When undertaking a correspondence course, the manager should first review the contents of the course to make sure it is applicable to his company and to his job. Wide variations exist in teaching content and methods. If what he learns is outmoded or inapplicable, the manager will find that he has wasted time and effort.

Committee Participation

Membership on a committee can be a useful development activity. However, the manager should be made a working member with full participation in committee assignments and discussions. Simply to observe the committee deliberations is rarely worthwhile.

As a participant in committee affairs, the man often can secure better insight and understanding of the different points of view represented. He can see better where his own unit fits into the total scheme and the importance of his contribution for over-all success.

SUMMARY

Most companies spend more money on people than any other item and give less attention to this critical factor than almost anything else. This failure can be overcome by sound development, which is the work managers do to help people improve their knowledge, attitudes, and skills. Development will take place most effectively if there is top management support and a sound basic organization. Each manager should be held accountable for developing his own people and for seeing to it that there is a balanced scheme of compensation to ensure proper incentive for developmental effort. The process of development begins with performance appraisal, which is the evaluation of current performance and potential for advancement. This can best be done on a group basis, using an appraisal form designed to measure the performance of work and results, with minor stress on personality characteristics. Following appraisal, each manager should counsel with his people to help them to recognize their strengths and weaknesses and to develop a plan for personal improvement. A manager can offer help in development by providing a good example, by coaching on the job, and by making opportunities for job rotation, attendance at courses and seminars, and committee participation.

PART FIVE

Management Controlling

CHAPTER 26

Management Controlling

> *It is always a great mistake to command when you are
> not sure you will be obeyed.* MIRABEAU

DEFINITIONS

The Function of Management Controlling

The work a manager performs to assess and regulate work in progress and completed.

The Activities of Controlling

Establishing Performance Standards: the work a manager performs to establish the criteria by which methods and results will be evaluated.

Performance Measuring: the work a manager performs to record and report work in progress and completed.

Performance Evaluating: the work a manager performs to appraise work in progress and results secured.

Performance Correcting: the work a manager performs to regulate and improve methods and results.

Assess: to weigh and appraise.

Regulate: to adjust; to return to a predetermined course.

Performance: the act of doing work.

Results: the outcome of performance.

Method: the way work is done.

THE LOGIC OF CONTROL

Once work is under way, it is necessary to have a means of checking up to make sure that performance is what we want and that results are satisfactory.   The whole process of checking up is a separate and identifiable kind of management work to which we have applied the term "control." This departs somewhat from the conventional meaning, for control has been taken to mean anything from guide or direct to measure.

The manager guides through planning, organizing, and leading; he directs people through decisions and motivating.   The term "measuring" is often used as a synonym for "control," but we find that, in itself, measuring is not enough to make certain that performance and results are acceptable.   Therefore, we have settled upon the use of the term "control" and have injected into it the logical meaning necessary to express the full scope of this function.   Let us examine the process of control in this sense.

If he is to check up, the manager requires some means of differentiating between acceptable and unacceptable performance.   The criterion he uses is his *performance standard*.   He must be kept informed of what is happening and he should not have to be present in person to find out.   The process of keeping him informed is *reporting*.   Even when he knows what is happening, however, he must still appraise the work that is being done, the methods used, and the results secured.   He accomplishes this through *evaluation*.   Finally, if either his results or methods are not satisfactory, the manager must rectify the deficiencies and provide for continued improvement.   He does this through *performance correction*.

TYPES OF CONTROL

The manager has two basic approaches to control.   Both are necessary and it is important to understand the difference if we are to use them effectively.   These are control by personal inspection and control by exception.

Control by Personal Inspection

"One picture is worth a thousand words" is true enough, and this holds also for the visual pictures we get by personally observing what is being done.   A professional manager may rely largely upon control by exception, but he finds that a certain amount of personal observation of what is being done is necessary for effective control. Personal inspection is most useful in case of emergency, to audit work that is normally controlled by variance, and to control operations for which performance standards cannot be developed.   The manager may want to make a personal inspection at the beginning, midpoint, and completion of large or continuing assignments.   Personal observation of people in action can provide a good basis for performance appraisal.

In Campbell Soup Company, a large food processor, quality of the product is of paramount importance. Campbell maintains its position by having a unique product which it tries to make superior in quality and flavor to competing products. Since no machine can do the job of tasting or can have as much discrimination as the human palate, the president and top executives of Campbell Soup periodically taste samples of food put up in some twenty-eight processing plants around the world. This is important and necessary personal inspection.

The prime disadvantage of control by personal inspection is that, if it is used exclusively, it limits the scope of the manager to what he can personally observe and appraise. Furthermore, his judgment tends to be in terms of whether or not the work is performed the way he would do it himself.

People want to inject something of themselves in the work they do, and overuse of personal inspection gives them the feeling that the boss is always peering over their shoulders, watching to see that they do it *his* way. This discourages initiative and independent action.

If one outstanding top executive habitually checks everything in person, the control will probably be good while he still has the capacity to do it. Inevitably, however, the job will outgrow him or he passes from the scene. When this is the case, the organization has no logical or formalized control system to replace the personal leader and chaos frequently results.

In the case of one New York manufacturing company, for example, the founder of the enterprise, an outstanding engineer, retained most of the effective control himself, even when the company had reached a sales volume of several hundred million dollars. A constant and unexpected visitor in almost every office and plant of the company, the highly capable chief executive kept most of the complex affairs of the corporation in his head. His knowing eye scrutinized key operating and financial reports carefully. If results were questionable or unsatisfactory, he outlined the discrepancy with the red pencil which he reserved as his personal brand. However many levels of organization it sifted through, the familiar red slash elicited attention and then fast corrective action. Effective as it was during his lifetime, when the strong personal leader died, it left the company without a sound and consistent method of maintaining control.

Control by Exception

Control by exception requires the manager to determine in advance what methods are to be used and what results he expects to accomplish. So long as the operation proceeds according to plan, he devotes little of his personal attention to it. However, if the operation falls behind in any respect, he is alerted by his control system and immediately can attend to the variance.

Management control frees the manager from the need to remain cognizant of detail. It gives him a tool for analyzing results so that he can anticipate and correct variances before they occur. Furthermore, it encourages people to use imagination and resourcefulness in the work they do. Because control by exception is more difficult and requires continuing effort, managers frequently fail to make effective use of it. However, properly employed, this is one of the most valuable tools a manager has to free himself from grinding detail so that he can focus on the work of management that lies particularly within his province.

Both personal inspection and control by exception are needed. In general terms, managers at lower levels make greatest use of control by inspection. Those at top levels rely to a greater extent on control by exception. The reason is that lower-level managers monitor directly the end results as they are being accomplished. At each level higher in the organization, accountable managers are this much further removed from the actual operating work. If an executive wants to observe operations in person, he will have to go down through four or five levels of organization to reach the field of action. While necessary and desirable in proper proportion, too much personal inspection by top-level managers will tend to weaken the accountability of those at lower levels.

THE ALLEN PRINCIPLES OF CONTROL

We have identified two basic principles which apply to control in all of its aspects. These are of particular significance with the rapid increase of automatic data recording and the use of the computer.

Principle of Least Cause

In any given group of occurrences, a small number of causes will tend to give rise to the largest proportion of results.

In any group, we can expect a few people to produce the most work, a selected few to account for most of the errors, and a relatively small number of employees to account for the largest number of accidents.

This principle is valuable in control because it enables us to focus the greatest part of our energy and resources on the few variables in a control situation that we can expect to yield the greatest results.

As an illustration, Ducommun Metals & Supply Company, a leading steel distributor, found that over 80 per cent of its business came from the sales made to only 10 per cent of its accounts. Obviously, these were the critical few that produced the largest proportion of results. The company's question was: How could it intensify this profitable effort and minimize the least profitable calls? The course of action that Ducommun adopted is instructive. First, the company made sure that salesmen gave greatest attention to the most promising accounts. To accomplish this, each salesman programmed and scheduled his calls; he decided what accounts had greatest potential and called on each of these weekly. He not only planned the call but also set an objective for the volume of sales that could be made on each call.

This principle is operative in many fields. Discount stores, for example, competing with conventional merchandising establishments, have learned to identify the critical few items in each line which can be stocked and sold most profitably. One of the large New York department stores carries 129 separate styles of men's white shirts. The prices of these range from $1.99 to $14.09. A competing discount chain carries 35 styles ranging from $1.49 to $6.99. While both approaches have their advantages and disadvantages, it is obvious that concentration upon the critical few gives the greatest promise of results.

To illustrate this principle further, in the automobile insurance industry there has been a tendency to make little distinction between low-risk and high-risk drivers. Allstate Insurance Company, a leader in the field, changed this by undertaking research to identify the critical few. The company established a correlation between the number of miles a person drives and his chances of having an accident. By offering the lowest-risk drivers a substantial discount, the company was able greatly to increase its underwriting of this preferred category.

Principle of Point of Control

The greatest potential for control tends to exist at the point where action takes place.

In many companies we have studied, the chief executive and top staff groups tend to receive detailed statements of operating information and they spend a great deal of time in evaluating and assessing these data. However, this is not the prime focus of control, for discrepancies are identified and corrective action must then proceed through the intervening layers of organization until finally it is exercised at the point where the action took place. A moment's logical thought will show that this is a slow, expensive, and ineffective way to control.

First-line managers who supervise operations, such as the functional supervisors of manufacturing and sales, directly regulate end results. They spend a large part of the company's money and are best placed to exercise direct control. Accordingly, greatest control effort should be applied at the focus of control, the first level of management, rather than at the top.

The more quickly first-line supervisors can identify variances, determine their significance, and do something about them, the more effective control becomes. At successively higher levels of the organization, managers should be concerned with consolidation of detail and review of operating results. Their attention should be directed largely to exceptions and not to a check of the on-going routine. Detail is better left to the first-line supervisor who is actually monitoring the operation.

This principle emphasizes the vital importance of providing first-line managers with accurate information as quickly as possible and giving them the tools they need to utilize these data effectively in control of their segment of the business.

CONTROL AND THE COMPUTER

The computer has great potential impact upon control and will correct some of the inadequacies of conventional control systems.

Inadequacies of Conventional Control

Conventional control has developed in terms of the control of specific elements of the business. In the past, we have concentrated upon cost controls, quality controls, the control of inventories, manpower, sales, and a round dozen more items. Development of performance standards and the reporting and evaluation of these factors most often have been the responsibility of functional groups, and the placement within the organization and the capability of these groups have had much to do with the type and effectiveness of the control that resulted. As a general rule, we find that the greater the functional concentration, the greater the tendency toward control bias.

To illustrate the dangers of functional imbalance in control, one large West Coast manufacturing company had an aggressive quality control group which developed a rigorous system for quality maintenance in every part of the production cycle. The costs of rejects and scrap dropped perceptibly, and the company pointed with pride to its savings of $123,000 the first year and $278,000 the second year of the program. During the second year, the company called in outside consultants to help with its proposed divisionalization. As a result of the organization study that was made, the total number of employees was cut by 20 per cent with a resulting savings of almost $1 million. After the reorganization was completed, the company did nothing about maintaining control of the organization but intensified its quality control program under the urging of the quality control manager. As a result, the lean, trim organization quickly grew fat and had to be trimmed back radically again within five years by a further organization survey.

An important requirement in the use of automatic data processing for control is that a systems approach be adopted. This should be geared not to static organizational groups but to the needs of the total organization. Hard and fast functional boundaries, which once set sharp lines of demarcation among the different departments of the company, must be breached so that there can be effective use of these new techniques. Here again the resistance is psychological. Managers resist change; they fear the computer for the sharp light it promises to throw on past inefficiencies, and also for the threat it brings of doing away with many once-important management and staff positions. If an automated approach to control is to work, it will demand of each manager that he understand and put first the needs of the total organization. This will require not only self-discipline, but also an intensity of education and orientation that we have not yet mastered.

To utilize the computer and electronic data processing most effectively in the control system, we should look first to the control needs of various levels of the organization, and then to the possibility of controlling the business as a whole with the aid of these new tools. Here we examine first the level of control.

The Level of Control

Control can be applied logically only if we have a clear perception of the control needs of the various levels of the organization. As is true with planning, *each manager should have his unique and identifiable control work to do, and this should not overlap or duplicate similar control work done by any other manager.*

Top management properly concerns itself with long-range plans which are developed to guide the over-all course of the business. To do its job effectively, top management needs control tools that will keep it constantly informed of progress against these plans. It should be noted here that the president and his top staff have smallest concern with the specifics of direct manufacturing and direct sales; rather, they need to have consolidations of data that will keep them constantly informed of the total course of the business. Top management should be concerned primarily with next month's problems and those of next year rather than those of today. For this reason, it needs to think largely in terms of alternatives, and the control data it receives should give it sound guidance in selection of the most desirable options to be followed.

First-line foremen and supervisors are accountable for the physical production and sale of the product and they need much more specific short-term data.

At middle levels, managers act primarily as interpretation points. They must translate the broad, general plans of top management into the specific item-by-item plans that will be carried out at the operating level. When control data are generated at the operating level, it is the job of middle-level managers to interpret and consolidate them so that top executives can see the total flow of the business.

With the advent of electronic data processing, it becomes much more feasible for every manager to see the business as a whole and to visualize his part in it. This broadened viewpoint will be of maximum value only when we learn to develop a control system that envisages the total needs of the company and not simply those of the accountant, the salesman, or the manufacturing man.

Controlling the Business as a Whole

If we are to control the business as a whole, we need a control structure that meshes closely with the planning structure we have already discussed. We have seen that the focus of effective planning is at the top levels of the organization, where the broad guidelines are established which channel the plans and action taken at lower levels toward the end results that are most advantageous to the enterprise as a whole. Since control is, essentially, a monitoring of plans already decided and put into effect, the first focus of control is at the first operating level, where the plans are being executed.

Just as planning is meaningless at lower levels unless it is established within limits that can be developed only at top levels, it is also true that top-level control will be ineffective unless it can be centered clearly *on those variances that lower-level managers are incapable of controlling effectively themselves.* In general terms, this involves those control items which involve two or more different components or which have impact upon the organization as a whole.

Controlling the business as a whole requires three basic steps:

1. *Sharing of the emphasis upon results with renewed attention to the methods by which those results are attained.* In the past, we have tended to concentrate upon controlling the results accomplished, relying heavily upon historical reporting for the purpose. Most control in-

formation, even today, is derived by measuring the work after it has been completed. However, we know that control of results, by itself, is not enough, for results are always past history. Once the action is completed, we can no longer regulate it. The best we can do is to anticipate and prepare to control the next cycle of the same action.

To achieve control, we must have a means of finding out how effective our methods are and what occurs as work is in the process of being carried out. In a four-stage production process, we want to be able to identify probable mistakes and deficiencies at stage one, not at stage four. In selling to customers, we need to identify changes in market and demand before the salesman calls on the customer, not after he has tried to make the sale and failed.

Here automatic data processing looms large, for it enables us to find out about things *while they are happening*. Customer rejection of a product feature can be reported in minutes, not days. A thousand quality complaints that once could be collected and analyzed only with weeks and months of effort can now be registered, reported, and acted upon in hours, often while the faulty process is in operation and can still be corrected.

2. *Emphasis upon quality of information, not quantity.* A common belief is that automatic data processing is valuable primarily because it generates more information than has been available in the past. While this is true, it is also well to keep in mind that it has been possible for many years to produce more information than managers could understand or use. Introduction of the computer bids fair to aggravate this situation instead of improving it unless we recognize one salient point: *Sound control depends upon the development of the minimum amount of information that will do the job, and reporting it quickly enough to be useful.*

The manager who is accountable for an entity of the business is in the best position to determine what information he needs, and *when* he needs it, to control his component effectively. In the past, unfortunately, most of this work has been assumed, in the manager's default, by the accounting or controller's department. The natural result is the provision of financial and accounting information which the manager often does not understand and finds it difficult to apply to his own area. The best answer is to delegate to managers the authority and responsibility for control which they have abdicated, or have never had, and require them to develop management controls in terms of standards based on approved plans, reports tailored to documentation of both results and the way those results are accomplished, and the accomplishment of the major part of control at the point where the action takes place.

3. *Development of a planning and control staff group.* Few business enterprises today are organized to implement these concepts of computer-assisted control; one important reason is our fragmentation of the planning and control process.

Typically, each function in the past has planned and controlled its own operations, acting largely within the framework of company policies and procedures where these have existed. Coordination has been accomplished most largely by middle-level managers and by committees. These agencies will no longer serve, however, as the human mind has limited capacity to ingest, understand, and analyze the vast amounts of information that must be comprehended if the business is to be treated as a total entity. The alternative that is rapidly emerging is to collect all pertinent control data at one central point, analyze them, and report them to fit the specific needs of each using unit. This, of course, is in contrast to conventional methods, where the information has been collected in bits and pieces and finally tied together at the top level for appropriate consideration and action.

SUMMARY

Controlling is the work a manager does to assess and regulate work in progress and completed. The control is the manager's means of checking up. While control by personal observation is often necessary, the most desirable method is control by exception. Here the Principle of Least Cause and the Principle of Point of Control are important to ensure that greatest control is applied where it will do the most good. Proper control should be furnished managers at each organization level to minimize overlap and duplication. With the advent of the computer, it is important for each manager to look to his part in controlling the business as a whole rather than an isolated segment of the total.

CHAPTER 27 *Performance Standards*

*If you have called a bad thing bad, you have done no
great matter; but if you call a good thing good, you
have accomplished much.* GOETHE

DEFINITIONS

Establishing Performance Standards: the work a manager performs
to establish the criteria by which methods and results will be evaluated.
Synonym for standard: yardstick.

Differentiating: distinguishing grades or levels of quantity, quality,
and other characteristics.

Satisfactory: a level of performance equal to or better than a predetermined requirement.

Unsatisfactory: a level of performance less than a predetermined
requirement.

THE LOGIC OF STANDARDS

A central problem in control is how to differentiate between good
work and poor work. The logical requirement of any good standard
is this: it must provide a *test* of performance.

Since a professional manager is required to maintain constant check
on work that is undertaken many levels below him, and often thousands
of miles distant, it follows that he must be able to test the quality and
quantity of performance without being on the spot himself.

For example, the president of a large company may be accountable
for the work done by forty to fifty thousand people, but he cannot see
much of this with his own eyes. Instead, he must rely upon performance standards.

Here we come to the heart of scientific management control, and we find, again, that it is as much a matter of psychology as of technology. If we can develop standards which are *understood and accepted* not only by himself but also by those whose work is being judged, the manager need then give but passing attention to work and results that meet the standard, and he can concern himself primarily with variances from the standard.

A further logical requirement is that the standard must be capable of testing the adequacy both of the manner in which the work is done and the results that follow from it. Over the long term, good methods tend to yield good results. By good fortune and genius, we may be able to follow poor methods and still get good results. However, the professional manager prefers to develop sound and effective methods in the knowledge that this will enhance the probability of good results.

THE IMPORTANCE OF STANDARDS

Although they are often dealt with in a cursory fashion, sound management standards have a deep and lasting impact upon the survival and success of the company and each of its parts.

Encourage Entrepreneurship

People prefer to command their own destinies. To illustrate, when General Lucius Clay became president of the Continental Can Company in 1950, he found that the company had grown quickly and successfully but that in the process it had tended to concentrate a high degree of authority—and accountability—at headquarters. Faced with the need for providing a new impetus for continued growth, the general saw one of his first tasks as "getting everybody thinking he's his own boss."

As was clear in Continental Can, this desirable end result can be accomplished only if people can be given substantial authority to make their own decisions; this, in turn, requires that some means be developed of segregating the work and results to be accomplished by individual managers. Again looking to the excellent example provided by the Continental Can Company, we find that if measurable performance standards can be established, each manager can, almost literally, be put into business for himself. Continental Can accomplished this through the preparation of detailed operating plans for each unit of the company. These, in turn, provided the performance standards against which each accountable manager could be judged and his performance compared with others.

It is true that performance standards require the manager to operate within the limits of specified guidelines; however, within those parameters, he can be delegated a large share of the authority necessary to take free and independent action.

Make Self-control Possible

Performance standards enable accountable managers to determine for themselves how well they are doing. Because he can read his own indicators, the accountable manager can identify deficiencies in work in progress and can catch his own errors before final results are accomplished and reported. This kind of self-control is more satisfactory to the manager concerned; it gives him a feeling of accomplishment and accords a dignity to his work it otherwise would not have.

Form a Basis for Effective Reporting

The reports managers receive frequently provide them with information that has little pertinence to what they are doing and provides little help in real control of their operations. Effective performance standards point precisely to the things which are of critical concern and identify the kind of information the manager needs.

Facilitate Self-development

Managers have little incentive to improve their performance unless they know the specific areas in which they are falling behind. Performance standards, properly developed, will help each manager to isolate and identify for himself those areas of management performance in which he is not meeting accepted requirements. With this knowledge, he can then come to focus on the specific activities he should carry out if he is going to improve as a manager. An important point here is that the standard will enable the manager to identify and correct his own performance and it minimizes the need for his superior to dwell constantly upon his deficiencies. Because the standards are impersonal, they provide an objective and noncritical basis for encouraging personal improvement in management.

IMPROVING USE OF STANDARDS

The development of performance standards can be a creative contribution to the company's survival and profitability, or it can be a waste of effort and even a detriment to accomplishment. Much depends upon recognition of three cardinal points.

1. *Psychological Factors Must Be Considered. The psychological factors that enter into the preparation of performance standards are at least as important as the mechanical considerations.* The first purpose of good standards is to make people want to excel. The runner who

covers the 100 yards in 12 seconds isn't doing very well. He knows it and so does everybody else. The standard here not only tells him how well he is doing, *it makes him want to improve*. To serve this important purpose, any standard must be designed so that it will identify and highlight outstanding performance and help to identify those who excel. If people know they will have an opportunity to shine, however briefly, in the spotlight of the boss's approbation and that of their teammates, they will put forth added effort to win this recognition.

The question often is asked: Isn't it enough for an individual to be able to identify his own accomplishment? Generally it is not, for if the individual fails to meet standard, all too often he will rationalize his failure. If he exceeds it, a substantial part of his reward lies in having others know about it. A few exceptional people are self-motivated to the extent that they need little or no external recognition. In real life, these individuals number so few that we cannot safely build our standards in terms of their attitude. And even here we tend to find that the self-motivated individual has a positive reaction to external recognition of his success and failure.

To see the broad implications of this factor, consider the case of the Buick Motor Division of the General Motors Corporation. Back in 1955 Buick was competing for top place in the passenger car market. Gearing to meet increased production requirements, the division fell behind in its styling and quality control, and found itself producing more automobiles than customers wanted to buy. To top it off, all too many of those who did buy were complaining about the quality of the automobile they had acquired.

General Motors Corporation has an outstanding control system which ensured that these deficiencies would be identified quickly. However, rather than merely tightening controls, General Motors carefully assessed the human factors involved. A new Division Manager was brought in. In General Motors, Division Managers are given large responsibility and authority. Operating in competition with the other Divisions of the company and with other automobile companies, each Division Manager has both internal and external pressure exerted upon him to excel. If he succeeds, his rewards in terms of money and recognition are large.

Working within this system, Buick put to work its precise and rigorous performance standards to identify the weak areas in quality and styling. Each deficiency was carefully evaluated, corrective action was initiated, and within a few years Buick had regained its lost ground and forged to the front once more.

2. *Individual and Group Needs Should Be Balanced.* People work for personal rewards; however, if the standard is so constructed that it

identifies only personal accomplishment, the individual will tend to focus completely on his own small part of the team play, often to the detriment of the over-all effort. The important and difficult requirement in establishing sound standards is *to be able to identify outstanding individual performance even when the team results are poor* and, at the same time, *to have a means of identifying and rewarding the team as a whole* when its total performance excels.

3. *Standards Are Necessary for Both Methods and Results.* While, as we have seen, good results tend to follow from good methods, it is vitally important that we know when poor methods are being employed. It is only in this way that we can identify the causative factors that lead to poor results so that we can correct them before the work being done is carried to conclusion. Conventional standards have emphasized results because in the past we have not been able to get information quickly or accurately enough to determine the effectiveness of our methods. With the computer and new electronic devices that are now available, the measurement of methods becomes eminently feasible.

SOUND PLANS PROVIDE THE LOGICAL BASIS FOR MEANINGFUL STANDARDS

With these considerations in mind, we now look to the establishment of effective standards. The logical and scientific approach to developing standards is based upon the assumption that we cannot know whether we have arrived at a destination unless we have first decided what that destination is; we cannot know if we are following the best method unless we have determined *what that method should be before we embark upon it.* This brings us to the basic requirement: management performance standards, whenever possible, *must be based upon the guiding plans* that were developed in the first place. Too often this does not occur because the work was unplanned. Where this is the case, we have no alternative but to complete the job, then to review it and determine whether the methods and results were satisfactory. Here we lose the most valuable aspect of the standard—its use by the manager to test his performance as the work proceeds, with the opportunity to identify and regulate deficiencies *before the whole job is finished.* Simple and logical as it is, this basic requirement is generally overlooked by all but the real professionals in management.

It bears repetition that we can best assess our results if we check our accomplishment against the plans we established to guide our action in the first place. Here the plan serves a dual purpose; first, it is used to determine what we should accomplish, how we should do it, and what it should cost; then, once action gets under way, the same plan serves as a criterion to help us determine our progress toward our goal and how well we are carrying out the steps we determined were necessary to get there.

ASSESSING RESULTS AND METHODS

Results are best gauged in terms of our accomplishment of objectives. How close do we come to meeting our goals and targets? What have we accomplished in sales volume, sales revenue, market position, and improved margins? What is our current position with respect to return on investment and cash and capital requirements?

We assess our *methods* by using programs and schedules, budgets, procedures, and policies as standards of performance. If we have determined beforehand what we can reasonably expect to accomplish within predetermined time periods, we can check what we have done and measure our progress against the program and schedule. If we fall behind in program or schedule, we know that our progress toward our objective is jeopardized and *we can take corrective action before the crisis is upon us*.

Budgets are valuable also in their second role of performance standards. The budget tells us how much it *should* cost to carry out our programmed activities within the time limits set by the schedule in our progress toward objectives. By constantly measuring our actual expenditures against this standard, we can achieve most effective control of costs.

When it is important that work be carried out in a standardized fashion, standards based on procedures give us the control we need. In the same fashion, if there are standing decisions which apply and must be adhered to in getting the job done, use of established policies and regulations as performance standards will ensure this uniformity of action.

PARTICIPATION IS THE KEY
TO ACCEPTANCE OF STANDARDS

As we have seen, performance standards may be technically perfect but practically useless unless they are both understood and accepted. If people are given an opportunity to contribute their ideas in the setting of standards, they will tend to accept them realistically and work in terms of them. If the standards are developed and applied arbitrarily, however, the natural reaction is resistance and rejection.

Here again our dual concept of planning provides us with the key to most effective participation: plans provide the best basis for standards.

If people contribute to the development of the initial plans, there will be little grounds for resistance when these same plans are used in the role of standards.

This is well borne out in the H. J. Heinz Company, a leading food manufacturer. In H. J. Heinz, the company proceeds on the philosophy that managers at the operating level are best qualified to establish the standards by which their work will be measured. Each factory, for example, develops and sets its own cost standards. In doing this, the accounting group in the factory begins the task of assembling the data on which the standards will be based about six months before they will actually be put into effect.

Working with the accountable managers involved, the staff group reviews standard fixed and variable overhead rates and materials yields, materials prices, and labor costs. The cost for each of the many products produced in the factory are weighted to provide the budget which later becomes the standard for operating performance.

In carrying out this rather complex job, the controller's staff plays an important part. Accountable managers are consulted and their recommendations and suggestions are considered carefully. The record of past variances is studied carefully and used as data in reappraising the new standards. This process is helped considerably by the continuing review of both standards and performance that all managers maintain on a continuing basis.

SUMMARY

A standard is the means of differentiating between acceptable and unacceptable work and results. Both the human and technical factors necessary to develop sound standards should be given adequate consideration. The basic requirement for management standards is that they be developed from the guiding plans that were established to guide the action in the first place. Properly done, this type of standard gives us a means of assessing what is done in terms of what *should* have been accomplished. To be acceptable, standards must be developed with full consultation and participation of the people whose work will be measured.

> *We have more useless information than ignorance of what is useful.* V. G. BLAS

DEFINITIONS

Performance Measuring: the work a manager performs to record and report work in progress and completed.

Record: to make notation of, to set down in writing.

Report: to convey information.

THE LOGIC OF MEASURING

If we are in London and something happens in New York which we need to know about, a notation of some kind must be made of what occurred and this information must be conveyed to us in London. Our knowledge of what occurred, our interpretation of what it means, and our understanding of it will depend almost completely on the information we receive. Geographically distant as are New York and London, virtually the same situation prevails when managers are separated by only a few levels of organization or are located in separate plants or offices.

Our logical problem is not just to get information back and forth. We must get the information that will tell us what we must know in terms we can understand. Once again we find that while the technology is important with respect to speed and accuracy, the matter of conveying *meaning* is more a matter of emotion and communication than anything else.

In the past, reporting has been mostly historical—a conveying of information about things that had already happened. Now, with the vast acceleration possible through use of the computer and related systems, we have the possibility of conveying information so quickly that accountable managers will have a much greater opportunity to use the information received while it is still pertinent to the work in process.

Three things are happening today: (1) Managers can maintain *current* check of performance against plan as action is executed; (2)

through operations research and simulation, alternative plans of action can be tested almost as quickly as basic conditions or assumptions change; and (3) integrated information systems enable managers to regulate the ongoing performance of even complex and intricate operations by commands issued from one central point. This is possible because managers are able to understand at any given time the flow of activity for the business as a whole and the status and interrelationships of each functional part.

ACCOUNTABILITY FOR REPORTS

Reports convey control information from the point where action takes place to the managers who are accountable for results. Reporting is usually thought of primarily as an accounting function. However, the preparation and use of reports are a basic responsibility of every manager. Properly prepared, reports can greatly facilitate the task of management. Timely, accurate reports enable a manager to remain abreast of operations and to make sound decisions concerning the work in progress. Reports, by telling him what has happened, also give him the best basis for planning for the future. Much of the control information a manager receives is part of a company-wide reporting system, established by top management to ensure that each manager has the proper information when he requires it. A standardized system not only speeds the flow of data but also makes possible consolidated reports covering the operations of different organizational units.

Within this system, each manager should see to it that he receives the information he needs to maintain constant check on the results for which he is accountable. The type and amount of data reported vary at different organization levels. Since first-line supervisors have the greatest opportunity to regulate directly the operation going on, the reports they receive should contain the largest amount of detailed control information. Accountability broadens at successively higher levels and is further removed from end results. As a consequence, reports prepared for top-level managers should be consolidations of data already reported to lower levels.

REQUIREMENTS OF EFFECTIVE REPORTING

With the growth, expansion, and decentralization of business and the greater accessibility of information, there has been a tendency to increase both the number and complexity of reports. The criterion of what can be used effectively, however, is not what is available but *what the human mind can absorb*. Here we find that a prime requirement of effective reporting is to tailor and streamline reports so that they provide the specific information a manager needs in a form that he can readily understand and apply to his own area of accountability.   Several factors are pertinent here.

1. *Check the Effectiveness of Planning*

Before analyzing the reporting system, it is necessary to look closely at the validity of the plans that are in use.   Since the prime purpose of the report is to tell us how well we are doing against established objectives, programs, budgets, and other plans, it is clear that the usefulness of the report will depend upon the planning already completed.   The more complete and accurate the plans, the easier it is to report the variances and exceptions as they occur.   If planning is sketchy or incomplete, there will be a natural tendency to manufacture, *after the fact,* some standard which will purport to show what should have been accomplished.   This robs the report of its value because after-the-fact analysis tends to concentrate on results and precludes proper assessment of the methods used to attain those results.

2. *Adopt a Stewardship Concept of Reporting*

Reports should analyze the stewardship of accountable individuals. As used by companies such as Standard Oil Company (N.J.), stewardship refers to the accountability of a manager for the facilities, materials, and people entrusted to his care.

Stewardship reporting literally measures an individual as manager of his own business.   It holds him to account for the cost of his operation, or even better, its profit or loss.   This kind of reporting is often difficult because it requires that reports be based, not exclusively on bookkeeping precepts, but on concepts of management accountability.   It requires that each manager be given a clear picture of the money value of his operation and the results that he is getting.

For many years, one large company maintained an extremely accurate and detailed reporting system.   This gave top management overall financial data in profusion about the results attained by the company as a whole.   Unfortunately, none of the reports showed how much it cost to make each product, or how much money an individual manager was spending or should spend.   Costs gradually inched upward, seemingly impervious to top management control measures.   Foreman training programs and cost-cutting campaigns yielded only mediocre results. The company was able to get its costs in hand only after it had revamped its common-pot accounting system so that each manager could be made to toe the line.

Stewardship accountability is possible only if a manager is delegated authority over money spent in his department or on behalf of his department; otherwise he cannot be held accountable for the expenditure. It therefore follows that a stewardship report should come to focus on controllable items of expense. If expense over which the manager has little or no command is reported, these items should be listed separately.

3. *Provide Meaningful Information*

The basic purpose of a report is to inform accountable managers how well they are doing; in other words, to show what is actually happening in the accomplishment of established plans. Simply to tell a manager what has happened as of a given moment in time is not very helpful. So far as possible, it should tell him not only what is happening now but also should bring to his attention a clear picture of related performance in the past. This calls for trend reporting so that the current accomplishment is shown in its proper relationship to previous experience.

To be realistic, the data upon which the trend line is based must be adjusted so that the basis for comparison is uniform throughout. When different departments of the company are involved, close scrutiny must be maintained to ensure that changes in the basic data reported from any one component are adjusted so that they are consistent with the over-all picture, or, if necessary, the basis for the trend line is changed in terms of a new common denominator.

Information will be most meaningful if each manager is provided with data that apply specifically to his own accountability. It is as pointless, for example, to give the president detailed information on plant burden costs as it is to feed the foreman a breakdown on general administrative expenses.

In Southern Counties Gas Company of California, a leading public utility, for example, top management ensures that it receives the information it needs in its primary function—that of planning, controlling, organizing, and leading the over-all activities of the company. Accordingly, top-level managers are primarily concerned with *totals of information* from the operating divisions of the company. At the lower levels of organization in Southern Counties, however, the primary focus is on reporting the specifics of information—the data each supervisor needs if he is to be kept informed as to how well he is doing in carrying out his day-by-day job. To burden top management with this operating detail would be pointless; to give the first-line supervisor the over-all consolidations would be meaningless.

Compare to this a large manufacturing company with headquarters in Cleveland. Here the president feels that he must know everything and demands a continuing flow of information. Completely documented and fully detailed reports funnel to his desk; he scrutinizes each in person and shuttles his red-penciled comments to accountable managers in an unending stream.   Remote from the actual scene of operations, he must have comprehensive explanations of operating detail that are a matter of firsthand knowledge to managers on the spot.   In this situation, managers who should be controlling the operation look to the chief executive for both control information and control instructions. They cannot be held to accountability for the work they do and exhibit general disinterest.   The chief executive, an outstanding individual, derives great pleasure from his personal command of the entire enterprise. There is virtually no possibility of change until he retires or dies.

In looking to the provision of meaningful information, we should concern ourselves with three primary points.

First, *the amount of data reported should be in proportion to the controllability of the expense.*   There is little point in reporting on disposition of money spent where there is little opportunity for corrective action.   Long reports of how budget appropriations were consumed, for example, are often useless.

Secondly, even if the volume of information is kept within bounds, those who can do most about it should still see it. *Decision-making information should be provided to the lowest organizational level where perspective exists for sound decision.*   Within the framework of company policy, the department manager should have authority to make practically all decisions which affect only his department.   However, if the decision reaches over into two or more departments, the authority and information necessary to make the decision should be delegated to a level sufficiently high to encompass all interests involved.

When this reporting approach is adopted it will be observable that more reports are required at foreman and superintendent level, and fewer at department level and higher.   What is more, reports at lower levels will tend to go into increasing detail, while those at higher levels will deal with the broad consolidations necessary for over-all judgment.

Thirdly, *if reports are to be meaningful, they must be understandable by the managers to whom the information is transmitted.*   A hazard here is reliance upon accounting and financial terminology.   This may have special significance to the accountant but only vague familiarity to the manager using the report.   If technical terms are necessary, the managers using the reports should be educated in their meaning.   If there is any doubt, it is best to attach an explanatory glossary or footnote to the report itself.

4. Make Reports Timely

In a fast-moving and competitive industry, an outdated report leaves management on the bleachers instead of in the ball game.

How can we speed up the reporting process? There are two major impediments. One is the desire to give managers a completely documented and detailed statement of operating and financial results. The second is to make these management control statements audit-accurate.

For purposes of control, a manager does not need a complete breakdown of each item of expense and of his sales and profit results. A control report is not a budget and should not attempt to recapitulate budget data. What the manager needs is an analysis of the performance for which he is accountable, with the variances highlighted so that he can focus his attention immediately on areas that require action.

If management insists on management and not bookkeeping reports, accounting people can satisfy them. Many timesaving techniques become possible once the fetishes of completeness and split-cent accuracy are sidestepped. For example, many key figures can be estimated before the transactions involved are actually posted.

Since the reporting data are always geared to the closing date, reporting is expedited by anything done to hasten the closing of the books. Positive steps here include planning all possible preliminaries so that they are completed before the closing date. Working papers can be prepared and many accounting statements finalized before the closing figures are entered.

With a little prior planning, all hands in the accounting department can focus their major effort for a few days on closing activities and let routine wait.

Faster reporting almost always requires changes in the accounting system so that it can better meet the requirements of management control. This is the point at which most attempts at improvement fail. Accounting systems can be modified only slowly because procedures are necessarily highly standardized, a large volume of work is handled under time pressure, and accuracy is important. When changes are required, accounting personnel should participate fully in the planning and should spearhead the effort required.

In a Southern food company, for example, the president hired a specialist to install a new budgetary control system. The expert reported directly to the president. It took him six months to set up a budgetary reporting system, but at the end of three years he still had not been able to get the accounting staff to change their procedures so that his system would work effectively. The president turned the mangled remains of the system over to the controller. Within a few months a less ambitious but still highly effective budgetary control system was operating.

Allegheny Ludlum Steel Corporation, conscious of this need, makes it clear that it is up to operating management to acquaint the accounting organization with the information it wants and why it is wanted. Given this background, the controller can then develop a concise, graphic, and timely reporting system geared closely to management's real needs.

This does not mean that every manager can be given independent authority to collect data and report them the way he thinks best. In Varian Associates, Lockheed Aircraft, Parke-Davis, and other leading companies, responsibility for collecting information is often quite highly decentralized, but the reporting and interpreting phases are centralized in the accounting, controller's, or other department. This helps speed up reporting, while ensuring that data reported are accurate and comparable.

Electronic equipment can be valuable in recording control information and speeding an accurate flow to higher levels in small and large companies. However, manual record keeping is not to be tossed out the window without carefully studying the mechanized alternative. It may be difficult to shift from one to another of the many possible cost-saving applications. When it is properly installed and manned by a trained staff, however, companies such as General Electric, Thompson Ramo Wooldridge, RCA, Ford, and many others have found data-processing and related equipment potent cost savers in process planning, scheduling, inventory measuring, reporting, and other activities.

While there is no panacea for slow, voluminous reporting, a concerted approach on all four points described can yield immediate and lasting results. If managers are to manage, they must *know*—fast and accurately—and this is the special province of an effective reporting system.

SUMMARY

Measuring is the recording and reporting of information about work in progress and work completed. Every manager must both send and receive reports to maintain effective communication. Particularly with the use of the computer, several key points should be followed in developing an effective reporting system. Basic is the need to report against planned accomplishment. This can best be done by holding every manager to stewardship for one segment of the business and keeping him fully informed of his progress in this stewardship. Reports should provide information that is understandable to the managers using them, in terms of their job requirements. Reports should be kept up to date so that they will spur timely action. Management and not accounting needs should be given first consideration in developing a management reporting system.

It is better to know nothing than to know what ain't so.
JOSH BILLINGS

DEFINITIONS

Performance Evaluating: the work a manager performs to appraise work in progress and results secured.

Variance: a departure from what was intended; a divergence, over or under.

THE LOGIC OF PERFORMANCE EVALUATION

His performance standards tell a manager where he *should be;* his reports tell him where he *is.* Now he must ask, "Is this satisfactory?"

If we are falling behind, are there good reasons for it? Must we learn to live with the new conditions or can we change things so that we can achieve the goals that we have set? The answers to these questions require a careful appraisal of the results achieved and investigation is necessary in order to determine why deficiencies occur.

WHO SHOULD EVALUATE

Once the data are in, the question arises as to who should compare the actual performance to the standard and who should determine the significance of variances that have occurred. The accountable manager is generally in the best position to evaluate his own performance and to take corrective action as the activity progresses. He not only should know his standards but also should have prompt access to the data which report his performance.

CHECKS AND BALANCES

But self-control is not enough.   In the interests of sound evaluation, we should note that the accountable manager is likely to be biased in his own favor.   He is prone to rationalize failures and discrepancies and to provide arguments for his own defense.

Effective checks and balances require two steps: (1) Assurances that the accountable manager has been fully informed and given the opportunity to take corrective action; and (2) further reporting of the variance, if it is still significant, to a higher level of management, or, if corrective action has been taken, reporting of both the variance and the corrective action, with an estimate of its effectiveness, to higher management levels.

In some companies deficiencies in performance are discussed only with the accountable manager and are carried no higher.   This is a mistake.   It is literally true that what the boss inspects the subordinate corrects.   While the manager on the spot should be given the first opportunity to improve performance, an impartial and objective viewpoint must be brought to bear to determine the effectiveness of the correction and also to derive from the action taken lessons that can be applied elsewhere in the company.

Checks and balances are best provided by introducing an independent viewpoint into the evaluation process.   This frequently can be done by use of staff departments.   Here Southern Counties Gas Company again provides an excellent example.   In Southern Counties, management emphasizes the evaluation of activities and the work being done, and not the individual and his personality.   Organizationally, Southern Counties has divisionalized geographically, with the division managers reporting to the chief executive office.

To implement the company control philosophy, the corporate specialized staff departments work both with the division and top management to develop control tools that will be most useful to the company as a whole.   Each corporate staff group, working with the divisions, develops standards of performance for accomplishment of that function within the division.

This requires the accountable manager and the staff man, working together, to analyze and discuss the key factors in effective performance and to agree upon acceptable standards upon which evaluation will be based.   It gives the division manager objective measures which he can use in all aspects of performance within his organization component.

Utilizing a program and schedule developed in conjunction with the division, each staff group evaluates the operations of the division within its functional area.   Reports go first to the division manager, who has first opportunity to determine the action he will take and to report it to the chief executive office.

More typical of independent evaluation is the use of internal audit groups. As utilized in many leading companies, this group commonly concentrates upon accounting and fiscal data. It reviews periodically the scope, adequacy, and accuracy of the records and procedures used and ensures that they are in conformance with established company policy and procedure.

REQUIREMENTS OF EVALUATION

The following items should have constant attention if the evaluation approach is to be most useful to accountable managers.

1. *Control by Exception*

Control should be in terms of exceptions, not routine. Major control effort should be applied to those areas which are in greatest need of attention—exceptions or variances. If we have already thought through what we want done, how we want it done, and what it should cost, there is little need for confirmatory reports to notify us that everything is going according to plan. We can assume this. It is more important to know what is *not* going according to plan because these discrepancies point up the relatively few areas in which effective corrective action can be undertaken.

2. *Determine Allowable Limits of Tolerance*

On most operations we do not expect results to coincide with our expectations to the last penny or the last quarter-ounce. We usually consider the results satisfactory if they come within reasonable distance of the goal we set. It is important to determine the allowable limits of variance beforehand. On a new operation we may want to accumulate historical evidence of our results to assess the degree of accomplishment. Once we can determine what tolerances are reasonable, we can establish these as the basis for our evaluation.

3. *Measure by Standards, Not Tolerance*

In most cases it is desirable to note and discuss all deviations from standard, even within the limits of tolerance. If this is not done, the tolerance tends to become the standard and we soon find ourselves establishing tolerances for tolerances. We can also throw our standards into disrepute by using two sets of standards and tolerances, one which we announce and the other which we use privately. It is better to secure agreement on one set of standards and tolerances and to adhere firmly to this.

SUMMARY

In evaluating performance, a manager appraises work in progress and the results secured. Here he compares actual performance to the standard, identifies the variances, and determines why variances occur. Effective performance evaluation involves checks and balances so that each variance will be assessed by an individual who is not directly accountable for it. The important requirements of evaluation are to provide for control by exception, to determine allowable limits of tolerance within which variances may occur, and to measure by the standard not by the tolerance.

CHAPTER 30

Performance Correcting

> *Never let your head hang down. Never give up and sit down and grieve. Find another way.* LEROY (SATCHEL) PAIGE

DEFINITION

Performance Correcting: the work a manager performs to regulate and improve methods and results.

THE LOGIC OF CORRECTIVE ACTION

The final step in control is to take the corrective action necessary to bring discrepancies and variances into line. Corrective action should be initiated by the accountable manager. He can do this most effectively if three conditions prevail.

1. He must understand and accept his responsibility; he must know what work he is expected to carry out.
2. He must agree to and accept the standards of performance by which he is judged; that is, he must know what results he is expected to accomplish and agree that they are reasonable and necessary.
3. He must have command over his own performance. If he cannot regulate the present operation and make the changes necessary to secure the results he wants without constantly checking with his superiors, he cannot be expected to carry out corrective action.

HUMAN PROBLEMS IN CORRECTIVE ACTION

Identifying what is wrong is one thing; getting people to do something about it is quite another. In correcting deficiencies and improving performance, the critical factor invariably is the human being involved. Interested, willing people will undertake correction without prompting; those who find no challenge in the work itself will have to be prodded continually to improve unsatisfactory situations. To ensure that accountable managers will initiate and carry through their own corrective action as completely as possible, the following points should be considered.

1. *Avoid Self-criticism*

Most of us are fallible, and know it; however, we are quite reluctant that the news be noised about. When we make a mistake, our natural tendency is to rationalize it. We must assume that it will be difficult to pin down people to precise accountability for deficiencies in their work.

In the face of these obstacles, what can we do? Our best recourse is to establish a control system that will enable people to come to agreement, before any work is actually undertaken, as to what constitutes satisfactory and unsatisfactory performance. In that way, their performance will be measured by a system which they will have helped develop and which will undertake correction of deficiencies in a manner agreed to beforehand. Participation and communication in establishment of standards, measurement, and evaluation are thus a necessary prerequisite to effective performance correction.

2. *Provide for Self-correction*

People want first opportunity to identify and correct their own mistakes. If we are in the wrong, we want to know it first ourselves, so that we can correct the situation before the policeman is at the door. However, it is important to note that, being human, we probably won't do much about it unless we know that there *will* be a policeman at the door if we fail to take corrective action.

If we are to correct our own work, there must first be persistent pressure for correction; we must be alerted continually that if we do not perform, we will be called to account. Secondly, we need tools of control that we can use ourselves. There is no point in commanding a man to swim if he does not know how to swim. The control system must give the manager accountable for correction the background he needs to see the immediate and continuing influence of the corrective action he takes.

3. *Correct First Things First*

The human span of attention is limited. Most of us are capable of attending to only one thing at a time. Instead of deluging managers with insistent demands that a host of small details be corrected, each manager should be alerted constantly to the important deficiencies that affect his own accountability and should be required to correct these first.

If we keep in mind that the scalar nature of an organization provides automatically for attention to matters of increasingly greater significance as we go up the line, it becomes clear that we should design our control system to focus management attention on the important things that can be corrected properly only at the appropriate point in each level of management.

4. Overcome Emotional Resistance

Before we implement correction, we can safely assume that there will be strong emotional resistance to what we are trying to accomplish. The remedy lies not in increasing the pressure; as we have seen, this will tend to result in greater resistance.   Rather, the two techniques of participation and communication should again be called into play to secure the understanding and acceptance of those whose work is to be controlled.

MANAGEMENT ACTION AND OPERATING ACTION

When corrective action is indicated, it tends to fall into a specific pattern.   First, we generally see the need for operating action.   The current operation is out of phase.   We take immediate action to bring it back to plan.   For example, perhaps we are falling behind in our deliveries.   We cannot get the goods out fast enough.   To correct the lag, we put another man on the job.   This operating action is taken on short notice.   It corrects an immediate situation.   It usually treats the symptoms, but there is every possibility we haven't corrected the underlying cause.

If we want operating action to be truly effective, we should back it up with whatever management action is necessary.   This means that a manager should continually review his objectives, programs, schedules, and budgets.   He looks to his organization and controls and to his leadership.

In the case of slow delivery, for example, he may discover that his schedules are too tight.   A readjustment may make the extra man unnecessary.   Perhaps the organization of the work is at fault, in which case a rearrangement may improve the flow and help him get more work done in less time.

When taking corrective action, every variance should prompt a check to ensure that the cause of the exception is not an inadequacy of our underlying management. In this way, we can use our controls to ensure that we are accomplishing the results we want, within the limits we have set for ourselves. This is the final test of professional management.

SUMMARY

Corrective action is the work a manager performs to regulate and improve methods and results. In doing this, managers are rectifying deficiencies and providing for improvement of the results that are secured. Effective correction requires that the manager avoid the onus of self-criticism. Provision should be made for self-correction so that the accountable individual will be able to correct things before they are called to his attention by his boss. Since human capacity is limited, corrective action must be taken in terms of the most important things first, with subsidiary effort relegated to the unimportant items. In all of correction, we can anticipate emotional resistance, and here participation and communication will provide the best antidote. In most variances, the direct action is operating action. Often we put out the fire and forget to look for the causes of the fire. Here appropriate attention must be given to the need for a renewed cycle of planning, organizing, leading, and controlling to eliminate or minimize the possibility of future occurrence of the same variance.

Bibliography

While not intended to be complete, the following will provide corollary reading for the individual interested in professional management. Differing viewpoints will be found in many of the works shown.

PART ONE—LEADERS AND MANAGERS

Allen, Louis A., *Management and Organization,* McGraw-Hill Book Company, Inc., New York, 1958.

Anshen, Melvin, and George Leland Bach (eds.), *Management and Corporations 1985,* McGraw-Hill Book Company, Inc., New York, 1960.

Appley, Lawrence A., *The Management Evolution,* American Management Association, New York, 1963.

Barnard, Chester I., *The Functions of the Executive,* Harvard University Press, Cambridge, Mass., 1956.

Berkeley, Edmund C., *The Computer Revolution,* Doubleday & Company, Inc., Garden City, N.Y., 1962.

Bethel, Lawrence L., Franklin S. Atwater, George H. E. Smith, and Harvey A. Stackman, Jr., *Industrial Organization and Management,* 4th ed., McGraw-Hill Book Company, Inc., New York, 1962.

Bowen, Howard R., *Social Responsibilities of the Businessman,* Harper & Brothers, New York, 1953.

Brech, E. F. L., *Management, Its Nature and Significance,* Sir Isaac Pitman & Sons, Ltd., London, 1948.

Childs, Marquis W., and Douglass Cater, *Ethics in a Business Society,* Harper & Brothers, New York, 1954.

Cordiner, Ralph J., *New Frontiers for Professional Managers,* McGraw-Hill Book Company, Inc., New York, 1956.

Davis, R. C., *Industrial Organization and Management,* 4th ed., Harper & Brothers, New York, 1957.

Drucker, Peter F., *The Practice of Management,* Harper & Brothers, New York, 1954.

Fayol, Henri, *General and Industrial Management,* Sir Isaac Pitman & Sons, Ltd., London, 1949.

Gulick, Luther, and L. Urwick (eds.), *Papers on the Science of Administration,* Institute of Public Administration, New York, 1937.

Koontz, Harold, and Cyril O'Donnell, *Principles of Management,* McGraw-Hill Book Company, Inc., New York, 1959.

Metcalf, Henry C., and L. Urwick (eds.), *Dynamic Administration: The Collected Papers of Mary Parker Follett,* Management Publications Trust, London, 1949.

Newman, William H., *Administrative Action,* 2d ed., Prentice-Hall, Inc., Englewood Cliffs, N.J., 1963.

Simon, Herbert A., *Administrative Behavior,* The Macmillan Company, New York, 1957.

Taylor, Frederick Winslow, *Shop Management,* Harper & Brothers, New York, 1911.

Urwick, L., *The Elements of Administration,* Harper & Brothers, New York, 1943.

Villers, Raymond, *Dynamic Management in Industry,* Prentice-Hall, Inc., Englewood Cliffs, N.J., 1960.

PART TWO—MANAGEMENT PLANNING

Abramson, Adolph G., and Russell H. Mack (eds.), *Business Forecasting in Practice,* John Wiley & Sons, Inc., New York, 1956.

AFSC Policies and Procedures Handbook, *Program Evaluation Review Technique,* Aeronautical Systems Division, Air Force Systems Command, Washington, 1962.

Bennis, Warren G., Kenneth D. Benne, and Robert Chin (eds.), *The Planning of Change,* Holt, Rinehart and Winston, Inc., New York, 1961.

Branch, Melville C., *The Corporate Planning Process,* American Management Association, New York, 1962.

Chamberlain, Neil W., *The Firm: Micro-Economic Planning and Action,* McGraw-Hill Book Company, Inc., New York, 1962.

Ewing, David W. (ed.), *Long-range Planning for Management,* Harper & Brothers, New York, 1958.

Jerome, William Travers III, *Executive Control,* John Wiley & Sons, Inc., New York, 1961.

LeBreton, Preston P., and Dale A. Henning, *Planning Theory,* Prentice-Hall, Inc., Englewood Cliffs, N.J., 1961.

Neuschel, Richard F., *Management by System,* McGraw-Hill Book Company, Inc., New York, 1960.

Thompson, Stewart, *How Companies Plan,* American Management Association, New York, 1962.

Tilles, Seymour, "The Manager's Job: A Systems Approach," *Harvard Business Review,* January–February, 1963.

PART THREE—MANAGEMENT ORGANIZING

Allen, Louis A., "Can You Eliminate Assistants?" *Dun's Review and Modern Industry,* December, 1956.

———, *Charting the Company Organization Structure,* National Industrial Conference Board, Inc., New York, 1958.

————, *Improving Staff and Line Relationships,* National Industrial Conference Board, Inc., New York, 1956.

————, *Preparing the Company Organization Manual,* National Industrial Conference Board, Inc., New York, 1957.

————, "The Art of Delegation," *The Management Record,* March, 1955.

————, "The Doctrine of Completed Work," *The Management Record,* December, 1954.

————, *The Organization of Staff Functions,* National Industrial Conference Board, Inc., New York, 1958.

————, "The Urge to Decentralize," *Dun's Review and Modern Industry,* December, 1957.

Bain, Joe S., *Industrial Organization,* John Wiley & Sons, Inc., New York, 1959.

Brown, Alvin, *Organization, a Formulation of Principle,* Hibbert Printing Company, New York, 1946.

Dale, Ernest, *Planning and Developing the Company Organization Structure,* American Management Association, New York, 1952.

———— and Lyndall F. Urwick, *Staff in Organization,* McGraw-Hill Book Company, Inc., 1960.

Haire, Mason (ed.), *Modern Organization Theory,* John Wiley & Sons, Inc., New York, 1959.

Hebb, D. O., *The Organization of Behavior,* John Wiley & Sons, New York, 1949.

Holden, Paul E., Lounsbury S. Fish, and Hubert L. Smith, *Top-Management Organization and Control,* McGraw-Hill Book Company, Inc., New York, 1951.

Kahn, Robert L., and Daniel Katz, *Leadership Practices in Relation to Productivity and Morale,* University of Michigan, Institute for Social Research, Ann Arbor, Mich., December, 1952.

Lawrence, Paul R., *The Changing of Organizational Behavior Patterns,* Harvard Business School, Division of Research, Boston, 1958.

March, James G., and Herbert A. Simon, *Organization,* John Wiley & Sons, Inc., New York, 1958.

Smith, George Albert, Jr., *Managing Geographically Decentralized Companies,* Harvard Business School, Division of Research, Boston, 1958.

PART FOUR—MANAGEMENT LEADING

Argyris, Chris, *Personality and Organization,* Harper & Brothers, New York, 1957.

Davis, Keith, *Human Relations at Work,* McGraw-Hill Book Company, Inc., New York, 1962.

Dooher, Joseph M., and Vivienne Marquis, *The Development of Executive Talent,* American Management Association, New York, 1952.

————, Elizabeth Marting, and Robert E. Finley (eds.), *Effective Communication on the Job,* American Management Association, New York, 1963.

Folsom, Marion E., *Executive Decision Making,* McGraw-Hill Book Company, Inc., New York, 1962.

Haire, Mason, *Psychology in Management,* McGraw-Hill Book Company, Inc., New York, 1956.

Herrick, Judson C., *The Evolution of Human Nature,* University of Texas Press, Austin, 1956.

Houser, Theodore V., *Big Business and Human Values,* McGraw-Hill Book Company, Inc., New York, 1957.

Hovland, Carl I., Irving L. Janis, and Harold H. Kelley, *Communication and Persuasion,* Yale University Press, New Haven, Conn., 1953.

Leys, Wayne A. R., *Ethics for Policy Decisions,* Prentice-Hall, Inc., Englewood Cliffs, N.J., 1955.

Marrow, Alfred J., *Making Management Human,* McGraw-Hill Book Company, Inc., New York, 1957.

Maslow, A. H., *Motivation and Personality,* Harper & Brothers, New York, 1954.

McGregor, Douglas, *The Human Side of Enterprise,* McGraw-Hill Book Company, Inc., New York, 1960.

Merrihue, Willard V., *Managing by Communication,* McGraw-Hill Book Company, Inc., New York, 1960.

Nichols, Ralph G., and Leonard A. Stevens, *Are You Listening?* McGraw-Hill Book Company, Inc., New York, 1957.

Redfield, Charles E., *Communication in Management,* The University of Chicago Press, Chicago, 1958.

Spates, Thomas G., *Human Values Where People Work,* Harper & Brothers, New York, 1960.

PART FIVE—MANAGEMENT CONTROLLING

Jerome, William Travers, III, *Executive Control—The Catalyst,* John Wiley & Sons, Inc., New York, 1961.

Malcolm, Donald G., and Alan J. Rowe (eds.), *Management Control Systems,* John Wiley & Sons, Inc., New York, 1960.

Rose, T. G., and Donald E. Farr, *Higher Management Control,* McGraw-Hill Book Company, Inc., New York, 1957.

Tucker, Spencer A., *Successful Managerial Control by Ratio-Analysis,* McGraw-Hill Book Company, Inc., New York, 1961.

Welsch, Glenn A., *Budgeting: Profit-Planning and Control,* Prentice-Hall, Inc., Englewood Cliffs, N.J., 1957.

The Louis A. Allen Common Vocabulary of
Professional Management

Accountability, Management: The obligation to perform responsibility and exercise authority in terms of established performance standards.

Activity, Management: The basic category of management work.

Administration: The total activity of a manager.

Analyze: To divide a complex whole into its constituents.

Approve: To accept as satisfactory.

Art: A skill exercised in terms of the individual personality of the practitioner.

Assess: To weigh and appraise.

Assist: To help by providing advice and service.

Assistant: Personal staff position.

Assistant, Administrative: A personal staff position which performs specified detail and routine activities related to both management and operating responsibilities which the manager might otherwise perform himself.

Assistant, Executive: A personal staff position.

Assistant, Line: A person or position that provides advice and service to one principal in all aspects of his responsibility and assumes part or all of the authority of that principal on specific delegation.

Assistant, Management: A personal staff position which provides help and advice to a manager primarily in the planning, organizing and controlling aspects of his responsibilities.

Assistant, Special: A personal staff position which provides specialized help in one kind of work.

Assistant, Staff: A personal staff position which provides advice and service to one principal in limited portions of his responsibility and does not assume his authority.

Assistant to: A synonym for staff assistant.

Associate: A line assistant who is delegated and exercises substantial portions of the principal's authority and responsibility on a continuing basis and who is held accountable for this work and these decisions.

Attitude: Reaction to things, people, situations and information.

Authority: The sum of the powers and rights assigned to a position.

351

Authority, Formal: Powers and rights which are delegated consciously to a position.

Authority, Informal: Powers and rights which are assumed by a person without conscious assignment of this authority to him by his superior.

Authorize: To give final approval.

Automation: The process of using machine power primarily to augment or replace human mental skills.

Budget: An allocation of resources.

Budgeting, Management: The work a manager performs to allocate resources necessary to accomplish objectives.

Centralization: The systematic and consistent reservation of authority at top levels of the organization.

Centric Group: A group in which the general level of personal concern tends to be greater than the general level of group concern.

Chief Executive: A position which has accountability for the overall management and operation of the enterprise as a whole.

Coaching, Management: The personal activity of a manager in instructing and helping employees to develop on the job.

Collaborate: To work together.

Committee: A body of persons appointed or elected to meet on an organized basis for the consideration of matters brought before it.

Communicating: The work a manager performs to create understanding among people.

Concept, Management: A general idea in management stated in a formalized manner so that it can be communicated in a standardized fashion.

Conclusion: A terminal point in thinking arrived at from consideration of established premises.

Consolidation: Bringing together at one physical location people, equipment facilities, or other things.

Control, Management: To assess and regulate work in progress and work completed.

Controlling Function: The work a manager performs to assess and regulate work in progress and completed.

Coordinate: To time, unify and integrate work as it takes place.

Decentralization: The systematic and consistent delegation of authority to the levels where work is performed.

Decision-making: The work a manager performs to arrive at conclusions and judgments.

Delegating: The work a manager performs to entrust responsibility and authority to others and to create accountability for results.

Develop: To build by successive additions.

Developing People: The work a manager performs to help people improve their knowledge, attitudes and skills.

Differentiating: Distinguishing grades or levels of quantity, quality and other characteristics.

Direct: To command.

Dispersion: Physical separation of people, equipment and facilities.

Divisionalization: The process of dividing large functional organization units into units grouped in terms of product, geography or some other basis.

Encourage: To stimulate people to do what has to be done through praise, approval and help.

Enterprise: Organized endeavor.

Executive: A manager in the higher levels of the organization.

Executive Vice President: A line assistant who reports to the chief executive.

Forecasting: The work a manager performs to estimate the future.

Function, Management: A group or family of related kinds of management work, made up of activities which are closely related to one another and have characteristics in common derived from the essential nature of the work done.

Function, Organizational: The total of positions encompassing one kind of work grouped to form an administrative unit.

Group Evolution: The systematic and continuous adaptation of a group of people working together to their internal and external needs.

Grouping: Putting related work together to form positions, units and other organization components.

Impel: To force or incite action by any necessary means, including compulsion, coercion and fear, if required.

Initiate: To begin something.

Inspire: The process of motivating through the leader's personality, his example, and the work he does, consciously or unconsciously, to infuse a spirit of willingness into people to perform most effectively.

Interpret: To explain the meaning of.

Job Rotation: The purposeful movement of an individual from one position to another on the same organizational level for purposes of development.

Judgment: The verdict arrived at after weighing of evidence.

Knowledge: Cognizance of facts, truths and other information.

Leader: A person who enables other people to work together to attain identified ends.

Leader, Natural: A person in a leadership position who enables people to work together for identified ends primarily by using his own innate, natural aptitudes, skills and personal characteristics.

Leader, Personal: Synonym for natural leader.

Leadership: Guidance and direction of the efforts of others.

Leadership Evolution: The systematic and continuing adaptation of a leader to the needs of the group he leads.

Leadership, Management: The work of planning, organizing, leading and controlling performed by a person in a leadership position to enable people to work most effectively together to attain identified ends.

Leading Function: The work a manager performs to cause people to take effective action.

Maintain: To keep in effective condition.

Management Development: The work a manager performs to help managers and candidates for management positions to improve their knowledge, attitudes and skills.

Manager: One who enables people to work most effectively together by performing the work of planning, organizing, leading and controlling.

Manager, Professional: One who specializes in the work of planning, organizing, leading and controlling the efforts of others and does so through systematic use of classified knowledge, a common vocabulary and principles, and who subscribes to the standards of practice and code of ethics established by a recognized body.

Mechanization: The process of using machine power primarily to multiply human physical skills.

Method: The manner or way in which work is done.

Motivating: The work a manager performs to inspire, encourage and impel people to take required action.

Objective: An end result; a goal or target toward which effort is directed.

Objective, General: The longest range and culminating end result, generally in a series of identified accomplishments.

Objective, Specific: An intermediate, shorter term end result leading to a general objective.

Objectives, Establishing: The work a manager performs to determine the end results to be accomplished.

Operating Work: The work a manager performs other than the planning, organizing, leading and controlling work that logically belong in his position.

Organization Chart: A schematic representation of organization structure, authority and relationships.

Organization Structure: The pattern work assumes as it is identified and grouped to be performed by people.

Organization Structure—Developing: The work a manager does to identify and group the work to be performed.

Organizing Function: The work a manager performs to arrange and relate the work to be done so it can be performed most effectively by people.

Performance: The act of doing work.

Performance Appraisal, Management: The work a manager performs to evaluate the performance and capabilities of himself and his people.

Performance Correcting: The work a manager performs to regulate and improve methods and results.

Performance Counseling: The process of discussing his performance with a person whose work has been appraised.

Performance Evaluating: The work a manager performs to appraise work in progress and results secured.

Performance Measuring: The work a manager performs to record and report work in progress and completed.

Performance, Satisfactory: A level of performance equal to or better than a predetermined requirement.

Performance Standards: The criteria by which methods and results will be evaluated.

Performance Standards, Establishing: The work a manager performs to establish the criteria by which methods and results will be evaluated.

Performance, Unsatisfactory: A level of performance less than a predetermined requirement.

Plan, Management: A predetermined course of action.

Planning Function: The work a manager performs to predetermine a course of action.

Policies, Establishing: The work a manager performs to develop and interpret standing decisions which apply to repetitive questions and problems of significance to the enterprise as a whole.

Policy, Management: A standing decision made to apply to repetitive questions and problems of significance to the enterprise as a whole.

Position: Work grouped for performance by one individual.

Prepare: To make ready for use.

Prescribe: To direct specified action.

Principle, Management: A fundamental truth that will tend to apply in new situations in much the same way as it has applied in situations already observed.

Procedure: A standardized method of performing specified work.

Procedures, Establishing: The work a manager performs to develop and apply standardized methods of performing specified work.

Profession: A specialized kind of work practiced through the use of classified knowledge, a common vocabulary and principles, and requiring standards of practice and a code of ethics established by a recognized body.

Program: A sequence of action steps arranged in the priority necessary to accomplish an objective.

Programming: The work a manager performs to establish the sequence and priority of action steps to be followed in reaching objectives.

Program Step: An individual action step that is part of a larger program.

Projection, Analytical: A forecast made by determining why events have occurred in the past and transferring this reasoning to analysis of probable future occurrences.

Projection, Mechanical: A forecast made by assuming that future trends will assume substantially the same characteristics as those of the past.

Radic Group: A group in which the general level of group concern of the members of the group tends to be greater than the general level of personal concern.

Recommend: To offer or suggest for use.

Record: To make notation of; to set down in writing.

Regulate: To adjust; to return to a predetermined course.

Regulation: A standing decision made to apply to repetitive problems and questions of significance to one component of the endeavor.

Relationship, Line: A relationship involving command authority with respect to end results.

Relationship, Staff: An advisory and service relationship.

Relationships: The conditions necessary for mutually cooperative efforts of people.

Relationships, Establishing: The work a manager performs to create the conditions necessary for mutually cooperative efforts of people.

Report: To convey information.

Responsibility: Work assigned to a position.

Responsibility, Reserved: That portion of a manager's work that he performs himself and does not delegate.

Results: The outcome of performance.

Review: To examine critically.

Schedule, Management: A time sequence.

Scheduling, Management: The work a manager performs to establish a time sequence for program steps.

Science: A unified and systematically arranged body of knowledge dealing with facts or truths and showing the operation of general laws or principles.

Selecting People: The work a manager performs to choose people for positions in the organization and for advancement.

Skill: The ability to put knowledge into practice.

Staff Advice: Counsel, suggestions, opinions and recommendations offered by a person in a staff relationship to other positions and units.

Staff, Personal: Positions created for the purpose of providing advice and service to one principal.

Staff Service: The process of doing work for other persons and units.

Staff, Specialized: Those positions and components organized primarily to provide advice and service in one specialized function to other units in the accomplishment of overall objectives.

Supervise: To direct personally.

Supervision, Span of: The number of people supervised by a manager.

Understanding: Comprehension of meaning.

Variance: A departure from what was intended; a divergence, over or under.

Work: Physical and mental effort.

Index

357